CHILD TRAFFICKING
An Unconscious Phenomenon

CHILD TRAFFICKING

AN UNCONSCIOUS PHENOMENON

DR. A. THOMAS WILLIAM
M.A. (S.W.), D.L.L. & A.L., Ph.D.,
Reader
Arul Anandar College (Autonomous)
Karumathur, MADURAI

KANISHKA PUBLISHERS, DISTRIBUTORS
NEW DELHI-110 002

KANISHKA PUBLISHERS, DISTRIBUTORS
4697/5-21A, Ansari Road, Daryaganj
New Delhi-110 002
Phones : 2327 0497, 2328 8285
Fax : 011-2328 8285
E-mail : kanishka_publishing@yahoo.co.in

First Published 2008

ISBN 978-81-8457-088-5

PRINTED IN INDIA

Published by Madan Sachdeva for Kanishka Publishers, Distributors, 4697/5-21A, Ansari Road, Daryaganj, New Delhi-110 002. Typeset by Sunshine Graphics, Delhi, and Printed at Nice Printing Press, Delhi.

Acknowledgements

This research work is the resultant product of many hands that guided, assisted and supported me in this endeavour. I sincerely acknowledge the constant encouragement and support extended by Rev. A. Thomas Amirtham, The Rector, Rev. Fr. Dr. G. Pushpa Raj, The Principal and the Jesuit Management of Arul Anandar College (Autonomous), Karumathur, Madurai.

Malcolm and Elizabeth Adiseshiah Trust, Chennai is greatly obliged for their financial support through out the research. **Dr. H.B.N. SHETTY**, I.A.S., The Executive Trustee is greatly acknowledged for his motivation in sanctioning the financial assistance on time and for all his prompt and timely communications.

I sincerely express my gratitude to Dr. A.J. Christopher, Reader, Dept. of Social Work, Sacred Heart College (Autonomous), Tirupattur, Dr. I. Devanan, Vice-Principal – Self-finance and Reader, Department of Rural Development Science and Mr. Ambudoss Arvind, Faculty in the Department of Rural Development Science for their constant encouragement and guidance. I extend my thankfulness to all the faculty members of Rural Development Science.

My kind remembrance to DR. Arul Gnanasekar, Good Hope, Tirumanagalam, Mr. Ayyankalai, MASW and the functionaries of all the NGO's, self help group members and the local people for their participation and support.

I am greatly indebted to the Children who had helped me by participating in the research process. My thanks go to all the field investigators and in a special way to Mr. Alex and Mr. Tamilarasan.

My special acknowledgement is due to Ms. Suganya, for feeding the data in the computer and helped in analysis.

My kind remembrance are due to my loving students Ms. Jayalakshmi and Ms. Priya for their assistance and support during data collection and submission of accounts.

Finally I acknowledge all the heartfelt thanks to those who read this material and offer suggestion to probe further in the field.

AUTHOR

Preface

This study on Child Trafficking focuses on the child labour perspectives of the phenomenon. Trafficking is a clandestine activity nowadays increasing in the alarming speed with vigour and velocity. The advent of technology, material culture, and growing complexities of socio-economic problems paves way increasing rate. While trafficking is a global problem spreading its wings regionally, nationally and internationally; it is an integral part of the process of international migration, it does assume specific regional and national dimensions. Unfortunately India is one of the main source, transit point as well as destination for trafficking activity.

Trafficking is a low risk high return and well organized criminal activity which fetches huge amount of income. It is estimated that human trade is the bigger trade in the world which is the third biggest money earning illegal trade. There are at least one million child prostitutes in Asia alone mostly, in India, Thailand, Taiwan and Philippines as estimated by UNICEF (2003).

The definition given by the United Nations General Assembly (1994) could give us a basic understanding about the menace. It viewed that: "Trafficking of persons is the illicit and clandestine movement of persons across national borders with the end goal of forcing women, girls and children into sexually oppressive and exploitative situations for profit of recruiters, traffickers and crime syndicates as well as other illegal activities related to trafficking such as forced domestic labour, false marriages, clandestine employment and false adoption".

Though various definitions and researches conducted both nationally and internationally there need to be conceptual clarity on the issue; as it is more complicated and complex. There are different approaches employed by the researchers to study trafficking. For many researchers trafficking means commercial sex business and for some it is human rights violation, etc. There could also be various dimensions to study trafficking such as migrational approach, bonded labour approach, child labourer approach, etc.

There are exhaustive research work done among trafficked women and girl children with the commercial sex dimension. It is the recent trend also that more number of girlsand women are trafficked for commercial sex purpose, child prostitution, sex tourism, pornography, etc. Indeed focusing on the child labour perspective is the need of the hour as only few studies are available in this regard.

The present study is conducted in Usilampatty Taluk of Madurai District, Tamilnadu. The one time infamous for female infanticide has now become the hub for traffickers and recruiters to traffick children for labour activities. The problem is worse as the socio-economic condition of the taluk is backward in nature added with no alternative livelihood except dry farming in most of the area. Murukku Company (Preparation of sweets and snacks in bulk and supply to retail vendors) is the entrepreneurial activity gaining momentum nowadays. The people migrate to various other parts of the country in search of employment, business, etc. One such migration taking place to establish units of Murukku Making in various states like, Andhra Pradesh, Orissa, Maharastra, West Bengal, Assam, Madhya Pradesh, Uttar Pradesh, etc.

The local private owners or the small business entrepreneurs finds the children of this area as money earning machines and take them on contract by exploiting the minds of the parents. The socio-economic deprivations add up to the vulnerability and the children become the easy prey to these traffickers.

With this back drop the researcher has taken up a study to identify the social and economical factors responsible, causes, the working conditions the ill-treatments and abuses such as beating, scolding, punishments, tortures, trade the Modus operandi, the consequences and trace the NGO's who are working for the prevention and rehabilitation of the victims.

To have a better understanding of the phenomenon various study reports are analysed to understand the nature, type, purpose, chain, national and international scenario, destinations, causes, consequences, various legal and developmental provisions, economics involved, source, approach, consequences, psychological aspects and the child labour perspectives' studies are examined

The study area Usilampatty taluk is located at the Western side of the Madurai district. It comprises of two Panchayat Union namely, Chellampatty and Usilampatty. The rampant and known villages for trafficking are identified by pilot visit and consultation with NGO's, Panchayat leaders and self help group members. Interview schedule was constructed based on the objectives covering personal profile of the children, family background, economic details, expenditure pattern, working condition, time of work, conditions of work spot, wage and salary, modus operandi, ill-treatment, psychosocial aspects, bad habits and future prospects. Through personal interview in the field using structured interview schedule the data was collected from 119 children respondents.

The collected data is anlysed using variables such age, sex, caste, type of industry, type of work, causes, ill treatment, bad habits, property, saving, debt, Causes, modus operandi, type of industry, the conditions of work the contract amount, the year of contract, ill-treatment faced, the bad habits acquired if any, and the future plan. The variable such as age, sex, education, caste, cause etc., arc crossed with other variables and presented. The cross tables gave a better understanding about the phenomenon.

While analysed it has been observed that the preferable age group for the traffickers is 13, 14 and 15 years old male children in Murukku Making company and similar age group of female children in cotton mills. In various other industries mostly male children are wanted. The various industries such as hotel, hosiery industry, appalam making, cement industry and biscuit company. These children also given various type of work such production, sales, marketing, packaging, helping and menial work.

It has been found that the parents themselves become the recruiter for their own children as they convince their children to get locked in the trafficking chain. It is quite astonishing that the community also participates in the process in a way that they also encourage such activity and almost all of them never perceive it as a problem rather they feel that it is a boon. As far as the causes are concerned though poverty is the predominant reason; the land holdings and income of the family shows a different picture. It is assumed that there are other reasons such as earn quick money, to meet the immediate needs, to get away from the clutches of greedy debtors are the factors hiding behind the cause poverty. The various other findings such as contract for a period of one to ten years; the amount of money paid ranges from Rs. 1000 to Rs. 12000 per year indicate the outraged mentality of the traffickers on one side and the vulnerability of the victims on the other. There are lot of ill-treatments such a oral, physical torture and punishment are given to these children for childish reasons and the children in the Murukku Company are the worst affected. There are physical, psychological and social problems and bad habits such as smoking, panparak, drug, drinking and tobacco are the negative consequences on the children due to trafficking. The dangerous indicator is that these children are very much susceptible to be re-trafficked.

The problem of child trafficking in Usilampatty taluk with labour perspective is observed as an unconscious and community participative activity it should be dealt with a integrated approach. The participation of various stakeholders such as parents, children, traffickers, elders, Panchayat representatives, NGO personnel and the community so as to change the attitudinal level first and then plan for preventive, curative and developmental programmes. There are various recommendations are given based on the findings of the study and on the discussion with NGO and other players in the field.

Prevention of trafficking could be done through addressing the root cause of the problem. The unawareness or unconsciousness of the people is deliberately lead to magnify the issue. Unfortunately the formal leaders and the influential persons add fuel by encouraging such activities by providing justification in the name of poverty, unemployment, failure of monsoon, etc. At this juncture, it is to be understood that the children are not the only breadwinners Ultimately the children are the suffers in terms of health, mental, educational and in total the personality. The aftermath effects and consequences are rarely felt by the parents and the community as sending children to Murukku Company is a very casual activity.

The attitude and mentality of the local people is to be tackled first instead of thinking in terms of developmental programmes. Changing the attitude must be the first priority; though it is a slow process but in the long run it is a sustainable one. The importance of childhood, alternate education for those who are already in the chain could bring better results.

Hope this research study could of immense use in understanding the issue, causes, consequences, and intervention to various stakeholders such as Government, NGO, Policy makers, planners, local administrators, researchers and academicians. The approaches such as P – approach (Prevention, Protection and Prosecution) and the R – approach (Rescue, Relief, Rehabilitation and Re-integration) should be upheld by various intervention personnel so as to light a lamp in the lives of the young and tender minds – the future nation; to promote a prosperous India.

Dr. A. Thomas William

Contents

Chapter 1

Introduction

"In this 21st century when the Rights of Children while almost universally recognized, they are abused systematically and daily throughout the world".

– Kofi. A. ANNAN
Former Secretary General, UN (2003)

"We cannot hide from the fact that migration can also have negative consequences. The Global Forum provides an opportunity to address these problems in a comprehensive and proactive way"

– Pan Ki Moon
Secretary General, UN (July 2007)

Trafficking is a growing phenomenon internationally, regionally and nationally considered as a contemporary form of slavery and a gross violation of basic human rights by the international community. While trafficking is a global problem and an integral part of the process of international migration, it does assume specific regional and national dimensions. India is one of the main source, transit point as well as destination for trafficking in women and children.

Today trafficking has emerged as a low risk high return well organized criminal activity. Human trafficking is the third biggest money earning illegal trade. There are at least one million child prostitutes in Asia alone mostly, in India, Thailand, Taiwan and Philippines as estimated by UNICEF (2003). Trafficking does not seem to have any boundaries irrespective of push and pull factors. Trafficking in human beings taking place in almost all the countries, only the magnitude differs.

United Nations General Assembly (1994) viewed that: "Trafficking of persons is the illicit and clandestine movement of persons across national borders with the end goal of forcing women, girls and children into sexually oppressive and exploitative situations for profit of recruiters, traffickers and crime syndicates as well as other illegal activities related to trafficking such as forced domestic labour, false marriages, clandestine employment and false adoption."

An elaborate definition advocated by United Nations is that "The recruitment, transportation, transfer, harboring or receipt of persons below the age of 18 years, (Legally or illegally), within or across borders, by means of threat or use of force or other forms of coercion, of abduction, of deception, of the abuse of power or of position of vulnerability or/ of the giving or receiving of payments or benefits to achieve the consent of a person, with the intention or knowledge that it is likely to cause or lead to exploitation."

It is pitiable that there is no authentic statistics available with regard to the exact number of persons being trafficked in our country, as there has been no detailed study/survey of the problem. It is a recent trend that more and more minors and children are being trafficked. It is very pathetic that there are about 4 lakhs child prostitutes in our country. More than 60 per cent of the victims belong to backward classes, scheduled castes and scheduled tribes. It is estimate that 15,000 children go missing every year in India.

In the year 2002 alone 6562 cases of kidnapping and abduction children for purposes that qualify as forms of trafficking were reported to the police. Of these, 37 cases were of kidnapping for adoption, 15 for begging, 4 for camel racing, 1092 for illicit intercourse, 4871 for marriage, 190 for prostitution, 16 for sale, 1 for selling body parts, 63 for slavery and 273 for unlawful activity. 1.19 per cent of these cases involved children below 10 years, 22.96 per cent involved children aged 11 to 15 years and 75.85 per cent involved those aged 16 to 18 years. Amongst other crimes related to trafficking; 147 cases were for procurement of minor girls, 15 for selling of minor girls for prostitution, 53 for buying of minor girls for prostitution and 660 for exposure and abandonment of children. (Crime in India, 2002).

Trafficking—Causes

- Poverty, though not the only reason but still remains one of the major factors.

- Unequal distribution of resources
- Illiterate or semi literate parents.
- Lack of awareness.
- Lower status of women and girls in the society
- Dysfunctional, Disorganized and Broken families
- Inadequate enforcement of law by the authorities.
- Natural disasters like floods, draught and war etc.
- Drug addict and alcoholic fathers in the family (as reported in various cases in rural Tamil Nadu) make the minor members, quite vulnerable to trafficking.
- Persons sexually abused are more prone to entering commercial sex work.
- Consumerist life style of the younger generation.
- Involvement of Crime syndicate.
- Increasing inter-state and international trafficking of women and children.
- Growing feminization of poverty.
- Growth of sex tourism, pornography in print, electronic and cyber media.
- Changing attitudes towards morality and sex.

Trafficking – Classification

Trafficking can broadly be categorized into the following.

I. *Sexual Exploitation*

(a) Forced prostitution.
(b) Socially and religiously sanctified forms of prostitution.
(c) Sex tourism.
(d) Pornography.

II. *Illegal Activities*

(a) Begging.
(b) Organ trade
(c) Drug peddling
(d) Arms carrying
(e) Smuggling
(f) Child soldiers

III. *Labour*

(a) Bonded labour
(b) Domestic work
(c) Agricultural labour

(d) Construction work
(e) Carpet industry, garment industry, brick kiln, fish/shrimp export as well as other sites of work in the formal and informal economy.
(f) Food Industry

IV. ***Entertainment and Sports***

(a) Circus
(b) Acrobatics
(c) Camel Race in some Arabian countries.
(d) Dance Troup
(e) Music Troup

V. ***Adoption***

(a) Inter country
(b) Intra country

VI. ***For and throught Marriage***

A large number of young girls are forced into prostitution through the "marriage route."

False Hopes

(a) Offering good jobs at high pay
(b) Children would acquire useful skill or trade.
(c) As a friend, meet with families and convince parents that their children will be safer and better taken care.
(d) Paying the yearly payment in advance.
(e) Offering jewels and Utensils.
(f) Offering good food thrice a day.
(g) Trafficking to foreign countries through "Musical Troupes" and "Club Sports Teams" ostensibly to give musical performance and play friendly matches. Through employment, travel, modeling and match making agencies.

The Reality

Though given many false hopes, in reality in children face lot of abuses. Several kinds of abuses, could be listed as below:

- Abducted or kidnapped.
- Purchased and confined against the will.
- Physically tortured.
- Sexually abused.

- Privacy and self respect outraged.
- Denied any form of legal redressal.
- Treated as some commodity and not a human being.
- Victim of an organized crime.

Conventions and Legal Measures – International and National

It is a huge list of various conventions, articles and legal positions to protect the children and to prevent, suppress and punish traffickers. Some of the important ones are listed below:

- Universal Declaration of Human Rights, 1948 (UDHR).
- Convention for the suppression of the Traffic in persons and of the Exploitation of Prostitution.1949.
- Convention of the Elimination of all forms of Discrimination Against Women, 1979 (CEDAW).
- The Convention of the Rights of the Child, 1990 (CRC)
- Worst forms of child labour convention, 1999 (C-182, R-190).
- The protocol to prevent, suppress and punish trafficking in persons, especially women and children, 2000.
- Article 23 of the constitution specifically prohibits trafficking in human beings)
- Juvenile Justice (Care and protection of Children) Act, 2000.
- The Child Labour (Prohibition & Regulation) Act, 1986
- Plantation Labour Act, 1951.
- The Mines Act, 1952.
- The Merchant Shipping Act, 1958.
- Cruelty to Women (Deterrent Punishment) Ordinance, 1983.
- The Immoral Traffic (Prevention Act, 1956 (as amended in 1986).
- Young Person Harmful Publication Act, 1956.
- Indecent Representation of Women (Prohibition) Act, 1986.
- The Criminal Law (Amendment Act), 1983.

Initiatives by Government of Tamilnadu

In Tamilnadu the approach is holistic in nature. The principles of rescue, relief, rehabilitation and re-integration of the victims are the four dimensions of the approach. There is a three tier system structure is in operation. At the State Level, State Level Co-ordination Committee under the Chairmanship of the Chief -secretary to combat trafficking is appointed. At the district level District Advisory Committee for the prevention of Trafficking. Village Level Watch Dog Committees numbering 8000 (VLWC) have been constituted.

The Director of Social Defense has been designated as the Nodal Officer prevention of trafficking. The special fund called "Tamil Nadu social Defense Welfare Fund for Women and Children" is constituted to cover children who are in vulnerable situation. 'Girl Child Protection Scheme', Cradle Baby Scheme' both launched in 1992. Mapping of risk and frequently occurring areas is initiated. CHILDLINE an emergency Toll free No: 1098 for children in distress is established in Chennai, Coimbatore, Madurai, Salem and Trichy round the clock. At present there are 8 Service Homes and 30 Short Stay Homes are available for rehabilitation and reintegration.

There are 18 Child Welfare Committees constituted at the district level throughout the state recently in the month of January 2004 to safeguard any child who is in need of care and protection. The Ministry of Women and Child Development, undertaken a detailed study of trafficking throughout the country and the same is in progress.

Significance of the Study

The adverse effect of monsoon failure one side the poverty on the other and the false promises and hopes by the agents and employers on the third - paved way for the rampant increase in child trafficking in Madurai district especially with reference to Usilampatty Taluk. The area is declared 'Backward' by the Govt. of Tamil Nadu - adds up more to the cause of child trafficking. Though number of laws such as Juvenile Justice Act, Child Labour Act and various other laws enacted; Government Machineries like Social Welfare Board, Social Defense, Juvenile Justice Board, Child Welfare Committees, Police and Judiciary geared up. Number of NGO's working for the prevention and rehabilitation work; the District and Village level committees are constituted – the magnitude of the child trafficking is on the increase. It has been observed by the previous preliminary study that almost all the villages in this taluk has more than 15 cases of Children each taken to other states. Not only boys but also girls are taken for odd and contract jobs.

Objectives

The objectives of the study are:

- To study and analyse the factors responsible for the problem such as social, economical, political, etc.
- To understand the working conditions such as hours of work, interval, place of work, salary or wages, type of work, etc.

- To measure the ill-treatments and abuses such as beating, scolding, punishments, tortures.
- To understand the Modus operandi.
- To assess the physical, mental, social and economical aspects of the children.
- To study the NGO's working for the prevention and rehabilitation.
- To understand the initiatives taken by the Government and
- To suggest measures for prevention, rehabilitation and reintegration.

Chapter 2

Trafficking Phenomenon

Introducation

"DON'T HIRE BUT EDUCATE CHILDREN."

– *Dr. Manmohan Singh* Prime Minister of India (2007)

Trafficking is considered an act of gross commercialization of innocent human lives, perpetuated by organized criminals. The world is so complex and tragic for human abuse in which children become a vulnerable class. India is considered as the sixth most dangerous place in the world for children according to the recent survey conducted by Reuters Alternet (2006).

In the Indian context, vulnerability is a product of inequality, low status and discrimination, and of the patriarchal authority unleashed on children, especially girl children (Anand, 2005).

Internationally trafficking in persons is considered as the third largest illegal business after drugs and arms (Human Rights Watch, 2003). The materialistic attitude of society fuelled by a mindset of artificial relationship views children as mere goods.

Trafficking of humans engrosses moving men, women and children from one place to another and placing them in a circumstance of forced labour. The practice includes forced sex work, domestic servitude, unsafe agricultural labourer, sweat shop labour, construction or restaurant work and various forms of modern-day-slavery.

With no freedom of choice and options to lead a life with dignity, hapless women and children are trafficked and exploited, and forced to lead a life plagued by indignity, social stigma, debt bondage and a host of ailments including HIV/AIDS (Nair, 2005).

The lack of sensitivity, responsiveness, lethargy, seriousness and commitment by the law enforcement agencies makes the situation more distressing. It is further worsened when the suit is so wide in the response scenario that the trafficked victim gets further victimized, violated and more often than not re-trafficked.

It is also interesting to note that may a time trafficking is paralleled with prostitution and this is one of the main reasons why the human rights violation inherent in trafficking is not correctly understood, while the traffickers who are actually the offenders go unnoticed. Therefore, as Anand (2005) reported there is a need to demystify the term 'trafficking' and understand its trends and dimensions within a human rights paradigm.

The tenth plan strategy of Rights-based approach for "Survival, Protection and Development of Children" is far from being realized at this stage(Gautam, 2006).

The process of trafficking is designed and manipulated by traffickers for their own ends for which they employ all kinds of means. Trafficking usually happens through well-organised networks in which family members, relatives, friends, community leaders, brokers, pimps, and owners of brothels, police, politicians, and the crime syndicates are involved.

India; serves as a source, transit and destination, where thousands of children are exploited every day. There is a stronger network and co-ordination found among the traffickers and that works in an integrated manner where in all the players are well collaborated protected. It has also been revealed that it is hard to intrude into the ferocious networking of traffickers in order to undertake some tangible measures.

To trace the objectives of trafficking research; most of the trafficking research are to identify vulnerable areas and target groups, to ascertain the causes of weak law enforcement and to help provide data for the creation of proper programmes and policies to check trafficking effectively (Manohar Sujata, 2005).

The Gargantuan Need

The need of the hour is to either enact new legislations or amend to the existing ones in a comprehensive way to provide for proper rescue and rehabilitation programmes for the victims and also to target the traffickers. The researches should lead to proper policies and comprehensive laws for the apprehension, prosecution d punishment of traffickers, proper action at the government as well as NGO level to prevent trafficking, the creation of programmes that empower the vulnerable, and proper measures to rehabilitate the restore the trafficked and exploited women and children of our country their dignity and worth as human beings/ (Manohar Sujata, 2005).

The complexity of the phenomenon, its multidimensional nature, its rapid proliferation, continued persistence and the confusion surrounding the concept has made the need for a deeper comprehension of trafficking; a top priority (Nair, 2005).

Though there are manifestations of entrenched discriminations based on age, sex, caste, class and ethnicity which are traditional these have their own repercussions in the violence against women and children and as a gamut to the inhuman commercial sex, abuse and trafficking has been observed by number of Initiatives at the grassroots level

The most offensive violation of human rights is trafficking. Perhaps not many crimes are as frightening as trading in human misery. Human rights guaranteed by the Indian Constitution are inalienable, non-negotiable and universal.

Trafficking in children is one of the worst and most brazen abuses of human rights. It is ironic that in the century that started with the re-affirmation of the commonality of values based on human rights and fundamental freedoms, such abuses still go unchecked (Nair, 2005).

Significance of Trafficking

The study will be of enormous worth to all those who are concerned in the anti-trafficking association. It will be even more helpful for framing appropriate laws and policies making. More importantly, it will raise awareness among the stakeholders about the issue and encourage public participation. There is no doubt that the spin-offs have been instrumental in creating a national momentum on anti-trafficking. A world free from trafficking would be ultimate mission of the study.

Researching un-chartered territory, especially to fathom the dark alleys of organized crime, transcending the boundaries of time and space, was a tremendous challenge (Nair, 2005).

The trafficking could also be understood in the human rights background as the gross human violation and especially the violation of child rights and hence a right based approach is also compulsory to ensure that the fundamental human entitlements such as social, economic and political well being and ensuring a complete childhood for children.

Unfortunately issues concerning children attract the least attention of the government, policy makers, the intervention personnel, police, judiciary and the like.

The all-India study conducted by Nair (2005) suggested that a team work of various professionals necessary apart from the legal frame work in our country. The various areas need to be focused are

- Facilitating programmes and initiatives for prevention, protection and prosecution
- Setting up a functional national network of government officials and activists to devise and implement anti-trafficking strategies
- Identifying good practices across the country that could be replicated elsewhere ,and the dissemination of the same and
- Carrying out awareness orientation and training programmes for concerned agencies as part of he research to make them accountable and committed to the causes.

Definition

The definition on trafficking should be exhaustive and elaborate so as to cover all the aspects of the phenomenon. The concept of human trafficking refers to the criminal practice of exploiting human beings by treating them like commodities for profit. Even after being trafficked, victims are subjected to long term exploitation.

The definition by the UN Protocol in paragraph (a) of Article 3 declared to Prevent, Suppress and Punish Trafficking in Persons, (2000) for women and children is "the recruitment, transportation, transfer, harboring or receipt of persons by means of the threat or use of force or other forms of coercion, of abduction, of fraud , of deception, of the abuse of power or of a position of vulnerability or of the giving or receiving of payments or benefits to achieve the consent of a person having control over another person, for the purpose of exploitation. Exploitation shall include, at a minimum, the exploitation of the prostitution of others or other forms of sexual exploitation, forced labour or service, slavery or practices similar to slavery, servitude or the removal of organs."

This definition was adopted by the UN Convention Against Transnational Organized Crime and fortunately or unfortunately India is also one among the signatory.

The three elements in this definition are:

1. Trafficking as an action with intention,
2. The means of recruitment and
3. The purpose.

The vulnerability can further be explained in terms of any situation in which the person involved has no real and acceptable alternative but to submit to the abuse involved (Jordan, 2002).

Trafficking – Need for Conceptual Clarity

Almost all the experts tried to incorporate each and every facet of the issue of trafficking while defining the problem. There are lot of efforts have been done to have a lucidity in defining the phenomenon. Though there are lots of definitions adopted; researchers devoted considerable amount of space to define the concept of trafficking. The definitions reflect the lack of consent on what represent trafficking.

Over decades, the concept itself has evolved to include many more attributes and features, so much so, that 'increasingly, it has been recognized that historical characterizations of trafficking are outdated, ill-defined and non-responsive to the current realities of the movement and trade in people and to the nature and extend of the abuses inherent in and incidental to trafficking (United Nations, 2000).

Different interpretations are reflected in the various definitions of trafficking prescribed by various authors. Debates, arguments and confusions appear to be centered on issues of consent and movement, of purpose and the unequal treatment of women and children.

The United Nations Protocol to Prevent, Suppress and Punish Trafficking in persons, Especially Women and Children, adopted in November 2000, is a part of the United Nations Convention Against Organized Crime and provide the first internationally recognized definition of trafficking (ESCAP, 2003). Besides giving a framework for further discussions it has proved to be guiding principle for a macro-conceptual understanding of trafficking (UNIFEM, 2003).

This definition deals with the exploitative conditions that may result from trafficking, including ideas that were earlier confined only to understanding prostitution. The positive aspects of this definition include the explanation of the means used for trafficking, its clarity on the issue of consent (one of the most debated issues in trafficking) and the different acts in the trafficking process that it elucidates. Concern, however, has been expressed that this first modern definition of trafficking is being elaborated in the context of prime control, rather than with a focus on human rights (United Nations, 2000). The definition is also viewed as on which confuses the lay persons (UNICEF, 2001). Thus the debate is still continuing post-2000, with other definitions being suggested and adopted by Coomarsamy (United Nations 2001).

The concept of trafficking can easily be expanded, limited or shifted to accommodate institutional objectives and context (ILO, 2002). The 2003 ESCAP report also accomplished that trafficking is a multidimensional form of exploitation wherein each dimension has its own legal and conceptual framework. There are many forms of trafficking, each with different implications, yet forming part of an interrelated web of varying contexts (ESCAP, 2003).

The array of trait and variables involved in the trafficking process and the different perception on the theme are also the rationale for there being no uniform method for classifying the forms of trafficking. For example, some suggested forms are defined on the basis of differences at the place of origin of trafficking victims, while some others focus on difference arising at the destinations. Some make the methods adopted by traffickers as the basis for the forms an still others use the criterion of purpose (DWCD, 1996; Friedman, 2001; HAQ Centre, 2001; ILO, 2001; Marshall, 2001; Matter, 2002; Depaul University, 2002; IDS, 2003).

Approaches to Understand Trafficking

Various approaches have been employed by different scholars in the field of trafficking. The nature of the issue is such that it is more complex and multi-faceted researchers approached it with different back drop and it ranges from simple socio-economic profile to complex magnitude and impact on the victim. Most of the approaches have overlapping elements (Nair, 2005). The various dimensions focused are exploitation of children and women, social implications, economic impact, health and nutrition of the children, development perspectives, anti-social activities, national productivity, impact on the future generation, violence, human rights perspective, child labour, commercial sex work, involving in criminal activities, forced labour, bonded labour, etc.,

Approaches to Trafficking

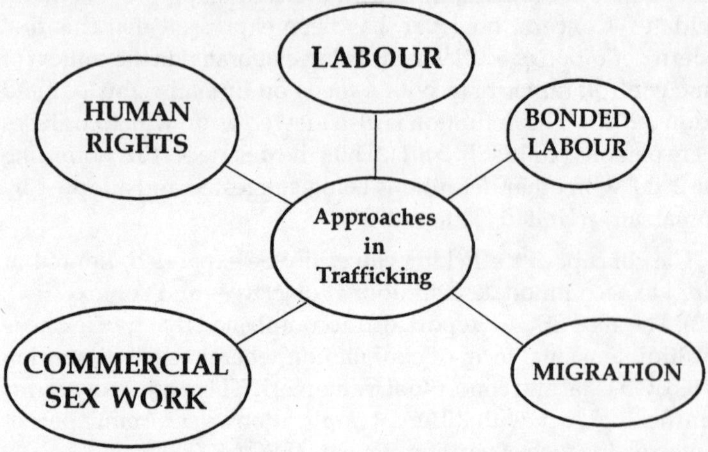

Human Rights Facet

Recently there was an elaborate study conducted by Nair (2005) interviewing 4006 respondents covering almost all the states in India using focused group discussions with large number of stakeholders and consultation involving all the players in the field such as judges, professionals, social activists and NGO personnel focusing the Human rights perspectives throws elaborate findings in the field. The report has also been presented in case studies based on various themes such as vulnerabilities that cause trafficking, prevention and other proactive responses, on trends and dimensions in trafficking, outline the exploitation and on law enforcement and other reactive responses to trafficking.

The reports on trafficking by press, police and NGO have given a clear and unequivocal indication that the buying and selling women and children for sexual and non-sexual purposes is an expanding activity, involving gross human rights violations. The warning that India is fast becoming a source, transit point s well as a destination for the traffickers is an immense cause for concern (Nair, 2005).

Some of the studies covered one or few dimensions and some covered only the children and few others focused on women. Only very few studies have conducted at the national level. Approaches and perspectives also influence the strategies that are designed for combating trafficking; Sanghera (1999) observed that in South Asia, trafficking is addressed as a problem of crime and violence against women, exploitation of children and child labour, or within a sociological framework. Only recently, attempts have begun to view it from human rights perspectives. Trafficking can be studied with a background as child labour, crime, migration, human rights, development, children's right and gender rights (Derks, 2000; Wijers, 2002). There are also studies available to trace trafficking in the light of commercial sex work either children or women involving (Shalini and Laitha, 1996).

United Nations: Rights of the Child

United Nations has strongly concerned that the status of children in many parts of the world remains critical as a result of:

- poverty
- inadequate social and economic conditions
- natural disasters
- armed conflicts
- displacement,
- economic and sexual exploitation
- illiteracy
- hunger
- intolerance
- disability and
- inadequate legal protection

The UN recognized that an integrated approach is very much required than that of legislation. To prevent violations of the rights of the child, that stronger political commitment is needed and those Governments should implement their laws and complement legislative measures with effective action by law enforcement agencies and in the administration of justice, and in social, educational and public health programmes.

It strongly recommended that, all relevant human rights mechanisms and all other relevant organs and mechanisms of the United Nations system and the supervisory bodies of the specialized agencies pay attention to particular situations in which children are in danger and where their rights are violated and that they take into account the work of the Committee on the Rights of the Child. It is imperative that the need for mainstreaming a gender perspective in all policies and programmes relating to children becomes compulsory. It also reaffirmed, as set out in the Convention on the Rights of the Child, that the best interests of the child should be a primary focus in all actions concerning children so as to ensure compete protection and bring out overall development.

Implementation of the Convention on the Rights of the Child

The various member nations should undertake:

- To implement the Convention fully, to cooperate closely with the Committee on the Rights of the Child and to comply in a timely manner with their reporting obligations under the Convention, in accordance with the guidelines elaborated by the Committee, as well as to take into account the recommendations made by the Committee in the implementation of the provisions of the Convention.
- To withdraw reservations incompatible with the object and purpose of the Convention and to consider reviewing other reservations.
- To ensure that the rights set forth in the Convention are respected without discrimination of any kind based on the child's or his or her parents' or legal guardians' race, colour, sex, language, religion, political or other opinion, national, ethnic or social origin, property, disability, birth or other status.
- To ensure that the education of the child shall be carried out in accordance with articles 28 and 29 of the Convention and that the education be directed to the development of respect for human rights and fundamental freedoms, for the Charter of the United Nations and for different cultures and to the preparation of the child for responsible life in a free society, in a spirit of understanding, peace, tolerance, gender equality and friendship among peoples, ethnic, national and religious groups, and persons of indigenous origin.
- To ensure that every child alleged or recognized as having infringed the penal law is treated with dignity in accordance with the principles and relevant provisions of the Convention.

- The United Nations, within the scope of their respective mandates, as well as intergovernmental and non-governmental organizations, the media and the community at large, to make the principles and provisions of the Convention widely known to adults and children alike in accordance with article 42 of the Convention and to encourage training on the rights of the child for those involved in activities concerning children.

The Committee on the Rights of the Child Should Initiate to Request the Secretary-General

- To ensure the provision of appropriate staff and facilities from the United Nations regular budget
- To effective the performance of the functions of the Committee
- To provide temporary support given by the Plan of Action of the United Nations High Commissioner for Human Rights
- To strengthen the implementation of the Convention on the Rights of the Child
- Promote voluntary contributions
- To provide human resources to assist the Committee
- To increase the workload due to the near universalization of the Convention, and
- Requests the Office of the United Nations High Commissioner for Human Rights to brief Governments regularly on the implementation of the Plan of Action
- To encourage the Committee, in monitoring the implementation of the Convention on the Rights of the Child, and
- To continue to pay attention to the needs of children requiring special protection.

The Girl Child

To protect the girl child the nations should promote various activities in order:

- To take all necessary measures and to institute legal reforms to ensure the full and equal enjoyment by girls of all human rights and fundamental freedoms, and
- To take effective action against violations of those rights and freedoms
- All the international and non-governmental organizations, individually and collectively, to set goals and to develop and effectively implement gender-sensitive strategies to

address the rights and needs of children, in accordance with the Convention on the Rights of the Child

- Specific needs of the girl children should be addressed such as education, health and nutrition, and to eliminate harmful cultural attitudes and practices against girls
- To eliminate all forms of discrimination against girls and the root causes of son preference, which result in harmful and unethical practices
- Enacting and enforcing legislation protecting girls from violence, including female infanticide and prenatal sex selection, genital mutilation, incest, sexual abuse and exploitation, and by developing age-appropriate, safe and confidential programmes, and
- To promote medical, social and psychological support services to assist girls who are subjected to violence
- To intensify efforts to raise awareness of and to mobilize international and national public opinion concerning the harmful effects of female genital mutilation and other traditional or customary practices affecting the health of women and girls
- To promote public awareness through education, information dissemination and training, involving, among others, public opinion leaders, educators, religious leaders, medical practitioners, women's health and family planning organizations and the media, in order to achieve the total elimination of these practices, and
- To support women's organizations at the national and local levels that are working for the elimination of female genital mutilation and other harmful traditional or customary practices.

Prevention and Eradication of the Sale of Children and of their Sexual Exploitation and Abuse, Including Child Prostitution and Child Pornography

There is a greater need for all the nations:

(a) To develop urgently, implement and enforce measures to eliminate the sale, trafficking, abduction and sexual exploitation or abuse of children, including through child sex tourism, keeping in mind especially the provisions of the Convention on the Rights of the Child and the concrete

measures outlined in the Vienna Declaration and Programme of Action and in the Programmes of Action adopted by the Commission in 1992 and 1993, as well as in the Declaration and Agenda for Action of the World Congress against Commercial Sexual Exploitation of Children

(b) To participate constructively in the negotiations on an optional protocol to the Convention on the Rights of the Child on the sale of children, child prostitution and child pornography with the aim of an early agreement on the text, recalling the mandate given to the working group by the Commission in its resolution 1995/78 of 8 March 1995

(c) To criminalize effectively commercial and all other forms of sexual exploitation and sexual abuse of children, including child sex tourism, while ensuring that the child victims of such exploitation or abuse are not penalized for such practices

(d) to prosecute offenders, whether local or foreign, and to ensure that a person who exploits a child for sexual abuse in another country is prosecuted by competent national authorities, either in the offender's country of origin or in the destination country

(e) To step up cooperation and concerted action, at the national and international levels, by all relevant authorities and institutions, especially those charged with law enforcement, with a view to combating the existence of a market that encourages such criminal practices against children and dismantling national and international networks trafficking in children

(f) And relevant United Nations bodies and agencies to allocate resources for comprehensive and gender-sensitive programmes to rehabilitate physically and psychologically child victims of trafficking and of any form of sexual exploitation and abuse, and to promote their social reintegration

(g) To work towards strengthening partnerships between Governments, international organizations and all sectors of civil society, particularly non-governmental organizations, in order to achieve these objectives, and welcomes the efforts already made in this respect

(h) To cooperate with and assist the Special Rapporteur and to

furnish all information requested, including by inviting her to visit their countries.

With Regard to the Special Rapporteur on the Sale of Children, Child Prostitution and Child Pornography

- To renew the mandate of the Special Rapporteur for a further three years
- To request the Secretary-General to provide the Special Rapporteur with all necessary assistance, and
- To urge all relevant parts of the United Nations system to provide the Special Rapporteur with comprehensive reporting to make the full discharge of her mandate possible, and
- To enable her to submit an interim report to the General Assembly at its fifty-third session and a report to the Commission on Human Rights at its fifty-fifth session
- To invite the Special Rapporteur to continue to cooperate closely with other relevant United Nations organs and bodies, and
- To convey to the Commission her findings on developments and her recommendations on the broad range of issues under her mandate.

It has been decided that with regard to the question of a draft optional protocol to the Convention on the Rights of the Child on the sale of children, child prostitution and child pornography:

1. To request the Secretary-General to transmit the report of the working group on the question of a draft optional protocol to Governments, relevant specialized agencies, the Committee on the Rights of the Child, the relevant Special Rapporteur and intergovernmental and non-governmental organizations and to invite their comments, *inter alia* on the scope of the optional protocol, in time for circulation prior to the next session of the working group, and invites the Committee on the Rights of the Child to consider being represented and the Special Rapporteur to consider being present at the next session of the working group;
2. To request the working group to meet for a period of two weeks prior to the next session of the Commission and to redouble its efforts with the aim of finalizing the draft optional protocol by the tenth anniversary of the Convention

on the Rights of the Child and, to that end, encourages the Chairman of the working group to conduct broad informal consultations;

Protection of Children Affected by Armed Conflict

(*a*) To consider acceding to relevant international human rights and humanitarian law instruments, and urges them to implement those instruments to which they are parties.

(*b*) To participate constructively in the negotiations on an optional protocol to the Convention on the Rights of the Child on the involvement of children in armed conflicts with the aim of an early agreement on the text and of the adoption of a higher standard of protection than the present one contained in article 38 of the Convention, recalling that the original draft used as a basis for the negotiations was prepared by the Committee on the Rights of the Child.

(*c*) In accordance with the norms of international humanitarian law, to integrate in their military programmes, including those for peacekeeping, instruction on responsibilities towards the civilian population, particularly women and children.

(*d*) And relevant United Nations bodies, including the United Nations Voluntary Trust Fund for Assistance in Mine Clearance, to contribute on an ongoing basis to international mine-clearance efforts.

(*e*) Urges States to take stronger action to promote gender- and age-appropriate mine-awareness programmes and child-centered rehabilitation, thereby reducing the number and the plight of child victims, welcomes increased international efforts in various forums with respect to anti-personnel mines.

(*f*) Recognizes the positive effect on children of those efforts, and in this regard takes due note of the adoption of the Convention on the Prohibition of the Use, Stockpiling, Production and Transfer of Anti-personnel Mines and on Their Destruction, opened for signature in Ottawa in 1997, and its implementation by those States that become parties to it.

(*g*) The amended Protocol II on Prohibitions or Restrictions on the Use of Mines, Booby Traps and Other Devices to the Convention on Prohibitions or Restrictions on the Use of

Certain Conventional Weapons which May Be Deemed to Be Excessively Injurious or to Have Indiscriminate Effects, of 1996.

All States and Other Parties should Undertake the Following Mission with Regard to Armed Conflict

(a) To respect international humanitarian law, and in this regard calls upon States parties to respect fully the provisions of the Geneva Conventions of 12 August 1949 and the Additional Protocols thereto of 1977, while bearing in mind resolution 2 of the twenty-sixth International Conference of the Red Cross and Red Crescent of 1995 entitled "Protection of the civilian population in period of armed conflict", and to respect the provisions of the Convention on the Rights of the Child which accord children affected by armed conflict special protection and treatment.

(b) To end the use of children as soldiers and ensure their demobilization, and to implement effective measures for the rehabilitation and reintegration into society of child soldiers, child victims in cases of armed conflict or foreign occupation, including victims of landmines and all other weapons, and victims of gender-based violence, through adequate education and training, and invites the international community to assist in this endeavour.

(c) As well as United Nations agencies, to ensure access of humanitarian aid and assistance to children affected by armed conflict.

The United Nations Reaffirms

(a) That rape in the conduct of armed conflict constitutes a war crime and that under certain circumstances it constitutes a crime against humanity and an act of genocide, and calls upon all States to take all measures required for the protection of children and women from all acts of gender-based violence, including rape, sexual exploitation and forced pregnancy, and to strengthen mechanisms to investigate and prosecute perpetrators.

(b) That all humanitarian responses in situations of armed conflict should emphasize the special reproductive health needs of girls and women, including those that arise from pregnancy as a result of rape, sexual mutilation, childbirth

at an early age or infection with sexually transmitted diseases, as well as human immunodeficiency virus/ acquired immune deficiency syndrome, and access to family planning services.

(c) The importance of preventive measures such as early-warning systems, preventive diplomacy and education for peace to prevent conflicts and their negative impact on the enjoyment of the rights of the child, and urges Governments and the international community to promote sustainable human development.

(d) The importance of special attention for children in situations of armed conflict, in particular in the areas of health and nutrition, education and social reintegration, and in developing emergency and other humanitarian assistance policies and programmes, and of enhanced coordination and cooperation throughout the United Nations system to this end.

(e) Its support for the recommendations of the General Assembly and the International Conference of the Red Cross and Red Crescent concerning the assessment and monitoring of the consequences of sanctions upon children, as well as those concerning humanitarian relief.

It has been resolved with regard to the draft optional protocol to the Convention on the Rights of the Child on the involvement of children in armed conflicts:

(a) To request the Secretary-General to transmit the report of the working group on the draft optional protocol to Governments, relevant United Nations bodies and specialized agencies, the Committee on the Rights of the Child, the Special Representative on the impact of armed conflict on children, and intergovernmental and non-governmental organizations, and to invite their comments on the draft protocol contained in annex I negotiated in plenary, as well as on annex II containing the "Chairman's perception" based on informal consultations, in time for circulation prior to the next session of the working group, and invites the International Committee of the Red Cross and the Committee on the Rights of the Child to consider being represented and the Special Representative to consider being present at the next session of the working group.

(b) To encourage the Chairman of the working group to conduct broad informal consultations with the aim of promoting an early agreement on the optional protocol and to produce a report thereon by the end of 1998 including, if possible, recommendations and/or ideas on the best way for the formal negotiations to proceed.

(c) To request the working group to meet in early 1999, primarily to consider the Chairman's report on the status of the informal consultations, which should be available well in advance, and to report to the Commission on Human Rights at its fifty-fifth session.

(d) To request the Secretary-General to give the necessary support to the working group to meet for a maximum of two weeks, if the working group decides that an agreement on the draft optional protocol is possible at that session.

(e) To reaffirm the aim of finalizing the draft optional protocol by the tenth anniversary of the Convention on the Rights of the Child.

It decides, with regard to the Special Representative of the Secretary-General on the impact of armed conflict on children.

- to recommend that the Secretary-General ensure that the necessary support is made available to the Special Representative for the effective performance of his mandate.
- to encourage the United Nations Children s Fund, the Office of the United Nations High Commissioner for Refugees and the Office of the United Nations High Commissioner for Human Rights.
- to provide support to the Special Representative, and to call upon other institutions and States to provide voluntary contributions for that purpose.
- to request the Secretary-General, in cooperation with States, international organizations and relevant non-governmental organizations, to consider modalities for organizing regional training programmes for members of the armed forces relating to the protection of children and women during armed conflicts.

Protection of Refugee and Internally Displaced Children

All States shall urgently plan programmes:

(a) To protect refugee and internally displaced children, through policies for their care, well-being and development, in such areas as health, education and psychosocial rehabilitation, with the necessary international cooperation, in particular with the Office of the United Nations High Commissioner for Refugees, the United Nations Children's Fund and the International Committee of the Red Cross, in accordance with their obligations under the Convention on the Rights of the Child and taking into account the 1994 guidelines on protection and care of refugee children of the Office of the United Nations High Commissioner for Refugees and the Conclusion on refugee children and adolescents.

(b) To ensure the early identification and registration of unaccompanied refugee and internally displaced children, to give priority to programmes for family tracing and reunification, and to continue monitoring the care arrangements for unaccompanied refugee and internally displaced children, taking into account the 1997 guidelines on policies and procedures in dealing with unaccompanied children seeking asylum of the Office of the United Nations High Commissioner for Refugees.

(c) To recognize that refugee and internally displaced children are particularly exposed to the risks of injury, exploitation and death in connection with armed conflicts, such as being forcibly recruited or subjected to sexual violence, abuse or exploitation, stressing the special vulnerability of households headed by children, and calls upon Governments and United Nations bodies and organizations to give those situations urgent attention, enhancing protection and assistance mechanisms, with the participation of women and youth in the design, delivery and monitoring of measures to protect them.

Elimination of the Exploitation of Child Labour

All the member nations should expedite various actions and programmes that have not yet done so to consider ratifying the conventions of the International Labour Organization relating to child labour, in particular the Forced Labour Convention, 1930 (Convention No. 29) and the Minimum Age Convention, 1973 (Convention No. 138), and those States that are parties to those conventions to implement them effectively, and urges all States, as a matter of priority:

- To eliminate all extreme forms of child labour such as forced labour, bonded labour and other forms of slavery.
- To eliminate progressively and effectively all forms of child labour contrary to accepted international standards, starting with its most grave and intolerable forms, by implementing national action plans with specific target dates, as well as supporting the forthcoming negotiations at the International Labour Organization for the early finalization of a future instrument aimed at eradicating the most intolerable forms of child labour.
- To recognize the right to education by making primary education compulsory and ensuring that all children have access to free and relevant primary education as a key strategy to prevent child labour, as well as making secondary education generally available and accessible to all, and in particular by the progressive introduction of free education.
- Systematically to assess and examine, in close cooperation with international organizations such as the International Labour Organization and the United Nations Children's Fund, the magnitude, nature and causes of the exploitation of child labour.
- To develop and implement strategies for combating such practices, giving special attention to specific dangers faced by girls.
- To strengthen international cooperation and coordination, through the United Nations programme of advisory services in the field of human rights, the International Programme on the Elimination of Child Labour of the International Labour Organization; and
- To promote various activities of the United Nations Children's Fund, as a means of assisting Governments in preventing and combating violations of the rights of the child, in particular the exploitation of child labour.

The Plight of Children Working and/or Living on the Street

- All States, while expressing grave concern at the large number of children working and/or living on the street and at the continued growth in incidents and reports worldwide of such children being involved in and affected by serious crime, drug trafficking and abuse, violence and sexual exploitation, including through prostitution, to continue actively to seek comprehensive solutions to the problems of children working and/or living on the street.

- Emphasizing that strict compliance with obligations under relevant international human rights instruments, including the Convention on the Rights of the Child, constitutes a significant step towards solving the problems of children working and/or living on the street.
- All States to ensure the reintegration of children working and/or living on the street into society and to provide, adequate nutrition, shelter, health care and education, taking into account that such children are particularly vulnerable to all forms of violence, abuse, exploitation and neglect.
- Encourages States to take the situation of children working and/or living on the street fully into account in preparing their reports to the Committee on the Rights of the Child, and
- Requests the Committee and other relevant treaty monitoring bodies, within their existing mandates, to give due attention to the question of children working and/or living on the street.
- All States to guarantee respect for all human rights and fundamental freedoms, particularly the right to life, and to take urgent and effective measures to prevent the killing of children working and/or living on the street and to combat torture and violence against them, and
- To ensure that legal and juridical processes respect children's rights in order to protect them against arbitrary deprivation of liberty, maltreatment or abuse, and
- The international community to support, through effective international cooperation, the efforts of States to improve the situation of children in need of special protection measures, including in urban settlements.

Children with Disabilities

The attention given by the Committee on the Rights of the Child, when considering the reports of States parties to the Convention on the Rights of the Child, to the subject of the rights of children with physical or mental disabilities to enjoy their lives with dignity and to their individual development and social integration, as well as the general debate on this issue.

The sixteenth session of the Committee in 1997, focused on the rights to life and development, self-representation and full participation and the right to an inclusive education, with the aim of preparing recommendations for the effective implementation of the Convention, and invites the Committee to continue its task in cooperation with the representatives of the relevant United Nations bodies and organizations, non-governmental organizations and the Special Rapporteur on disability of the Commission for Social Development.

All States parties to adopt, in accordance with article 23 of the Convention on the Rights of the Child, all necessary measures to ensure the full enjoyment in equal conditions of all human rights and fundamental freedoms by children with disabilities, especially ensuring the effective access of such children to education and health services, to develop and implement legislation prohibiting discrimination against these children, and to include these measures in their reports to the Committee on the Rights of the Child.

Migration and Trafficking

The governments (countries) have been slow to adapt migration; the result is burgeoning of illegal immigration, social tension, discrimination, loss of faith in government, and the empowerment of criminal networks. Earlier eras witnessed migration on a similar scale. At the turn of the 20th century, approximately three per cent of world's population was on the move. A hundred years later, the United Nations estimates that there are 191 million international migrants, a roughly similar ratio.

As we enter into the new age of mobility, people will move across borders in ever-greater numbers. In their pursuit of opportunity and a better life, they have the potential to chip away at the vast inequalities that characterize our time—and accelerate progress throughout the developing world. We cannot hide from the fact that migration can also have negative consequences. The Global Forum provides an opportunity to address these problems in a comprehensive and proactive way so that the benefits from migration are fully realized both in developing and industrial countries (Hindu 11th July 2007).

Magnitude

The magnitude and the velocity of trafficking increases with increasing poverty and unemployment prevalent in places and countries such as Nepal, Bangladesh, Pakistan etc., where the worth and dignity of the individual is at its lowest. This heinous crime, which transports people from the above mentioned countries for the purposes of domestic servitude, unlawful industrial and agricultural work, illegal adoption, forced begging and the sex industry, denies their victims' dignity, often subjecting them to torture and abuse (Ali, 2005).

Recent Growth in Trafficking

Some of the major causative actors to the recent increase in trafficking of women and girls have been identified by Sanghera (1991). While elements of some these factors existed previously as well, this study has revealed that there is a marked intensification in the above trends contributing thus to the growing magnitude of trafficking in and from the region. These factors are:

- The feminisation of poverty;
- The break down of traditional social and economic structures and the atomization of household members into units of labour;
- Increasing insecurity of food and livelihood for a vast majority of the marginalised population in the region;
- The rapidly growing need to migrate for work ;
- Growth in the feminisation of migration due to women bearing greater economic burden of the household;
- Increasing segmentation and diversification of the market on account of globalisation and an expansion in the market demand for those services which require women's and children's labour;
- An increased demand for cheap, vulnerable and easily exploitable categories of labour such as that of women and children due to heightened competition and falling rate of profit in the global market;
- An increase in unregulated, invisible and underground sites of work in the informal sector of the economy, and hence increased difficulty in monitoring human rights violations, enforcing labour standards or targeting violence and abuse;

- Recognition of the tremendous increase in the margin of profits accruing from the trade in women and children;
- A growth in the activity of traffickers and the entry and consolidation of organised crime syndicates in the arena of trafficking of women and children;
- A general increase in the level of corruption among agencies responsible for enforcing law and order, as well as a growing nexus between organised crime and certain segments of law enforcement;
- Rampant rise in consumerism;
- Increased criminalisation and brutalisation of society and intensification of crimes against women and children such as rape, acid attacks and battery;
- Rapid growth in modern transport, technology and communications.

In regards to the purposes for which women and children in the region are trafficked, the following were identified by the study:

- prostitution/sex work
- forced marriage
- domestic work
- agricultural labour
- construction work
- carpet industry,
- garment industry
- work in the formal and informal sectors
- forced begging
- camel jockeying
- adoption trade
- organ harvesting

Most of these sites have already been identified by previous studies though it does appear that trafficking into forced begging, forced marriage and invisible work ghettos in the informal sector has escalated. The sex industry continues to dominate as far as trafficking of women and girls is concerned, and there appears to be a general consensus that increasingly younger girls are being plugged into the sex industry. However, it is to be noted that this 'conclusion' is not based on any rigorous research of the sex industry in South Asia but emerges primarily out of anecdotal evidence and tentative observation.

Changing Trends in Trafficking

With regards to the overall trends in trafficking of women and children in the selected South Asian countries the following tentative observations may be made on basis of the assessment (Sanghera, 1991):

- There is an increase in the trafficking of women and children alongside an increase in illegal and undocumented migration within the region.
- There is an increase in trafficking from countries of South Asia to other regions and countries of the world including the Gulf states, Southeast Asia, Hongkong, Europe and North America.
- Increasingly fewer victims of trafficking are in fact being kidnapped or abducted; an overwhelming majority is actually led away under deception and/or false promises and is therefore active participants in their own trafficking during the first leg of the process[1] which includes recruitment and transportation.
- The routes, methods and activities of traffickers are becoming increasingly more organised and there is a greater penetration of organized crime syndicates in the trade and trafficking of women and children within and from the region.

Increased Vulnerability of Women and Girls

The causes of this gender-based vulnerability are not new but an intensification has been reported by many observers in the course of this study. The growing vulnerability of women and girls is associated to an growth of the following phenomenon:

- The status o serious insecurity for food and livelihood
- Areas facing a serious political crisis or armed conflict
- Regions suffering from natural disasters or environmental crises
- Resulting in *en masse* displacement and dispossession of local populations
- Minimum or lack of education and income generating skills,
- Status of Widowed, divorced or abandoned
- Victims of abuse and violence
- Disintegrated support systems
- Broken families due to death, disease, displacement or migration

- Families are facing a severe financial crisis such as loss of income, serious illness
- Problem of indebtedness

These are all women and girls who would like to improve their living conditions and that of their families. It is important to note that in all of the above instances the vulnerability of women and girls is connected to deepening crises at their home base on the one hand and the subsequent acute need to find alternate and viable means of livelihood on the other.

Statistics

There is a greater need for creation of a reliable database at an all-India level as there is a wide gap observed between the official data and data given by other agencies such as NGO and research organizations due to the clandestine nature of trafficking.

It is not an easy job to collect data about the trafficked children. Although trafficking is not a new issue, trafficking persons are almost invisible to the eye of the statistician. Moreover global reliable statistics are impossible to complete, it is estimated that trafficking affects about 1.2 million children each year and it has reached alarming highest in recent years as observed by various researchers. Everyday children are trafficked across the country and through out South Asia, with India being the Source, Transit and Destination points. India being both a consumer and a supplier, there is both internal and external movement children within the country and across borders (CACT, 2006).

TRAFFICKING - INTERNATIONAL OVERVIEW

Trafficking – Southasian Response

Most of the South Asian region countries which are affected by the problem of trafficking have made a commitment at a national level to combat the trafficking of women and children.

Thus, India, Nepal, Bangladesh, Pakistan and Sri Lanka have each formulated some policy or plan of action to address this problem. Of these, Nepal, Bangladesh and India are perhaps the most proactive in attempting to combat this problem. It does need to be stressed that countries of origin in particular, such as Nepal and Bangladesh have exhibited notable commitment in the very recent past in this field.

To varying extents, most countries of the region have ratified the relevant international Conventions such as:

- UN Convention on the Rights of the Child (1989)
- The Convention on the Elimination of all Forms of Discrimination Against Women (CEDAW)
- The Convention for the Suppression of Traffic in Persons and of the Exploitation of the Prostitution of Others (1949)
- The ILO Conventions No. 29 on Forced Labour (1930), and
- No. 138 on Elimination of Child labour (1973). In addition,
- The Fourth UN Conference on Women in Beijing (1995)
- The World Congress Against Commercial Sexual Exploitation in Stockholm (1996), and
- Two International Conferences on Child Labour in Amsterdam and Oslo (1997).

These instruments have provided avenues and impetus to the South Asian states to make good their commitment to promote the human rights of the children and women on whose behalf they have become signatories to these international conventions.

Trafficking from neighboring countries contributes for only 10 per cent of coerced migration to India. Among this portion approximately 2.17 per cent are from Bangladesh and 2.6 per cent from Nepal. The share of inter-state trafficking is estimated at 89 per cent (ADB, 2002). Studies by Rozario (1988), Ganthia (1999), SAP (2001) and Haq (2000) endow with details about the internal trafficking rotes in India and the location of interstate flesh trade triangles.

Bangladesh

Bangladesh has a 4,156 Km border with 30 districts on the Indian side. India has twenty official checkpoints manned by the Border Security Force. Being few and widely dispersed, they are ineffective in maintaining vigilance over movements across the border. Crossing the border between Bangladesh and West Bengal is a daily routine for many. Illegal entries by traffickers are a matter of common knowledge and it is a generally accepted idea that they are protected (Nair, 2005). A number of businesses have developed to facilitate these cross-border movements and each trip may cost no more than Rs. 50 per person (ADB, 2002). A well organized bride system also helps people to cross over the flat terrain (BNWLA, 1998). Further, a multiple passport system, 'facilitates easy entry to Bangladeshi girls into Kolkata brothels and a close nexus exists between traffickers and border village communities (DWCD, 1996).

Nepal

The Indo-Nepal is long and porous with only 14 legal entry points along the entire stretch which leads to extensive illegal cross-border movements. Under the 1950 Treaty with India, citizens of each country are guaranteed equal treatment, including the same privileges in the matter of residence, participation in trade and commerce. This means in practice that there is no immigration control for Nepalese traveling or migrating to India and hence no records are maintained (ADB, 2002). The ADB study on Nepal lists the districts through which this movement takes place and identifies the entry and exit points as well as the major border regions used by traffickers between Nepal and India.

The SAARC Convention on Trafficking

In the last five years there have been some important steps taken to address the issue at a regional level. Presently, certain international conventions are being invoked to address the rights of children and their labour in hazardous sectors within the region; many of these sectors include sites to which girls and children are trafficked. At the same time, regional instruments are being put in place (the Rawalpindi Resolution of 1996 and the SAARC Draft Convention of Trafficking of Women and Children) to specifically address the problem of trafficking.

Heads of states of South Asian countries have committed to addressing the problem of trafficking with the objective of eliminating it within the near future. This commitment was first reflected in the 1997 SAARC Summit in Male, Maldives, through a declaration which stated:

> Expressing grave concern at the trafficking of women and children within and between countries, the Heads of State or Government pledged to coordinate their efforts and take effective measures to address this problem. They decided that this should include simplification of repatriation procedures for victims of trafficking. They also decided that the feasibility of establishing a Regional Convention on Combating the Crime of Trafficking in Women and Children for Prostitution be examined by the relevant Technical Committee.

Upon input and feedback from concerned stakeholders and NGOs the SAARC Draft Convention on Trafficking was further discussed at the Colombo SAARC Summit in 1998. It is expected that the Draft Convention may be finalised at the upcoming SAARC Summit. The process of input into the SAARC Convention continues in an active and varied manner. At least three major separate platforms have been discussing the Draft Convention and suggesting changes. The first one has been spearheaded by the Resistance Network currently sponsored by UBINIG in Bangladesh. Several member organisations of this network met in August 1999 to provide further input into the Convention and discuss lobbying strategies to push for an acceptance of the recommendations.

The second forum is not an organised network but was put together to specifically address some of the glaring lacunae in the SAARC Draft Convention. This forum, represented by NGOs, Lawyers, policy makers, social workers and concerned individuals has had two meetings in the recent months in Goa and Delhi repsectively. The third initiative to affect changes to the Draft Convention was jointly spearheaded by UNIFEM and the office of the UN Special Rapporteur on Violence Against Women, Ms. Radhika Coomaraswamy. Three experts met in Colombo on July this year to review the Draft and suggest changes.

Notwithstanding minor differences in suggested language and logistics, all of the three initiatives have come up with the same major recommendations in their separate meetings:

- That the title of the SAARC Convention be expanded to cover trafficking not only for the purpose of prostitution but for other purposes as well.
- That a distinction be made between women and children in view of the fact that as adults citizens the agency of women to voluntarily work in certain industries and work sites such as prostitution be recognized.
- Commercial sex work per se is tantamount to abuse for children and minors.
- That women's preference, choice and autonomy be taken into account in formulating policies and programmes for rescue, repatriation and reintegration.

In addition to the above key suggestions for change, guidelines for implementation and enforcement of the clauses contained within the Convention as well as a recommended preamble to the Convention have been formulated by the three groups. One of the forums suggested that the title be gender neutral and read as 'Trafficking of Persons' instead of 'Women and Children'. The Resistance Network plans to hold a parallel Peoples' SAARC Forum at the time of the upcoming SAARC Summit to lobby for the suggested changes as well as to raise public awareness of trafficking and related issues of security of food and livelihoods within the region.

In addition to the above declaration which directly addresses the issue of trafficking, the SAARC body has also resolved to abolish all child labour by the year 2010 and hazardous aspects of child labour by the year 2000; prostitution has been identified as hazardous work for minors. Furthermore, the Beijing Platform of Action of the Fourth World Conference on Women (1995), which has been supported by all the SAARC countries addresses the issue of trafficking by making a strong plea for stepping up international and regional cooperation for concerted action by all parties and agencies, and for allocation of adequate resources to address the issue.

The international significance of drafting of a SAARC Convention of Trafficking at the behest of the South Asian States cannot be underestimated. Through this initiative the SAARC region has undertaken a very crucial first step globally, to come up with a regional response on the trafficking of women and children. Credit for his is also due to the vibrant and active lobbying on the part of several NGOs and women's organisations within the region and the support provided to this initiative by INGOs and the UN agencies.

However, as it presently stands, the SAARC Convention on Trafficking has some major flaws, and if the suggested changes mentioned above are not incorporated then the new regional Convention may not be particularly effective in addressing the problem of trafficking. Therefore, there is a pressing need to intervene in the process of finalisation of the SAARC Convention via effective lobbying strategies, and to advocate for the recommended changes. These recommendations are commensurate as well with the changes being suggested to the Protocol on Trafficking of Women and Children which is subsumed under the proposed new draft of the UN Convention on Organised Crime.

MAGNITUDE OF TRAFFICKING – INTERNATIONAL LEVEL

The nature of the operation is clandestine that the extent of the phenomenon is complex to calculate and it is equally tricky to gather data on it. The trade is secretive, the women are silenced, the trafficker's are dangerous and not many agencies are counting (Haughes, 2000). Among the most quoted figures are the United Nations estimates that 4 million people a year are traded against their will to work in some form of slavery, many of them children and that in the last 30 years , trafficking in women and children for sexual exploitation in Asia alone has victimized more than 30 million people.

A world wide survey conducted by US based organization that trafficked people worldwide : South-East Asia, 2,25,

S. No.	*Region*	*Total Trafficked*
1.	South-East Asia	2,25,000
2.	South Asia	15,000
3.	USSR (Former)	1,00,000
4.	East Europe	75,000
5.	Latin America	10,000
6.	Africa	500 million

Source: Congressional Research Service CRS, 2001.

The International Labour Organisation conducted a study in 2002 estimated that children are engaged in various forms of activities worldwide and reported that in Trafficking there are 1.2 million are in the prey; in forced and boded labour there are 5.7 million children are placed, in armed conflict 0.3 million children, prostitution and pornography 1.8 million and illicit activities there are 0.6 million children are positioned. It is alarming to note that every year one to two million people are trafficked globally and among them half a million are from South and South East Asia (Eichenberger, 2002).

INTERNATIONAL LABOUR ORGANISATION AND THE ISSUE OF CHILD LABOUR

Introduction

It is the beginning of the 1990s, the issue of child labour has become the spotlight which gained grave interest, in developing as well as in developed countries. As a result, practical action against child labour in the form of policies, programmes and projects has been building up on an unprecedented scale. There are various factors have contributed to this development.

First, an often-felt perception that the exploitation of child labour has become more serious and could well continue to do so in several parts of the world.

Second, a concern that, by employing children at an age and in conditions that do not conform to universally accepted standards, some countries might gain a comparative advantage in international trade over those which more strictly apply such standards.

Lastly, a stronger commitment to the cause of human rights, and the rights of children in particular, by civil society in many countries gained impetus.

There are various Players involved in the struggle against child labour has thus gained momentum and a wide variety of actors including governments, NGOs, trade unions, employers' organizations, and international organizations, to name just a few. Important lessons can be learned, especially in the framework of the ILO's International Programme on the Elimination of Child Labour (IPEC). The experience gained can provide valuable guidelines for policy formulation and the development of programmes and projects targeting child labour particularly in its most extreme forms.

Policy Development

Until recently, child labour was viewed in many countries with a sense of apathy. Largely perceived as a natural by-product of poverty, child labour was rarely a direct focus of government policies. This attitude has largely changed over the last few years and many countries have developed explicit policies and accompanying programmes of action dealing with the problem of child labour.

There is sometimes a tendency to confuse the terms, policies, programmes and projects. They are, of course, closely linked but it is important to define them clearly. A policy on child labour is a public commitment to work towards the elimination of child labour, setting out objectives and priorities and designating the authorities and institutions responsible for implementation. Policies in turn are implemented through programmes consisting of a comprehensive and coherent set of interventions. Projects, finally, constitute the building blocks of programmes. They are limited in scope and time and usually focus on a very specific objective and target group.

The Need for a National Child Labour Policy

The development of a concrete national policy on child labour is important mainly for two reasons. First, it demonstrates a clear commitment of government and society to attack the child labour problem in a systematic way. Second, it provides a coherent framework and sense of direction for the various actors and programmes and projects in the field. A clear national policy against the exploitation of children, reflected in both legislation and administrative regulations as appropriate, is the fundamental basis and point of departure for any action on child labour.

Several countries, for example Bangladesh, Brazil, India, Indonesia, Nepal, the Philippines, Tanzania, Thailand and Turkey, have already adopted national policies and programmes of action.

India was one of the first, formulating a national policy on child labour more than 10 years ago. Others have done so in the last few years.

A national policy on child labour can stand on its own or be part of a more comprehensive policy framework setting forth development or economic benchmarks to be achieved. Brazil, for example, derived its child labour policy from a comprehensive statute on Children and Adolescents (ECA), enacted in 1990, which sets out a catalogue of child rights based on a constitutional article. Indonesia has included child labour as an issue in its latest five-year development plan for 1991-99 (Repelita VI)

The development of such a policy is first and foremost the responsibility of government. However, in order to be an effective guide for action, it has to take into account the experiences and positions of a wide range of actors, such as workers' and employers' and their organizations and other non-governmental organizations.

Policy Elements

The following are the elements commonly found in any National policy and programme of action against child labour

- Definition of national objectives regarding child labour
- Description of the nature and context of the problem
- Identification and description of the priority target groups
- Description of the intervention approaches to be used
- Designation or creation of an institutional authority.

Defining National Objectives. Clarity about the goals to be achieved is essential to any policy. Most national policies affirm the objective to, *(i)* eliminate child labour, and *(ii)* actively work towards this end by means of prevention, removal and rehabilitation. Policy objectives can, of course, only gain relevance if based on appropriate legislation. In a number of countries, the establishment or refinement of child labour and minimum age laws therefore went hand in hand with the formulation of national child policies. India, for example, defined its national policy in the same year (1986) it formulated a comprehensive Child Labour (Prohibition and Regulation) Act which regulates the minimum age for admission to employment in specified sectors and occupations. In other cases, policy moves preceded legislative activities. In the Philippines, for example, legislation was reviewed after the plan of action on working children (1987) called for a strengthening of child labour laws.

Describing the Nature and Context of the Problem. The availability of timely and reliable data on the extent of child labour by region, sector, gender, etc. is an essential requisite for this. In order to assist countries in these often difficult and time-consuming tasks, the ILO has established two specific data collection instruments:

(i) a statistical survey methodology on child labour, and
(ii) a rapid assessment technique.

The survey methodology was developed to obtain a comprehensive set of statistics on the child labour situation in a country and generate data on specific core variables. It was first tested in India, Indonesia, Senegal and Ghana and has subsequently been successfully used in other Asian and African countries. The rapid assessment technique was designed to obtain relatively quickly a stock of qualitative and quantitative information with a view to develop action programmes. Information derived from this process could be at the basis of the government's policy statement on the problems to be tackled. It will in turn determine the approaches and instruments to be used in practical action programmes and projects.

Identifying and Describing Priority Target Groups. An important step in elaborating a national child labour policy is to identify potential target groups and to indicate priorities among them. While the total elimination of child labour should be the overall goal, it makes economic sense to concentrate scarce resources on the most extreme forms of child labour first.

These will, of course, vary from country to country, but they might include debt bondage or other slavery-like arrangements, prostitution and trafficking of children, and work under hazardous or otherwise abusive conditions which seriously endanger the physical and psychological development of a child. Box 1 gives a brief overview of the different priority areas for action in selected countries, as stated in national plans.

Choosing and Describing the Intervention Approaches to be Used. As the following sections show, single-issue approaches and narrowly focused projects seldom achieve a sizeable effect if not embedded in a larger, multi pronged strategy, encompassing the development of appropriate legislation and its enforcement, and action in such areas income-generation and employment promotion, education, welfare and advocacy of children's rights.

Having set clear priorities, the national policy and programme of action should encompass action that prevents child labour, interim measures that seek to protect children who are working and activities aimed at removing children from dangerous work, combined with rehabilitation efforts. The distinction between these fields of action can be blurred sometimes and some activities may follow objectives which aim, for example, to rehabilitate as well as prevent. In general, however, prevention, removal, rehabilitation and protection will include the following action:

Prevention: Action that halts children taking up specified types of work before reaching a certain age, such as identifying the geographical areas, social groups or situations from which a consistent flow of these children tends to come, identifying the push and pull-factors and systematically addressing both through activities with a long-term impact.

Removal: Action that immediately, or through phases, takes children out of dangerous situations, such as releasing them from bonded labour, removing them from a hazardous workplace and providing them with shelter and immediate care in specifically established reception centres.

Rehabilitation: Action that puts children, who have suffered from the work performed, back on their normal development path. This may include medical care, counselling and special educational and vocational preparation programmes. Rehabilitation efforts should always lead to the provision of a meaningful alternative activity, usually the attendance of school.

Protection: Action that is undertaken at the workplace to reduce or eliminate the impact of hazards while keeping the children at work.

IPEC experience suggests that it is easier and less expensive to prevent child labour than to withdraw children from work and rehabilitate them. This applies in particular to children working in hazardous conditions. They and their workplaces are often hidden from public view and attention. Many rehabilitation efforts thus naturally focus on groups of child workers easier to reach and thereby miss out on the worst forms. Where rehabilitation is difficult and costly because of a large array of obstacles, preventive action becomes even more important. National plans should take account of that and emphasize prevention.

Designating the Actors. Most initiatives against child labour today still come from non-governmental organizations. However, the burden of the campaign against child labour is far too heavy for NGOs to carry alone. Broader social mobilization is required. Government and the social partners need to contribute their share.

Three fundamental types of action against child labour can be provided only by the *government*: *(i)* child labour legislation and appropriate enforcement mechanisms; *(ii)* a national child labour policy that sets public priorities and reaches out to engage all the important social actors; and *(iii)* a publicly funded system of basic education that ensures universal attendance and quality schooling. Education is perhaps the most powerful of all tools against child labour and ways will have to be found how to coordinate effectively a national child labour policy and educational policies.

Workers' organizations are the logical leaders for discovering and denouncing child labour abuses at the local, national and international levels. They can become credible advocates for the protection of children against workplace exploitation by documenting concrete cases of child labour and its effects on the children involved.

Trade unions are also in a good position to communicate to large numbers of adult workers and their families the importance of promoting the education of their children, of protecting them against work hazards and of keeping them as much as possible from premature engagement in the labour market. Notable amongst the various anti child labour activities workers' organizations and national and international trade union federations have carried out over the last few years are surveys on child labour, awareness campaigns, the provision of schooling for children, and collective agreements on child labour.

Employers and their organizations also have an indispensable role to play in the fight against child labour. Obviously, the best way for individual enterprises to contribute in this field is to adhere strictly to the minimum age provisions of national labour laws and regulations. Where the employment of children is not legally proscribed, they can ensure, in particular, that child workers are kept away from any dangerous substance or machinery and that their working hours and schedules do not hinder or affect school attendance and performance. In a number of countries employers' organizations at the national and international level have assisted their members in these important tasks, especially by raising awareness of the human, economic and social costs of child labour.

There are many other reasons for employers and their organizations to be interested in child labour issues. Child labour degrades the human capital necessary to achieve sustainable economic development. Former child workers, especially those who have not benefitted from any schooling and have been working for years in hazardous conditions, can hardly become productive adults.

If child labour is allowed to continue today, badly needed skills might be in short supply tomorrow. Moreover, the use of child labour can ruin a company's reputation. This is especially true in the case of large, often multinational enterprises, where child labour, for example in subcontracting arrangements, can damage a carefully built-up brand image from one day to the next and have strong repercussions on profit and stock value.

Other non-governmental organizations (NGOs) at the local, regional, national or international levels have an equally decisive role to play, particularly when it comes to assisting specific target groups. In many countries NGOs have been at the forefront in the struggle against child labour, often operating a wide range of direct support programmes at the community and the local levels. Close proximity to, and insider knowledge of target groups, have allowed them in many instances better than any other group to develop and conduct concrete activities which meet the need of working children and their families.

Independence and creativity can be other hallmarks of NGOs involved in child labour issues. NGOs have often played a crucial role in discovering and publicizing concrete cases of abusive child labour and in denouncing the shortcomings in government action, in particular failure to enforce relevant laws and regulations. Some NGOs, however, are hindered by their smallness and lack of managerial skills. Sometimes they are only informal groups built on the vision and drive of a single individual. Care has therefore to be taken not to overburden them and to ensure that managerial capacities are commensurate with the tasks entrusted to them.

In addition to the above-mentioned groups, there are, of course, other groups and institutions which have an important role to play in the struggle against child labour. Their weight and influence will vary between countries but in general they may include *parliamentarians, universities* and *research institutes, teachers, religious leaders* and the *media*. Particularly the media have often played a pivotal role in uncovering child labour and bringing it to the forefront of national and international attention.

Creating the Necessary Institutional Capacity. Child labour issues cut across the work of numerous governmental and non-governmental agencies and organizations. Responsibility for work on child labour is often diffuse. Defining and implementing a national policy against child labour thus requires the creation of an institutional mechanism within the government apparatus with responsibility for:

- Setting priorities in close partnership with the representative organizations of employers and workers and other relevant Groups of civil society.
- Promoting and coordinating the activities of various ministries and other governmental institutions concerned with child labour.
- Encouraging the participation of the private sector and ensuring that measures taken by the public and private sectors complement each other, and
- Supporting practical action in the form of programmes and projects against child labour.

Over the last few years, broad-based advisory bodies or national task forces on child labour have been established in a number of countries where child labour has been recognized as a priority policy issue. In IPEC-participating countries, institutional capacity has been built up in the form of National Steering Committees (NSCs) which have been created as independent bodies, mostly under the Ministry of Labour. Including a broad range of governmental and non-governmental agencies and organizations, the NSCs have proved to be effective vehicles for the development and implementation of coherent strategies on child labour. In many cases, NSCs have become official national coordinating bodies for child labour.

Projects and Programmes for Development

Over the last few decades, enormous projects against child labour have been carried out, in all parts of the world. Important lessons could be derived out of these experiences. The following sections concentrate on some of the worst forms of child labour, the problems faced and the approaches used.

Child Labour in Hazardous Industries and Occupations

Though defining which work or occupation is hazardous is not an easy task; The ILO Minimum Age Convention No.138 stipulates that the minimum age for admission to employment or work which may jeopardize the health, safety and morals of young persons should not be less than 18 years (or 16 in case full protection can be ensured and adequate instruction be given). It furthermore requires ratifying countries to determine what kinds of work exactly fall into this category.

Almost all countries have now incorporated the principle of prohibition of child work in hazardous conditions and activities in their national legislation, or defined the conditions under which children may work. In some countries the definition of hazardous work is extremely restricted. For example, it may be confined to underground work, work in industrial painting or work involving the use of white lead and lead sulphur. In other countries the scope is somewhat broader. It may cover, for example, various occupations in transport, industrial workshops, factories and plantations.

Most of the legislations and regulations of various countries prohibit children working in industries and other related activities such as:

- underground or underwater work
- work on construction sites
- work involving machinery in motion
- work involving the manufacture, preparation or handling of chemicals or other hazardous substances
- work in places of public entertainment, such as bars and nightclubs.

Work-related Hazards and Risks

Taking a closer look at the dangers many child workers may face, one can generally distinguish between physical and psychosocial work hazards. Physical work hazards are those which seriously endanger the normal child's health and normal physical development or even place children's lives in immediate peril. Various characteristics of the work performed can be at the source of these dangers. The most obvious ones are contact with or use of chemicals or other hazardous substances or work processes which are intrinsically dangerous because of the likelihood of accidents, injury or disease.

In many instances, it is not one hazard but a combination of hazards which make a specific work situation dangerous to children. In glass-making, for example, one can identify a whole range of occupation-specific hazards such as high temperatures, open flames or exposure to dust.

In addition to hazards related to the production process of certain goods or services, many enterprises, particularly but not exclusively in the informal sector, expose their workers to general hazards arising out of poor working conditions or a degraded working environment. These could include lack of sanitation, poor lighting, loud noise, or excessive working hours. Table 1(Annex 1) provides an overview of some examples of child labour in hazardous occupations and its possible consequences.

Hazards also arise from the context in which children have to work. Child labour may have serious non-physical consequences due to psychosocial hazards, especially when it is burdensome or abusive. Some children, for example, are vulnerable because of their work situation and not so much because of the nature of their occupation. Divorced from natural links to their family, often totally dependent on their employers, deprived of education and play and largely invisible to the outside world, many child workers are seriously stunned in their social and psychological development.

It is, by now, well known that work hazards that effect adults affect children even more seriously. As children are still in the process of growing up their normal development can be severely endangered by conditions that might not constitute such a peril to adults. Children suffer more from exposure to hazardous substances because of their weight and body size and insufficiently developed mechanisms for detoxication. Young workers also have a lower heat-tolerance and are more susceptible to noise-induced hearing loss. Due to their more limited working capacity, children are, in general, more prone than adult's to occupational injuries due to inattention, fatigue, poor judgment and lesser knowledge.

Various interventions at different levels are needed in order to effectively tackle the problem of child labour in hazardous occupations and industries. Roughly speaking, most of the activities can be grouped in two categories, namely the preventive approach and the rehabilitative approach.

Prevention Measures

Prevention is a cornerstone of virtually all country programmes working towards the elimination of child labour, whether it is of a hazardous nature or not. It usually takes a long-term perspective and includes policies, laws and programmes that combat poverty, provide basic services, develop human resources, administer justice and regulate the behaviour of business and industry with a view to stamp out child labour. Sustainable and long-term results will be achieved only when new generations of children are effectively prevented from entering hazardous occupations. Investment in prevention has proven to be the most economical method in the long run.

There are several essential steps in protecting children from work hazards. First and foremost it is important to identify dangerous work and the children currently or potentially engaged in it. Government and the general public have to be informed and mobilized in order to secure broad-based social support.

The importance of awareness-raising in prevention activities cannot be overestimated for experience over many years and in all parts of the world has clearly demonstrated that,

(a) Significant public pressure is needed to ensure and support government action against child labour, and

(b) Awareness among the key actors, i.e. children, their parents and communities, as well as employers, about the serious consequences of hazardous work at a young age, provides the essential basis for its eventual abolition.

Much hazardous work is not visible to the public, and often even the families of child workers in dangerous occupations and industries are not sufficiently aware of the dangers.

Another obvious and essential starting point is the adoption of appropriate laws and regulations defining the minimum age for admission to hazardous work and the conditions under which children may or may not work. Such laws are important not only because they provide a legal basis for action in the best interest of the child but also because they can have inspirational value and encourage initiative. In many countries, large numbers of children working under hazardous conditions are not covered by child labour laws. Where they are covered, enforcement of the laws is often weak so that many violations either remain undetected, or are insufficiently sanctioned.

Preventive programmes and projects can, of course, be successful only if the population groups at risk are provided with viable alternatives and options, such as affordable good-quality education and the justified expectance of adequate job opportunities for school leavers. Relevant educational offers in the form of universal, free public schooling will ultimately be the most effective instruments for the elimination of child labour.

Experience in different parts of the world has shown that school attendance has a major effect on reducing the number of children in hazardous work.

First, most detrimental forms of child labour are inconsistent with regular school attendance. In cases where it is combined with part-time work it may at least reduce excessive hours of work which often account for the bulk of strain put on a young child worker.

Second, educated persons are more aware of their rights and so less likely to accept hazardous working conditions.

Third, educated persons, it has been proven, have fewer, better educated and healthier children when they become adults, a factor which should contribute to the overall reduction of child labour in hazardous occupations in future generations.

Child labour is a product of poverty and the difficult income situation of families is usually at the basis of the parents' decisions to send their children to work. Strong economic growth and development are important beneficial factors to any preventive strategy of child labour. However, growth in itself does not necessarily take care of a country's child labour problem, not even of its worst forms.

A number of countries which have achieved substantial growth rates in the last few years have seen child labour drop, but not to the dramatic levels one might expect and many children remain trapped in obviously hazardous conditions. In order to tackle child labour effectively the benefits of growth will have to be distributed more equitably and income disparities will have to be reduced. Only if poverty alleviation and full productive employment are accorded top priority among the developing country's priorities will a basis for the elimination of all forms of child labour be created.

The Essentials of Rehabilitation

The abolition of hazardous child work will take time, and preventive approaches will bear fruit only in the long run. For this reason, rehabilitation assumes an important role in the short to medium term. Rehabilitative actions tend to reach out to individual children who are already in the labour market, either providing them with certain services intended to protect them from the hazards they face or providing them with alternative options subsequent to their removal from work.

Eliminating children from work is not an easy task. Viable alternatives have to be offered, especially in terms of education and training, and the foregone income on which the child labourers' families often depend has to be substituted by other sources. In order to facilitate the removal of child workers from hazardous work, a number of projects have offered economic incentives such as cash grants or in-kind payments.

It is imperative to understand that an ILO study which surveyed a variety of these programmes found that economic incentives work best when combined with other activities, e.g. income-generating activities for the child workers' parents. However, rarely can the level of grants and payments match up to the lost income and many children have returned to work after the subsidies ceased.

A child's withdrawal from work has to be accompanied by a whole range of supportive measures. Care has to be taken to ensure that the attempts to remove children from one sector or industry do not push them into industries or occupations which may even be more hazardous or exploitative. In addition to education, training and health services, former child workers need to be provided with intensive counselling, a safe environment and often legal aid. In many cases, so-called "drop-in centres" have been set up as a first-call station, often run by NGOs, which offer professional services from social workers, family or child therapists and psychiatrists.

In India various measures and approaches have been initiated by number of NGO's and other agencies. It could be number of components combined together or an integrated approach. To mention few:

- Identifying child labourers
- Enrolling them in specially designed education schemes or in government schools
- Integrated strategy which combined a public campaign with community involvement
- Offer of adequate education programmes and a steady dialogue with employers
- Could be persuaded personally
- Village meetings to renounce the use of child labour.
- Nnon-formal education while the are introduced to
- Cooperative poultry farming for parents in order to compensate for the lost income.
- Establish independent small family farms with the help of small bank loans.

If it has not been possible or initially partially possible to remove children from hazardous occupations,

- Special protective programmes have been established as a transitional measure to minimize the dangers these children face or to upgrade their skills.
- Health dangers may be reduced with regular medical examinations and assistance.
- Non-formal education or vocational training can be offered in the evenings or on weekends; or
- Employers can be encouraged to improve their workplaces or work organization.

- Child workers are shifted to less dangerous tasks.
- Distributing safety equipment (gloves, masks, goggles, safety shields) to more than a thousand child workers in hazardous occupations.

Essential to the success of these protective measures therefore is the need to emphasize their transitional character and to package them in larger programmes leading to the eventual removal and provision of alternatives.

Two projects are illustrative in this respect. In the Philippine capital Manila the Smoky Mountain Project helped scavenger children working on a garbage dump in a most distressing social milieu through a phased approach of protection and removal measures. In the first phase it provided immediate care and protection, subsidized meals and first aid in a drop-in centre, while in the second phase it aimed at removing child workers from scavenging and rehabilitating them with a range of measures which included vocational training, non-formal basic education, health care and income-generation activities. In three years it assisted about 1,200 child workers and removed 160 from the dangers at work and placed them into school.

In the Brazilian states of Pernambuco and Bahia, a workers' organization followed a similar approach by providing rescue and education to children in hazardous agricultural work in a fruit-producing region. The trade unions conceived a scheme which offered non-formal education to child workers and trained them in skills that would help them find better jobs in the future. As the project progressed, it succeeded in withdrawing children from work and enrolling them in schools. Close contact with the parents and the awareness and commitment of the whole community were seen as essential in ensuring long-lasting results.

Commercial Sex and Trafficking of Children

Prostitution and trafficking of children have emerged in recent years as a major global concern. Both developing and developed countries are facing the problem, although the situation in the former is greater in intensity. Facilitated by globalization and modern communications means and technologies, the sexual exploitation of children is becoming increasingly transnational in scope.

Commercial sexual exploitation of children is defined as "sexual abuse by the adult and remuneration in cash or kind to the child or a third person or persons. Child prostitution, pornography and trafficking of children for the purpose of sale into the sex trade are the most common forms of abuse." Overall, the majority of victims are girls although in some countries boys may at least be equally affected.

It goes without saying that the commercial sexual exploitation of children is not only a particularly hazardous form of child labour but also a violent crime. It flouts the basic notion of humanity and strips away the dignity and freedom of society's most vulnerable members. Its impact can be disastrous. Child victims of commercial sexual exploitation are robbed of their childhood, deprived of a normal development and often have to face extreme forms of physical and psychological abuse which leave long-lasting scars. Many get infected with sexually transmitted diseases and HIV/AIDS or are beaten or tortured.

Because commercial sexual exploitation is often invisible or only marginally visible, it is very difficult to obtain accurate data on the problem and therefore to quantify its extent. It is estimated that each year more than one million children are tricked or drawn into the multi-billion-dollar sex trade. The nature and scope of commercial sexual exploitation of children vary from one country to another. Generally, Asia and Latin America are regions known for the highest incidence of child prostitution and child trafficking. In recent years, however, Africa and Eastern Europe have emerged as new regions of concern.

Various factors facilitate and lead to the commercial sexual exploitation of children at the national and international levels. Poverty and ignorance are probably the most important ones. Poor families searching for means to increase their meager income are often easy victims for exploiters. Powerful criminal groups dominate the sex business in most countries and many children are tricked into the trade, unaware of the cleverly concealed real intentions of recruiters.

Parents in rural areas, for example, may be told that their children will be put into respectable jobs in town, such as work in a restaurant or as a shop attendant but instead the children end up in brothels. In some countries, children from specific groups of the disadvantaged and poor such as indigenous populations or lower castes face a particular risk to be lured into the sex trade. The increased commercial sexual exploitation of children in recent years has also been fuelled by the demand for ever younger prostitutes based on the misconceived notion that sex with children will prevent the danger of HIV infection. Further contributing factors may be the alienation effects of rural-urban migration and an array of traditional discriminatory practices against the girl child in many parts of the world.

Given this broad context, commercial sexual exploitation of children requires multifaceted responses. Interdisciplinary strategies with long-term impact are needed, at the national as well as international levels. While prostitution and trafficking of children have long been ignored as quiet evils, growing awareness has been building up over the last few years and a number of important steps have been taken to tackle the problem. Many governments have now entered into strong commitments against the sexual exploitation of children and are assisted in their efforts through international cooperation and technical assistance arrangements with IPEC and other programmes.

Measures to be Taken

Since the child prostitution is a very complex nature of the problem suggesting action programmes is not that much easy as the commercial sexual exploitation of children is severely complicated by vested interests of those profiting from the practice and by the illegal nature of the problem. However, activities of governments, NGOs and committed individuals have shown that successful action against it is possible by mobilizing all key actors in the society to show concern and come up with innovative measures. As in the case of action against other forms of child labour, success crucially depends on closing society's ranks against the scourge, through close cooperation between the partners involved, complementarities of measures and a coherent coordination of overall action.

Activities generally aim at

1. Preventing children from being lured, coerced and trafficked into commercial sexual exploitation,
2. Withdrawing the victims from the trade and providing them with rehabilitation, repatriation as well as social and economic reintegration programmes, and

3. Creating public awareness and mobilize public support against all forms of commercial sexual exploitation of children.

In order to be effective, practical action will have to be based on two basic pillars such as a national policy on prostitution and trafficking of children and appropriate legislation. The policy could either stand alone or be a component of an overall policy framework against child labour as such. Most countries in which the sexual exploitation of children is a significant problem have formulated such a policy.

In the Philippines, for example, an Indicative Framework for Action to Attack Child Labour was adopted during a national planning workshop sponsored by ILO/IPEC in 1994. The workshop brought together a wide range of government representatives, NGOs, trade unions, employers and researchers in the field. Victims of child trafficking and children trapped in prostitution were identified among the four priority target groups in this framework for action. Similar events also led to the inclusion of the subject as a priority area in national child labour policies also in Nepal, Cambodia and other countries.

An important precondition for policy formulation and project targeting is a thorough analysis of the causes of the problem, it's extent and the groups involved. The collection and analysis of such information should be an ongoing process due to the multiple facets of the problem, illegality and the fast-changing environment surrounding this exploitative practice. National focal points could be established to process and disseminate the gathered information.

Protection of children from commercial sexual exploitation depends on effective laws and policies and their implementation at the national and local levels. Most countries now have some form of legislation against the sexual exploitation of children. It may be a specific law or may be part of the general criminal code. Most often, however, it is not the existence of applicable laws but the effective enforcement of these which poses a formidable problem. To strengthen law enforcement, the quality and training of police force, the judiciary and other law enforcement personnel must be improved. Legislation should focus on the criminalization of the conduct of customers and intermediaries and should not penalize the child victims.

Given the transnational nature of prostitution and trafficking, cross-border and international cooperation among law enforcement agencies are needed. Extradition agreements and mutual assistance arrangements could be expanded to facilitate the transfer of alleged criminals to face charges in the country where the exploitation has taken place. In this context, laws should be harmonized between different countries, including the age criteria for child protection. Children who are trafficked across borders are especially vulnerable because they are isolated by language and culture and do not have legal papers. Special legal provisions for their care and return to their home countries could therefore be considered.

Prevention

The best way to approach the problem of child prostitution is to prevent it. Preventive action in this field largely relies on awareness-raising and other activities which inform the public about the harmful consequences children face in the sex trade. In order to be effective, preventive action will have to target a number of different groups at the same time, such as society in general, children and families at risk, the business sector and the media.

Role of Local Community. Traditional cultural values which discriminate against women and girls in some societies may facilitate a girl's entry into the sex trade. The stigmas linked to these values may aggravate the plight of child victims of exploitation, rendering rehabilitation more difficult. Experience has shown that the impact of traditions that perpetuate this exploitative practice can be reduced or eliminated by educating society about their harmful effects on children. Here, as elsewhere, community participation is essential. In many countries, it was concerned communities that took the first step in self-defence of their girls, e.g. through community watch-dog programmes and local child protection committees working closely together with law enforcement agencies.

Often, it was rather unconventional means which succeeded in raising the population's awareness of child abuse. In Kenya, for example, an NGO toured a number of districts staging a theatre play performed by school children which depicted the daily life of working children, including child prostitutes and domestic servants. Thought-provoking debates after the performance spurred the involvement of teachers, parents and community leaders to engage actively in the identification of child labour and child prostitution in their communities.

Role of Family. As the basic unit in the society the family plays an important role in the protection and prevention of commercial sexual exploitation of children. As pointed out earlier, poverty and economic hardship have led some parents in effect to sell their children into the sex trade, often with the mistaken belief that the children are entering a respectable job.

In cases where parents of child prostitutes have been informed about their child's real occupation, many seem unaware of the potential, sometimes life-threatening risks faced by the children in such a situation. Educating parents on the fate or hardships faced by children employed in the sex market could reduce dramatically the number of parents willing to even consider such sale or other regrettable agreements with recruiters.

Promotion of child rights in family education and new approaches to family development assistance such as the introduction of innovative, and cost-efficient social security plans are other important steps to be considered to tackle this problem at the family level.

Role of Business Sector. The rise of sex tourism has increased the occurrence of transcontinental commercial sexual exploitation of children. The tourism industry has increasingly condemned that part of the industry which abuses and exploits children. However, much more needs to be done. Sex tourism should be discouraged more strongly and the service sector, including travel agencies and national tourism promotion boards, could act more responsibly on this issue. Industry-wide campaigns could be launched to reduce this grave abuse.

This may include the dissemination of information through distribution of leaflets at the departure or arrival airports and the incorporation of warnings against the commercial sexual exploitation of children in guidebooks.

Role of Media. The media plays an important role in disseminating information and raising awareness on the problem. But the media can also aggravate the plight of child victims of commercial sexual exploitation by insensitive coverage or general lack of understanding of children's rights. Therefore, codes of ethics and professional guidelines, the promotion of specialist children's correspondents and training on child rights for journalists could be considered to make the media a more effective ally in the fight against child prostitution.

Rehabilitation

Sexually exploited children may face various psycho-social problems such as loss of self-respect, depression, aggression heavy violence and develop post-traumatic stress symptoms Rehabilitating these children is extremely difficult because they may lost hope and trust in others, particularly adults. The emotional abuse many of them have experienced can be extreme, preventing their return to a normal way of life. Many sexually exploited children are said to be suicide-prone.

When planning rehabilitation measures, these obstacles to rapid results have to be fully taken into account and one needs to be aware of the fact that rehabilitating former child prostitutes may entail a very long process.

The right methodology coupled with an appropriate training of rehabilitation personnel is often the key to success. The priority of any measure should be to reduce the child victims' vulnerability in the future so that they do not fall back into the grips of exploiters. It could consist of the provision of shelter and food, legal aid, medical care, counselling, and social and economic reintegration. The latter may include education and vocational training to give the children a means to earn their livelihood and develop marketable skills. In this process, access to child-friendly services should be promoted. For victims of HIV/AIDS, support facilities, subsidies, medical care and accommodation could be provided.

Given the emotional impact of prostitution and trafficking on children, the restoration of family and friends, home life and self-esteem is very important. Real rehabilitation comes only with reintegration into the community and society. However, the stigma attached to children who have fallen victims of such exploitative practices and many a community's lack of understanding makes the reintegration of these children into society difficult. Greater emphasis needs to be placed on working with families and communities to accept and support children who have been sexually exploited.

The increasing transnational nature of the commercial sexual exploitation of children affects almost all countries today and India is no exception. To combat and find practical solutions for this transnational problem, regional and worldwide cooperation is indispensable. Bilateral and multilateral action and agreements could be considered to monitor commercial sexual exploitation of children, to detect the exploiters and trace the children affected, to facilitate prosecution, and to assist the recovery of children. Technical cooperation should also be promoted to share knowledge and experiences on this issue.

Bonded Child Labour

Though slavery belonged to the past; there are still millions of victims of slavery especially children in the new forms of it such as debt bondage. Adults as well as children are affected and often the victims are the sons and daughters of adult workers themselves in bondage.

The international community is viewing this issue as a Prominent one. In 1992, the ILO in collaboration with the United Nations Centre for Human Rights organized a regional seminar on child bondage in Islamabad, Pakistan. ILO/IPEC has made child bondage one of its top priorities and is supporting various action programmes in different countries. Regularly the ILO Committee of Experts on the Application of Conventions and Recommendations raises the problem of bonded labour, including that of children, and by repeating each year the request for complementary information keeps the issue on the agenda of governments.

Furthermore, it is proposed that the new international standards on the elimination of the most intolerable forms of child labour, scheduled for discussion at the International Labour Conference in 1998 and for adoption in 1999, should call for ratifying member states to suppress immediately all forms of slavery including debt bondage and serfdom.

Forms of Bondage

The UN defines debt bondage as "the status or condition arising from a pledge by a debtor of his personal services or of those of a person under his control as security for a debt, if the value of those services are not respectively limited and defined".[(Endnote 3)] Bondage in the case of children is found in three principal forms according to whether it consists of a hereditary debt, an occasional debt or an advance on salary.

Hereditary Debt Bondage. A child can be in bondage due to the simple fact of being born to parents who are slaves themselves. The family, riddled with debts, is unable to refuse their employer taking the child to do what he or she wishes. This system is usually found in rural communities which are more or less isolated from public view, as in large agricultural estates, plantations, forest exploitation, stone quarries, mines and brickyards.

Occasional Debt Bondage. The child is a member of a non-bonded family but due to extreme poverty the parents are not able to collect enough money to face exceptional expenditure such as a marriage, a funeral or serious sickness of a family member. The child is placed in bondage in exchange for a sum of money to pay the bill. The growth mechanism of the initial debt rapidly transforms a temporary situation into a permanent one.

Bondage by Advance on Wages. In some cases workers are not able to survive with their families on their wages and ask their employer for an advance on their future wage. The overall amount of advances and interest can become so substantial that the worker sees no other solution than to place a child on a gage at his employer's abode.

The sum borrowed is sometimes only a small amount and it is not always money which is lent. It could also be goods such as a working utensil, an animal, medication, food, or a service such as transport to a region where the worker envisages finding work. The borrower only having at his disposal his labour force or that of his children, gives this in exchange.

The crucial point in this transaction is that the lender, who will be the employer of the child, commonly takes advantage of his position of power to leave undetermined the duration of labour of the bonded child. As costs for food and medication are often added to the debt, a vicious circle is easily created where because of ill-defined rewards debt cannot be repaid, no matter how long and how much the child works.

The "effectiveness" of bonded labour is based on several aspects. First, there is the highly unequal and almost captive relationship between worker and employer. Debt bondage often occurs in regions with semi-feudal land ownership structures where landless peasants have no other choice but to accept any kind of work, however badly remunerated or hazardous the work may be.

One of the major problems confronting action against child debt bondage is its invisibility. There are primarily two reasons for this. First, bonded child workers are difficult to locate. They may work in small workshops with difficult access, remote quarries, building sites, agricultural estates far from residential areas or as domestic workers where entrance is often prohibited due to the fact that the workplace is a home and considered as private property.

Second, in the case of bondage, the employer is more than an employer, he is the proprietor of the child worker, just as one could be the proprietor of an animal or a machine. Fearing repression from the employer/proprietor, bonded child workers generally remain silent. Even in those cases where bonded children were freed they have often for years been unable to talk about their experiences and have retained a deep distrust of adults in general.

To keep the bonded children at their service the proprietors also need the silence of the public. They therefore usually see to it that all contact between the workers and possible investigators is prohibited and that no information is allowed to filter out. In some cases the proprietors may have supplementary protection, which is at the same time part of the machinery of recruitment and control of the slaves, namely the intermediaries. There can be three categories of intermediaries: the recruiters, the transporters and the surveyors.

The Recruiters and their Networks. Throughout the villages or slums they may visit the most poverty stricken, especially during the periods of financial difficulty. A loan may be proposed to the family by attracting them with the possibility of reimbursement through the labour of one of their children. The recruiters, acting, for example, on behalf of an enterprise active in mining or forest exploitation, may offer to pay the travel expenses to the place of work and to be reimbursed later.

Sometimes the child is taken away without payment of any advance, merely with the promise of feeding him and letting him acquire some skills in a particular trade. In many cases, the recruiters do not operate clandestinely. They might even be well known to the families, sometimes to the extent where the parents consider them sympathetic and trustworthy.

The Escorts. The greater the distance between the family and the place of work, the more the child will have difficulty in fleeing or being rescued by his family. This does not mean that children in bondage are automatically taken hundreds of kilometers away from home: in the plantations, the stone quarries or brickyards, children in bondage often live with their parents at the workplace.

This physical proximity of the family is far from being the usual lot of bonded children. There exist, for example, escorts who are simply charged with putting the children on a train or a truck and seeing that they arrive at the destination. In cases where inspections cannot be avoided, especially when national borders have to be crossed, escorts pose as members of the family of the children in their charge.

The Surveyors

A child in bondage is an income asset and the proprietor usually requires the uninterrupted physical presence of the child at the workplace. The more workers in bondage on a site, children or adults, the more the surveillance of the workers will be strict and organized. The surveyors' task is to prevent any escape attempts or communication with the outside world. In many cases, groups of private police, usually armed, watch over the workers.

In such a clandestine environment it is impossible to get precise figures on the extent of the phenomenon of child debt bondage. However, from existing documentation, one can confidently draw the following conclusions with certitude:

- The extent of the child debt bondage system is immense and the victims can number in the millions.
- It exists in a large number of countries.
- Its victims are almost exclusively from poor rural populations and minority social groups, notably indigenous peoples.
- It is often exercised in connection with other criminal acts such as kidnapping, the trafficking and selling of children or child prostitution.
- It is illegal everywhere but it is often sustained by an insufficient political will to fight it.

Practical Solutions

A number of international conventions explicitly condemn slavery, including child bondage. Most national legislations prohibit slavery. However, certain legislations whilst prohibiting slavery or forced labour are not adapted to this specific form of slavery. In fact only two countries have equipped themselves with laws expressly aimed at bonded labour; these are **India** in 1976 and Pakistan in 1992.

As in the case of other forms of child labour, even when the appropriate legislation is in place, enforcement of the law presents the real problem. On top of the usual difficulties which governments face in enforcing child labour legislation, bonded child labour poses a particular problem because of its hidden character and the often powerful vested interests at the root of the system.

It is at the national level that the suppression of slavery can be achieved for it requires not only measures which are within the jurisdiction of each government, but changes in social practices at times profoundly anchored in national history and culture. Such changes cannot be brought about without the committed contribution of various stakeholders.

It is to be concluded that the International bodies and organizations through their prolonged efforts and guidance incorporate various nations in the cause of elimination of child labour and the exploitation of children in various forms. The Nations on the other hand called to coopearate with various NGO's and other agencies in an integrated way to find ways and means in a sustainable way involve various players and stakeholders in protecting and promoting the status of children so as to give them the right to childhood.

* : (adopted from ILO)

It is estimated by the US that trafficking involves one million people across international boarders every year (Hindu, 2004)

India along with Thailand and the Philippines has 1.3 million children in its sex-trade centers (Shahare, 2005).

According to ILO estimate 15 per cent of the country's estimated 2.3 million commercial sex workers were children, while the UN reported that an estimated 40 per cent were below18 years.

Indian Estimates

The Indian statistics on trafficking is concerned commercial sex exploitation is generally taken into reference. In India also it is difficult to estimate the actual statistics (Gupta, 2003). In order to obtain a near estimate the adult and child sex workers in India are quoted; but there are also a considerable number of trafficked children are engaged in sweet making, domestic work, hotels and restaurants, match industry, quarry work and ready made garments. Hence the statistics showed by various researchers show a high degree of discrepancies and the possibility of arriving at an authentic data is remote.

These researches also identify geographical belts of exploitation, like for instance, the pink triangle between Agra, Jaipur, Delhi, Andhra Pradesh, Bihar, Karnataka, Madhya Pradesh, Rajasthan, West Bengal, Uttar Pradesh and Maharastra emerge to be the foremost states from where trafficked persons are supplied with the metro cities being the most frequent destination points. Razario et al (1988) sketched various sellers and market centres and found the interstate movement for prostitution to be high between Mumbai and Karnataka. Karnataka contributed to 45.6 per cent of the commercial sex workers in Mumbai, while interstate movement in the case of women in Bangalore was as high as 72.11 per cent. On the contrary 93.60 per cent of the commercial sex workers in Hyderabad were belonged to Andhra Pradesh (Mukherjee and Das, 1996).

Most of the studies reveal that approximately 30 to 90 per cent of women and girls are under 18 years of age at the time of their exploitation (Ganitha, 2003, SOS, 2001, Ganitha, 1999; Mukherjee and Das, 1996; UMCA, 1995; UNICEF, 1994).

FROM NEPAL AND BANGLADESH TO INDIA

Women trafficking are also an important and serious area that has to be looked into as there is no authentic data available due to the complexities in regulations which also varies from country to country. The only possible way is to get data from the agencies working in the field especially NGO's (ADB, 2002). The combined estimates for Nepal and Bangladesh range from 500 a year to 10,000 girls (UNDP, 2002) to 5000 to 7000 girls being annually trafficked (Tumlin, 2000) to more than 2,00,000 over a period of seven years (SOS, 2001). An average age of girls trafficked from Nepal to India ranges from 14 to 16 years in the 1980's to 10 to 14 years in 1994 (UNDP, 2002).

There are number of women from neighbouring countries trafficked to India. It has been reported that there are 1000 to 10, 000 women found in Kolkata brothels, 70 per cent were from Bangladesh (ADB, 2002). There are also 1,00,000 to 1,60,000 Nepali girls in Indian brothels, with about 5,000 to 7,000 girls being sold every year (Joshi,

2002). Reuters reported that there are 3000 women in Kolkata brothels are from Bangladesh ad another 10, 000 Bangladeshi women are in brothels in Mumbai and Goa. The percentage of trafficked women from Bangladesh is 13.5 per cent in Kolkata, 0.2 per cent in Mumbai ad 2.6 in Delhi (Joshi, 2002). In another study it has been reported that there in Mumbai brothels are 42 per cent women from Bangladesh (SOS, 2001).

Trafficking and Indian Response

India pays close attention to the problem of trafficking through its Department of Women and Child Development as well as through the National Commission for Women whose past president was a fervent crusader for victims of trafficking into the sex industry. Within the overall profile of trafficking in South Asia, India is a country of transit and destination. There is as well a considerable degree of internal trafficking as also some trafficking from India to the Gulf states and to Southeast Asia.

Most of the studies, data, and activity in the field of anti-trafficking work in the country has focussed on trafficking into the sex industry. However in India, some of the various states have undertaken their own initiatives in addition to interventions being designed at the central level. Therefore, West Bengal, Maharashtra, Uttar Pradesh, Bihar as well as some of the southern states have their own stated policies on trafficking of women and children especially into the sex industry. Certain interventions on the part of U.P, West Bengal and Bihar include cross border components as well with Nepal and Bangladesh.

As in the case of Nepal and Bangladesh, no reliable statistical data are available on the number of women and minors in the various red light areas of Indian cities , much less on the victims of trafficking. However, according to a survey done by the Central Social Welfare Board (CSWB) in 1991 in six metropolitan cities of India indicated that the population of women and minors in the sex industry in these cities would range between 70,000 and 100,000.

It also revealed that approximately 30 percent of them were below the age of 18 years, and nearly 40 percent of them were inducted into the trade when they were minors. Furthermore, more than 70 percent of the women and children in prostitution were illiterate. The CSWB survey also found that 60 percent of the women and girls in the sex industry belonged to culturally, socially or economically marginalised communities such as Scheduled Castes, Scheduled Tribes, and Other backward Castes.

According to other sources especially from the world of media, the number of sex workers in the Kamathipura red light area of Mumbai alone is supposed to be close to 100,000, whereas another 100,000 women are said to be engaged in prostitution in Calcutta. However, since the methodology whereby this statistical data is arrived at is questionable, there however is considerable merit to the assertion that the sex industry in India absorbs a vast number of women and girls, and the demand for more and younger workers by this industry continues unabated.

From the standpoint of the legal and policy framework, trafficking of women and children, sexual violence and discrimination, as well as abuse of child labour are stipulated as punishable offences. Some of the major laws in this regard are:

- The Constitution of India states that the Right against exploitation is a fundamental right. Under Article 23, traffic in human beings and "beggar" (bonded labour), and other forms of forced labour are prohibited. Any contravention of this provision is a punishable offence.
- The Immoral Traffic (Prevention) Act of 1956 (ITPA), supplemented by the Indian Penal Code (IPC) prohibits trafficking in human beings, including children, and lays down severe penalties. The ITPA and IPC prescribe punishments for crimes related to prostitution. A special feature included in the Act as amended is that the presumption of guilt is laid on the accused in cases where children or minors are found in a brothel and are proven to be sexually abused upon medical detection.
- The ITPA provide for enhance punishments for offences in regards to minors. Under Section 5 of this Act, inducing or taking a child or minor for the sake of prostitution is punishable with rigorous imprisonment for a term of not less than 7 years extendable up to 10 years and a fine.
- It has been reported by the that the states of Andhra Pradesh, Tamil Nadu, Karnataka, Maharashtra, and Delhi have been enforcing this Act with considerable efforts compared to other states in the country.
- The Juvenile Justice Act of 1986, provides for he care, protection, treatment and rehabilitation of neglected or

delinquent juveniles, including girls. The enforcement of IPTA, IPC and the Juvenile Justice Act is the responsibility of the states.

- Under Section 13(4) of IPTA it was recommended that the Central Government appoint a number of police officers as trafficking police officers and they shall discharge such functions and exercise powers in the entire country. Discussions have been held with the Central Bureau of Investigation and willingness expressed but concrete action remains to be taken.
- Two new draft bills have been proposed by the National Law School after being commissioned to undertake a review of the ITPA. The first Bill is the Prevention of Immoral Traffic Act and the Rehabilitation of Prostitute Persons Bill, 1993, and the second Draft Bill is entitled the Prohibition of Immoral Traffic and Empowerment of Sexual Workers Bill, 1993. The first one seeks to mitigate sufferings of victims of trafficking and the second one aims to combat trafficking and to confer rights on sex workers with a view to prevent exploitation and protect health and hygiene in sex work. Both these Bills have been referred to the National Commission for Women and are pending comments and further action.
- In pursuance of the Supreme Court Directives of 1990, the Government of India constituted a Central Advisory Committee on Child Prostitution. The recommendation of this Advisory Committee have been sent to the concerned Central Ministries/ Departments and state governments for appropriate action. A desk has been set up in the Department of Women and Child Development (DWCD) to implement the recommendations of the Advisory Committee.
- State Governments have also been advised to set up State Advisory Committees, Advisory Boards of social workers and NGOs in red light districts, conduct regular raids and take measure for protection and rehabilitation of trafficked victims.
- In 1997, under the directives of the Supreme Court, a Committee on Prostitution, Child Prostitutes and Children of Prostitutes headed by the Secretary, DWCD was set up. This Committee looked into the problems of prostitution and

trafficking of women and children in order to evolve suitable programmes.

- Protective Homes have been established by the Government under Section 21 of ITPA for girls and women detained under this Act. Currently there are 80 such protective homes which provide custodial care, education, vocational training and rehabilitation including arranging marriages for the inmates.
- A network of short stay homes under the sponsorship of DWCD and juvenile homes under the Juvenile Justice Act has been established for the protection and rehabilitation of victims. Medical services and counseling are made available at these homes.
- The Central Social Welfare Board provides financial assistance to NGOs to run Development and Care centres for children of prostitutes.
- To support future NGO projects and strategies for intervention on the problem of child prostitution and to formulate policy guidelines, the DWCD and UNICEF held six regional workshops covering all states and UTs in 1996.
- The National Human Rights Commission (NHRC) has also constituted a core group to study the problem of child prostitution in Delhi and Karnataka in order to formulate preventive and rehabilitative strategies.
- Recognizing that the influx of women and girls into prostitution is connected to the low status and income of women in society, the government is implementing various programmes of training and income generating activities (DWCRA, SEP, CCEVT, STEP, etc.). In addition a 40 percent reservation has been provided to women under the Integrated Rural Development Programme (IRDP). As a special measure of affirmative action, the Rashtriya Mahila Kosh has been set up to provide *micro-credit* to poor women in the informal sector. The Mahila Samridhi Yojna has been instituted to enable women to exercise greater control over household savings.

Various State Government's Initiatives

As mentioned previously, several State Governments have also initiated independent programmes to address the problem of trafficking and its linkage to prostitution.

- Several Devadasi rehabilitation and training schemes have been initiated by the Government of Karnataka. A component of this includes moral education and social upliftment.
- The Government of Andhra Pradesh has sanctioned a project in 1997-98 for the rehabilitation of victims of prostitution who are HIV positive.
- The government of Maharashtra has set up special juvenile homes with facilities for counseling, vocational training and health unit for child prostitutes infected with the HIV.
- The Government of Madhya Pradesh has initiated a scheme called Jabali in 1992-93, to encourage NGOs to take up welfare activities for women and child victims of commercial sexual abuse. This scheme targets those social groups in particular who have traditionally engaged in sex entertainment and prostitution as occupational caste groups.
- State governments have also demonstrated their active engagement with this issue by organising raids and rescuing 'victims' of prostitution. The famous raid in Mumbai in February 1996 wherein 484 victims including more than 200 girls from Nepal were rescued and sent back is a case in point of this activity.

From the above activities and interventions on the part of Central and State governments in India, it would appear that considerable gains have been made to not only stem the tide of trafficking but in fact to reverse it. However, the reality of the situation is quite the contrary. In fact the Report of the Committee on Prostitution of the DWCD candidly states, " Inspite of the many interventions for prevention, law enforcement, rescue and rehabilitation, there does not appear to have been much impact on the prevalence of commercial sexual exploitation of women and children except in the case of the Devadasi system".

Several reasons can be assigned to this major lacuna which visible in the field of expected results in respect to government interventions. Many of these will be discussed in a latter section, but some of the specific reasons have to do with a lack of seriousness on part of the law enforcement machinery and the administrative structure in addressing this problem. Furthermore, lack of coordination between departments and ministries, insufficient awareness and understanding of the issues, marginalisation of the issue of trafficking on the national and state agendas, inadequate resources, and often vested interests supported by a system of bribes and benefits, result in limited or even inappropriate responses on the part of the government to address the issue of trafficking.

Causes

There is a consensus found among the reasons for trafficking in many of the research studies. While several studies view vulnerability factors to be the foundation of trafficking, others state that, "they merely exacerbate the vulnerability of marginalized ad disadvantaged groups and render them increasingly more amenable to a variety of harm (Sanghera, 2002). The vulnerability factors related to the socio-economic and political contexts of people that are interlinked and can be divided into two categories - personal circumstance and socio-structural forces (Raymond et al 2002; Depaul University, 2002). These factors are generally scheduled in the background of commercial sex work. Mukherjee and Das (1996) identified 57 factors which play the role of causal agents to push women and girls towards prostitution (SEVA, 2003).

Psychological

Persons with low self-esteem and lack of self-control are reported to be especially vulnerable to trafficking (UNDP, 2002). Low levels of literacy, awareness and information are risk factors. Economic deprivation and associated conditions are also listed as factors that lead to vulnerability. Almost all the reviewed studies and reports affirmed that a high percentage of trafficked people belonged to low income groups. The greater the degree of impoverishment, the higher the risk of falling victim to trafficking has been observed by many researchers (Mukherjee and Das, 1996; Warburton and Maria, 1996; DWCD, 1998; UNDP, 2002). Differently able people or women who may suffer from disfigurements are also considered vulnerable (Ganitha, 2003).

Vulnerability Factors

Disorganized home environment such as marital discord, physical abuse, sexual abuse, drug abuse, family pressures, large families, families facing uncertain times, gender discrimination within the family, desertion by husband, husbands acquiring a second or a third wife, broken family, children in substitute care - are all considered to make people vulnerable to trafficking. Studies by the

CAUSES

SOCIAL

- POVERTY
- UNEMPLOYMENT
- FASHION AND MEDIA TRENDS
- ILLITERACY
- ATTITUDINAL
- LOWER STATUS
- DISASTER
- BROKEN FAMILIES
- ADDICTED FATHER

ECONOMIC

- ECONOMIC DEPRIVATION
- LOW INCOME
- DEBT
- AGRI-FAILURE

PSYCHOLOGICAL

- LOW SELF ESTEEM
- LACK OF SELF CONTROL
- STRESS
- TENSION

CONTRIBUTORY

- POVE
- LACK OF POLITICAL SENSITIVITY
- NO PROPER PREVENTION MEASURES
- LACK OF ENFORCEMENT OF LAW

Central Social Welfare board and others have shown that most trafficked women are unmarried, divorced, separated or widowed (Karmakar, 2001). The involvement of any of the family member in commercial sex work also increases vulnerability (Warburton and Maria, 1996).

With regard to women and girls the economic fluctuations, less opportunities to find employment are the prominent reasons identified by Sakthiprakash (2005) and hence they accept offers even if it is outside to their place. Sexual exploitation is a tool used globally to maintain class and gender inequalities and it is supported by the culture of poverty.

With regard to the socio-structural factors that sway and decisive these state of affairs are industrialization and globalization, economic crisis, economic decline, disruption or underdevelopment, economic policies such as privatization, liberalization, the withdrawal of subsidies and the commercialization of agriculture. The increasing rate of unemployment and disintegrating social networks also increase the vulnerability of trafficking of women and girls.

Dowry could be an another contributory factor as the whole family has to spend a lifetime earning on their daughters marriage and its related ceremonies like child birth, gifts during first Deepavali, Pongal, etc. could contribute in migration of girl children from their home town to an unknown area to earn more money and thereby settle in life.

The development of communication technologies are better utilized by crime syndicates to make the trade flourish.

Other factors include the erosion of subsistence agricultural practices, the loss of traditional livelihoods and inflation. Labour market demands and policies also influence vulnerability. In a global market, women and girls are increasingly being hired as service providers (Nair, 2005).

Poverty, unemployment, large family size especially with more number of girl children and illiteracy often force families to send their daughters along with know or unknown brokers to seek gainful employment to meet the needs of the family (Sakthiprakash, 2005).

There are also political reasons identified by various scholars and researchers. These can be listed as conflicts that cause disruption and instability, immigration policies and human rights violations by the state. Poor governance, limited law enforcement or implementation of labour standards also exacerbates vulnerabilities (ADB, 2002). Environmental Calamities and disruptions also added to their level to amplify the issue.

Construction of roads and highways, urbanization, industrialization has accelerated the migration process and in turn it contributed to a greater extent for trafficking. A culture of consumerism and materialism distorts family needs and individual desires (NCW, 1997; Raymond, 2002). Discriminatory practices and social exclusion exacerbate the vulnerabilities of groups like scheduled tribes, scheduled castes, other backward castes, ethnic minorities, tribal communities, undocumented migrant labourer and stateless people or people in refugee camps.

In another study, early marriage, the lack of choice in mate selection and the socialization of women into persons who remain servile and bear injustice silently render women more vulnerable (ADB, 2002).

Feminization of poverty and migration has also augmented women's vulnerability to traffickers (Sanghera, 1999). Motivated by the pressing need for gainful employment and by the scarcity of jobs

VULNERABILITY FACTORS

FAMILY →
- MARITAL DISCORD
- PHYSICAL, SEXUAL AND DRUG ABUSE
- FAMILY PRESSURES
- GENDER DISCRIMINATION
- BROKEN FAMILY
- DESERTION BY HUSBAND
- DOWRY
- CHILDREN IN SUBSTITUTE CARE
- INVOLVEMENT IN COMMERCIAL SEX WORK OF ANY OTHER IN FAMILY
- EXTRA-MARITAL RELATION

SOCIO STRUCTURAL →
- INDUSTRIALIZATION AND GLOBALIZATION
- ECONOMIC CRISIS
- ECONOMIC DECLINE
- UNDERDEVELOPMENT
- PRIVATIZATION
- LIBERALIZATION

POLITICAL →
- CONFLICTS CAUSING DISRUPTION AND INSTABILITY
- IMMIGRATION POLICIES
- HUMAN RIGHTS VIOLATIONS
- POOR GOVERNANCE
- LIMITED LAW ENFORCEMENT
- UNEQUAL DISTRIBUTION

in their home bases; women, girls and children are easy prey to the designs of deceitful agents offering 'choices'.

Enabling Factors

There are three important factors considered as trafficking triangle have been drawn by Alison Phinney (2001) are the space created by demand, supply and impurity with which trafficking occurs. According to her, 'sex trafficking' is driven by a demand for women's and children's bodies in the sex industry, fuelled by a supply of women who are denied equal rights and opportunities for education and economic advancement and perpetuated by traffickers who are able to exploit human misfortune with near impurity (Phinney, 2001).

Invisibility of the issue, the relatively low risks involved, insufficient or inadequate laws, minimal chances of prosecuting, poor enforcement, ineffective penalties, corruption and complacency, the failure of governments to implement policies and provide adequate services for victims all play a role in perpetuating trafficking (Warbutton, 1996; DWCD, 1996; Refugee Reports, 2000; Phinney, 2001; UNDP, 2002; Nimala Niketan, 2003).

A view that is often not highlighted is that, people who protest against trafficking are in a minority. It is very difficult to fight because everyone is unified – all are involved in trafficking in one way or the other.

There is seldom or no apposition from the families since there is though not high income is involved (HRW, 1995). In the context of the sexual exploitation of children 1996 workshop conducted by DWCD found that the absence of reliable data leads to some people emphasizing the speculative nature of the problem. This creates a lack of significance about the issue, which provides a chance for the misdemeanor to boom.

The Push and Pull Factors

The push and pull factors involve in migration is contextually adopted for the factors responsible for trafficking labour too especially with regard to children. The available employment opportunities outside their nativity, economic disparities, high unemployment, and disruption of traditional livelihoods, failure of monsoon, mechanization in agriculture, low paid wages, seasonal employment, irregular payments make the family force the children to fall in line with the trafficking chain. On the contrary the greener pastures in neighboring places or states pull them towards it. There are also complexities such as different political contexts and the geographical dimensions of the problem, ideological and conceptual differences and approach; the mobility and adaptability of traffickers in the different situations, and needs of trafficked persons, the inadequate legal frame work and insufficient research and coordination on the part of the stakeholders involved at the national, regional and international level experienced by various researchers.

It is also to be taken seriously that many a time the missing children are not examined from the perspectives of possible trafficking and on the other hand tracking trafficking overlooks the issue of missing children (Ali, 2005).

Push and Pull Factors of Trafficking

PUSH FACTORS

- ECONOMIC DISPARITY
- HIGH UNEMPLOYMENT
- TRADITIONAL LIVELIHOOD DISTRIBUTION
- FAILURE OF MONSOON
- MECHANISATION AND AGRICULTURE
- LOW WAGES
- SEASONAL EMPLOYMENT
- IRREGULAR PAYMENT

PULL FACTORS

- POVERTY
- THREAT TO LIVELIHOOD
- EMPLOYMENT
- ADDITIONAL INCOME
- VISITING NEW PLACES
- FOOD
- RECREATION
- PEER INFLUENCE
- LUXURIOUS LIFE

Major Causes

The major causes identified are the sexual services and domestic services are the only option available for the most of the women and girls. In order to care for the family and children, care of the elderly and young many women are the sole breadwinners of the family. In many cases, with rapid globalization and inflation in economy women want to be more self reliant and independent economically. The mixture of old tradition and new ideas, and new western influence, phonographic photos for the coverage of books ramp shows with sexy look satisfy these girls economically and lures them to help in accepting the offers of the traffickers. The young women also take it as a way of breaking traditions as the manifestations of liberty or freedom.

Contributory Causes

There is a lack of enforcement of law, corruption, no proper prevention measures are the causative factors to trafficking. Lack of political sensitivity to tackle the situation of forced commercial sex work and abuse are can also be listed under causes. Moreover patriarchal norms, tradition values and customs which legitimize the unequal power relation between men and women exacerbated by several factors such as increase in unemployment, poverty, stress, tension and financial crisis have added fuel to the crime. In addition to that fashion and media trends are also one of the major causes for trafficking. The new culture of minimum expenses and maximum profit either directly or indirectly motivate the women to engage in such activities.

Vulnerability

The victims belong to the low economic strata and lack economic opportunities Children who have low educational level, lack of employability are at risk as they have limited options for employment. These factors when compounded by gender, racial or ethnic discrimination, or insecurity caused by armed conflict and civil strife, create the ideal environment for trafficking networks to thrive (Siwal, 2005).

Poverty

Poverty is considered as the predominant factor which plays a major role in the issue of trafficking. The most obvious reason for exploitation and abuse is the poverty. The children in sexual exploitation network are reportedly belongs to rural area and live in poverty. Poverty makes the people more vulnerable and force individual to fall fry into the clutches of traffickers.

Broken Family/ lack of Parental Care

Children belong to broken family become susceptible to trafficking web. When the caregivers or guardians are not there they become more vulnerable for exploitation. Children without parental protection, or those placed in institutions often lack close relationship with the community and hence at risk. It has been reported by ILO that the orphaned children are much more vulnerable than the non-orphan children.

Causes for Women or Girls in Trafficking

The girl child could be disposed off in times of adversity for a paltry sum fall prey to vicious mechanization of local agents and traffickers due to relative alienation in lieu of a better world promised through marriage or job (Mallick, 2004).

Socio-cultural domain, traditions and superstitions and male chauvinist society are predominant among the causes. The caste system, lack of social awareness, dowry, child marriage, economic exploitation, unfair distribution of wealth, lack of economic justice, unequal land holding system, no role for the women in the economic decision, denial of women's rights lack of training, skill education and employment, lack of political commitment, lack of adequate law, ineffective implementation and enforcement on the laws and policies etc are considered as causes.

Source

A substantial body of newspaper reports as well as the information from voluntary agencies suggests that apart from Nepal and Bangladesh; some more poverty-stricken districts within India are also subject to trafficking. It is alarming to note that Trafficking from the Commonwealth of Independent States' countries is also on the rise. This is a significant indication of the complex organized nature of the crime.

Process and Organization of Trafficking

Vital to the organization of trafficking are the victims who become highly profitable, low risk, expendable, reusable and resalable commodities' (Richard, 1999). This trade in human beings as chattels and the treatment of their bodies as commodities becomes possible because of the incremental link between body and money. According to Troung (2001) this is a reflection of the ongoing, cultural decomposition of the human being through a gradual removal of its sprit, personhood, and vitality down to bare body parts.

Different Stages Perceived

Various scholars have noticed the stages of trafficking starting from canvassing to reaching the destinations. It is different to different places and the purpose for trafficking is done. For the purpose of labour the stages are simple and for commercial sex and criminal activities the stages are little more complex and clandestine. Nevertheless; there is a broad agreement on the stages of trafficking throughout the literature surveyed.

The stages can be listed as recruitment of people from a village or city, transportation to a designated location transit point possible shift to a central location, move to the ultimate destination, sometimes the trafficked persons are shifted several times before they arrive at their final destination, where the sale takes place. The different elements involved in this process create an impossible number of permutations and combinations of locations. Thus, most research on trafficking, including this study, resorts to case studies in an attempt to reflect its variations. However, at the regional level some patterns in these processes can be discerned (ILO, 2002).

Trafficking Chain

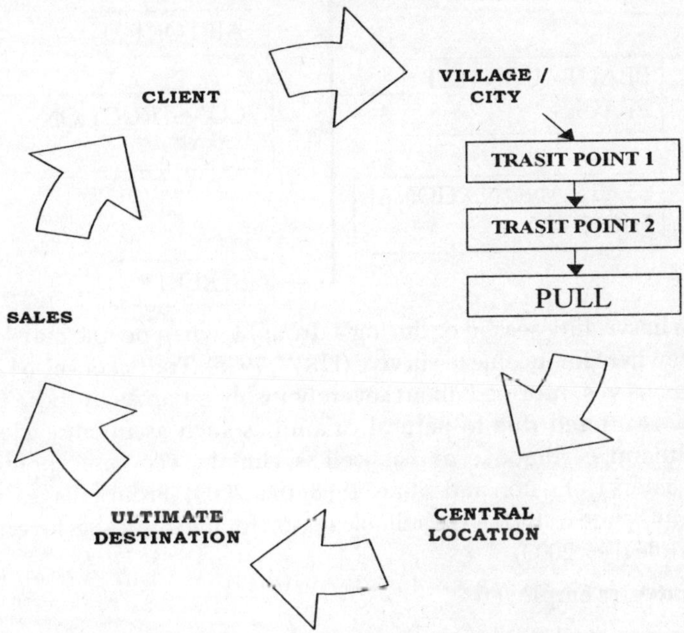

Place of Selection

The victims are reportedly recruited at places like cinema halls, bus stops, railway stations, airports, streets and even within homes.

Other places mentioned are cafeteria, restaurants, beauty contests and beauty parlors. State and national highways, quarry and construction work places, and areas where locals are displaced without proper rehabilitation may also be sites for potential victims.

Suitable Season

Research studies accounted that traffickers choose special times for recruitment. They take the advantage of difficult periods, either before

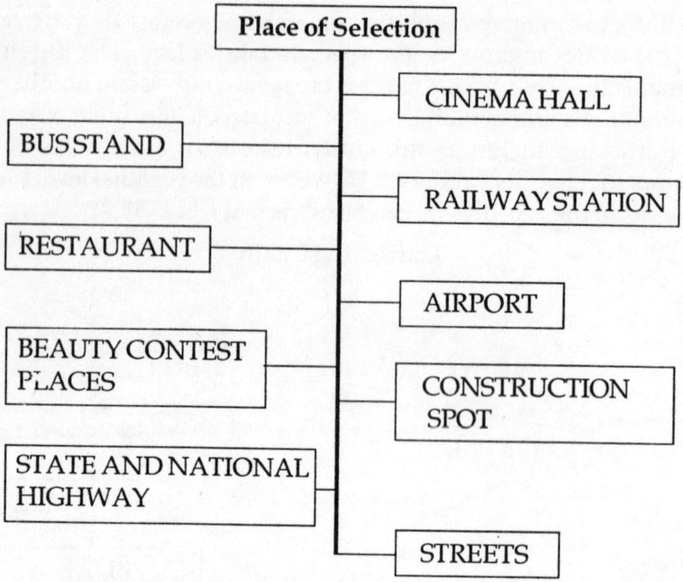

the harvesting season or during a drought, when people may look elsewhere for income to survive (HRW, 1995). Traffickers also keep themselves informed about severely insolvent areas or those that have suffered due to natural calamities such as flood, cyclone, Tsunami, earthquake, and as well as climatic, economic, political disasters (Johnston and Khan, 1998; ISS, 2003). From villages and countryside festival is the suitable season for the traffickers to recruit people (ISS, 2003).

Strategies employed

Various methodologies and techniques are employed by the traffickers to abduct people. The simple and easy way is to persuade with greenery future in terms of employment and earnings, false promises and hopes on the positive side and arouse their sentiments, emotions and feelings in terms of their dark future by projecting their weakness in terms of social and economic status.

The range of the strategies reportedly used varies from persuasion, material inducements, befriending and deception and to extremely violent actions like drugging, kidnapping and abduction. In the south Asian region, offers of marriage without dowries are welcomed, making it easy to arrange fake marriages. The trafficked victims are also reported that they are lured with fake job offers or false marriage offers.

It has been reported that the children are coercive, forced, deceived, use of fraud, debt bondage to force the victims in situations of slavery, forced labour or servitude where they are deprived of fundamental human rights (Amnesty organization, 2003).

METHOD OF RECRUITMENTS

- EMPLOYMENT
- MORE EARNINGS AND QUICK MONEY
- FALSE PROMISES AND HOPES
- AROUSE THEIR SENTIMENTS
- EMOTIONAL FOCUSSING OF MEAGER SOCIAL STATUS
- ADDING FEAR QUOTING THEIR LOW ECONOMIC POSITION

Studies on prostitution offer some information on the recruitment techniques that are used (Rozario, 1988; ATSEC, 2001; SOS, 2001; Joshi, 2002; ADB, 2002). In a CSWB study, 11.90 per cent of the respondents listed deception by someone as a cause for entry into prostitution (Mukherjee and Das, 1996). According to another study 11 per cent of the trafficked women are lured, while 11 per cent were abducted ad 9.2 per cent were sold or resold (Rozario, 1988).

Traffickers approach women and girls in groups as it helps them to win their trust (Sangroula, 2001). In India, recent news stories show a trend of traffickers using marriage bureaus, placement agencies ad tutorial agencies as a front for luring people.

Recruitment Personnel/Procurers

Recruiters for the most of the time are neighbors, family friends, relatives of friends, acquaintances returning from abroad, women who have migrated or who have been trafficked, and women friends returning from abroad, husbands, fathers, boyfriends or lovers. Some recruiters can be gay men who were trusted by women because of their sexual orientation (Raymond, 2002). They can also be drug peddlers, masons at construction sites, even band leaders in dance or live bars (ISS, 2003). More specific recruiters include motorcycle pilots as in Goa (GRG, 2003) or labour contractors (ISS, 2003). They use friends and acquaintances to recruit or rely on word of mouth. Terms like dalal or dalai are used to refer to traffickers (Nirmala Niketan, 2003; Gupta, 2003).

Specification of Traffickers

Traffickers are habitually young men and middle-aged women who are significantly older than the young women or young men or children they recruit. Some are naives operate as agents who are from home countries or regions to receiving regions and generally have links with the villages to which the victims belong. Procurers on an average are reportedly substance abusers or gamblers.

In case the victims are women; the traffickers are many a time older women who are either former prostitutes or are themselves in forced prostitution, truing to escape abuse and bondage by providing a substitute. Often traffickers speak several languages (Giri, 1999,:

Tumlin, 2000) and may have multiple roles. For instances those who help people migrate for trafficking may also be the people who facilitate other less exploitative forms of migration as in the case of refugees (Tumlin, 2000). The use of words like 'mafia' or the depiction of traffickers as villain outsiders do not correspond to most traffickers (Blanchet, 2002).

Important Players

There is a range of players said to involve in Organized trafficking 'along the road from acquisition to exploitation' (ILO, 2002). Trafficking networks may involve the police, visa and or transport officials, railway and bus authorities and employees, taxi/auto rickshaw drivers or rickshaw pullers (DWCD, 1996).

There are also other roles that the Traffickers operate in various levels which are classified as financiers or investigators, procurers or recruiters, organizers, document forgers, corrupt public officials or protectors, brothel operators and the owners and managers of sex establishments, escorts, guides or travel companions and crew members (Richard, 1999; Scholenhardt, 1999; Raymond, 2002). There is also the category of an initial spotter which is called choghat or arkathi in Bangali (ISS, 2003).

Scholenhardt (1999) presented few more additional categories in the context of smuggling and trafficking, especially for cross-border operations. These categories are: informers, enforcers, supporting personnel and specialists, debt-collectors, money-movers, and transporters who gather information on matters such as border surveillance, immigration and transit procedures, delivery systems and law enforcement activities.

DWCD (1996) identified two kinds of traffickers: primary and secondary. Pimps and procurers are the primary traffickers. The latter is said to operate behind the scenes with connections in government circles that are used to provide protection to the trafficking trade.

Operation Network

Trafficking can be done through organized international and local networks, or by occasional traffickers. Thus traffickers may operate alone or in small gangs or as part of organized crime groups (Richard 1999; Kelly, 2001; Icduygu and Toktas, 2002).

Operation Network of Trafficking

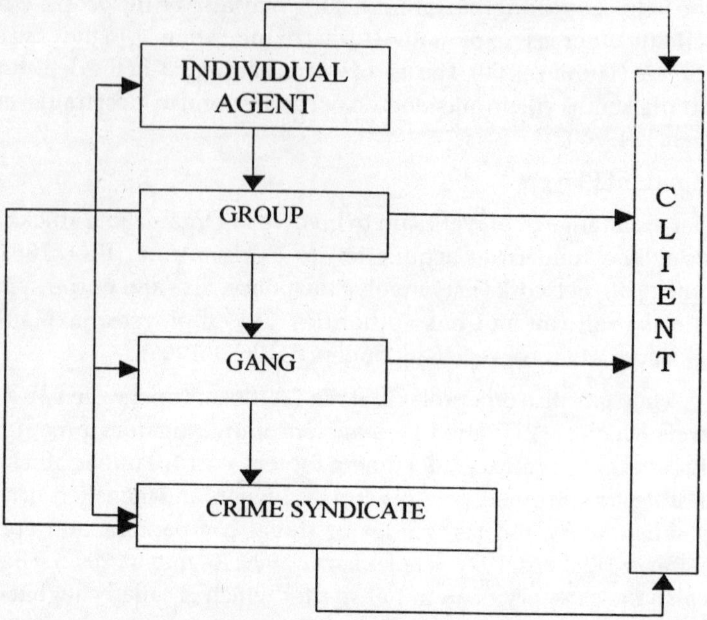

Gangs and criminal groups are reportedly the dominant modes of trafficking in South Asia (Govt. of Sweden, 2001; Nirmala Niketan, 2003). A women's research indicated the presence of an organized system of trafficking of girls for profit, which accounts for the greatest number of girls brought, transported and sold within and outside India (Shalini and Lalitha 1996). But for the traffickers it is the independent operation which dividends more profits than the organized network, where the traffickers have less freedom and make smaller profits.

Crime Syndicate and Trafficking

An organized crime group is defined by the United Nations Convention on Organised crime (2000) as s structured group of three or more persons, existing for a period of time and 'acting in concert with a aim of committing one or more serious crimes or offences established in accordance with this convention in order to obtain directly or indirectly a financial or other material benefit' (UN, 2000).

Richard (1999) found that the contribution of organized crime groups in trafficking in the international context and noted that in most cases, trafficking operations are sophisticated and global in scale, and facilitated by modern technology. There are only a few exceptions where trafficking is a localized cottage industry. The data that is available on the involvement of organized crime groups in the text on trafficking in India amounts largely to unsubstantiated references. The involvement is often indicated only by case studies covered by news reports (Ghosh, 1993; Nair, 2002). Traffickers operate within zones which are marked and do not usually violate that zone norms. Consequently, when moving from one zone to another, entirely different sets of people take over the activities (ISS, 2003). They also frequently change their area of residence to not only to keep away from the police, but also to widen their field of business.

Trafficking Routes

The routes are often highly complex, ranging from trafficking within one country and cross-border flows between neighboring countries to inter-continental and globalized trade (Tumlin, 2000). The general understanding is that the movement of trafficked people is from less developed areas to more developed regions. Thus the flow of trafficked women and children moves from the south to the north, from countries in economic, social and political crises to more socially and politically stable countries, or from rural to urban areas.

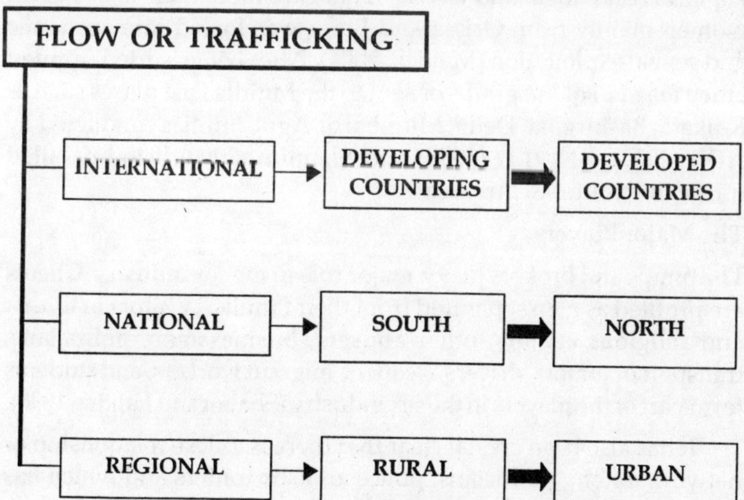

At the international level people have been trafficked from south-east Asia and South America to the United Kingdom, Italy and US.

They are also trafficked to the Middle-East. Some cases of trafficking from India to South-East Asia have been reported. Delhi and Mumbai are said to be the main transit zones for international movement (Haq, 2001). Some studies, however, also trace trafficking movement between affluent areas. The children come from relatively poorer areas and are trafficked to relatively richer one (Soma Wadhwa, 1998).

Routes are usually divided into origin, transit and destination points and some reports also mention collection and dispersal points. In the same way, nations are categorized as supply, transit or destination countries. Some countries may belong to more than one category. *India unfortunately becomes the representative of all the three categories such as; source, transit point and destination.*

Studies identified routes and discussed the problems faced in finding effective solutions to cross-border trafficking. Nepal and Bangladesh are the two main suppliers of trafficking victims for India. There have been news reports that after the disintegration of USSR women from Russia and other CIS countries, like Uzbekistan are being trafficked into India (Times of India, 24th June 2002).

Once trafficked women entering into India, they are generally kept in West Bangal and Orissa. There are more than 40,000 tribal women mainly from Orissa and Bihar was forced into economic and sexual exploitation (Mallick, 2004). After being 'sorted/graded ' they may be sold to pimps or sent to the Middle East places such as Kolkata, Bashirghat, Delhi, Mumbai or Agra. Studies conducted by ADB (2002), BNWLA (1998) and Shamim (2000) listed detailed trafficking routes in this area.

The Major Players

The pimps and brokers play a major role in the sex industry. Clients are profiled as men separated from their families, visitors in tourist and religious centers, other abusers, businessmen, politicians, transport operators, drivers, cleaners, migrant workers, and students form part of the players in the sex industry (Shalini and Lalitha, 1996).

It has also been crystal clear that there is a close relationship or network among politicians, police and sex traders and which has been reported in the newspapers more frequently (Indian express, 16 & 30th May, 2003; Hindustan Times, 17th June, 2003; The Hindu, 17th Feb. 2003; Statesman, 13th May, 2003).

Victims in Trafficking

Children as Victims

The data obtained through studies indicates that children are becoming more susceptible to trafficking because of decreasing focus and increasing complexity. Often being unacquainted of their rights, economically and socially disadvantaged populations have become easy prey to the trafficking trade. Migrating populations are also vulnerable to exploitation by traffickers. The trafficking trade needs to be probed further as such gross violations of human rights continue to be a low priority area for law enforcement agencies.

The violation of women's reproductive rights, the right of female infants and fetuses to life, domestic violence against women, custodial violence against women, violence against women in public places and the violation of women rights to decision-making to land assets and other resources (Warbutton and Maria, 1996; Sanghera, 1999; Karmakar, 2001; ADB, 2002; Raymond *et al.*, 2002).

If their families or guardians push women or girls into trafficked circumstances, many do not believe this as harmful, as they are measured as chattels of their father or guardians and further protection from their community would be inappropriate (ADB, 2002).

There are cases of male relatives making regular visits to collect the earnings have also been reported in the Nirmala Niketan College study (2003).

Spatial Location of Vulnerable Groups

With regard to the spatial or geographical location of vulnerable groups economically backward areas in India have been identified as hot spots (DWCD, 1996; Sanghera, 1999; Murthy and Sankaran, 2001). Contrary to the general perception a study from Orissa found that developed areas with improved infrastructure have invariable been the source as well as the destination of trafficking in women though 80 per cent of the victims belonged to landless households and families dependent on wage labour for survival (Pandey, 2002).

There is further examination of the spaces may be needed to fully understand and explain vulnerability.

High Risk Children

The following are the high risk groups that been identified by the researchers such as the street children, children living in slums, orphans and disabled children, children living in brothels or in countries practicing religious and cultural prostitution, children who have been in abuse or molestation, those born to AIDS victim, children in custodial and educational institutions away from families, children of bonded labourers and those working as domestic help have (SWCD, 1996)..

Commercial Sex Trade/ Women or Girls in Prostitution

There is a close relationship between trafficking and sex trade when the women and girls are victim. The trafficked girls are used in sex work, pornography, cyber sex and sex tourism. The industry is characterised by social stigma, economic exploitation, corruption, crime, drug, and all other related illegal activities. With all the powers and structure the government is finding it difficult to deal with it (Lim, 1998).

The large-scale accumulation of capital takes place through a progressive appropriation and decimation of women's and children's bodies, sexuality and entire beings (Raymond *et. al.*, 2002).

A mega survey conducted by CSWB in 1990 on prostitution in six metropolitan cities in India is a worth mentioning study where in one can understand the magnitude of the issue. The total commercial sex workers in all the cities accounted for 1 lakh (Mukherjee and Das, 1996) is very much alarming. Similarly in 1992 Association for the Rescue of Fallen Women reported that there are 8 million commercial sex workers in India and in addition to that the call girls accounted 7.5 million is worth mentioning.

The UN Special Rapporteur on the sale of Children, Child prostitution and Child Pornography (1996) cautioned that all the reports indicate a dramatic escalation of the number of sexually exploited children all over the world (Baker, 1999). Children are preferred as they are more likely to accept practices which older prostitutes may refuse. There are also myths relating to them that strengthen this reference for child prostitutes (Nair, 2005). It is believed that sexually transmitted diseases, including HIV infections, can be cured and virility can be increased by having sex with young girls. Younger girls are also preferred because they can put in more years as sex workers (Nirmala Niketan, 2003).

The capital city Delhi has recorded to the range of 10 to 15 thousand female prostitutes (Gupta, 2003).

It is a recent phenomenon that the women and girls are trafficked through one step pattern where in the girls are trafficked straight away from their original places especially from villages and sent to metropolis and abroad as there is a high demand for younger new women and girls and this method is gaining momentum and dominate in the days to come (UN, 2000).

It is also pathetic and traditional that few communities like *devadais* and *jogin*_induct_their young girls into the trade and men folk start pimping for their own family members. Even in such practice it has been observed that girls are coerced in few cases to enter into the profession shows their unwillingness (ISS, 2003; SAKHI, 2003; IDS, 2003; Gathia, 1999; Giri, 1999; DWCD, 1999).

Most of the girls and women entering into sex trade are from socially, economically and politically backward communities. It has been reported that nearly half of the population are from Scheduled Caste and Scheduled Tribe communities (DWCD, 1988). The plights of the children of these women are reported to be miserable (Nirmala Niketan, 2003).

Children in Sex Trade

There is a high demand for children in the sex trade due to myths, beliefs and chance of less risk to HIV/AIDS, and for variety and enjoyment. Children who have direct interaction with customers often feature among those who were sexually exploited by tourists. The Most disturbing of all the above is the increasing number of underage girls who are trafficked to work in the sex industry (Sakthiprakash, 2005). These children are reported prevalent in Rajasthan, Goa and Kerala. Mumbai is believed to be the biggest centre for pedophiliac commerce in India (Nirmala Niketan, 2003).

Child sex trafficking is one of the most inhuman crime against children. As Asia Observed pointed out the girls once sold to brothels are immediately forced into commercial sex work. If they refuse, they are locked in isolation, beaten up by brothel keepers, starved, and raped by the gang. Victims are subjected to sadistic brutality along with sexual harassment leading to scratching and bruising which facilitate the entry to HIV (Pushpa Karuna, 1998).

Children are highly preferred by traffickers due to the belief that younger girls are less likely to be the carriers of the AIDS virus. The myth that sex with virgins will cure sexually transmitted diseases also stimulates the requirement.

Tourism is one of the biggest and fastest growing industry worldwide. The negative side of the business such as the adverse effect it could produce in the area of social, economical, cultural, environmental and human rights are not viewed seriously. This may because of the high end revenue received by the business. The ugly and alarming face of the tourism is the growing connections between the crime syndicate, trafficking. Though tourism alone cannot be held responsible for the trafficking and sexual exploitation of children, it provides a platform for an easy access to children thus increases risk of trafficking and child abuse (CACT, 2006).

A study conducted in 2002 estimated that children on the eastern coast of India found that children are brought to the trade on giving, false promises such as better job, good income, various comforts of life, etc., It has been reported that 40 per cent of the children are forced to enter into the trade and money lenders had enforced the parents to sell their children to repay the debts (Equations, 2002). There are number of players work hand and gloves including adult sex workers, pimps and other middle men, rickshaw pullers, van pullers, and petty traders who have contact with street children bring them to tourist lodges and hotels as per the demand of the customers (Equations, 2003).

In a recent study conducted in Chennai it has been reported that the overwhelming majority of the trafficked girls enter into the trade at the tender age of 11-14 years and among them vast majority have first sexual experience at the age of 12 years. All of them have undergone sexual harassment and humiliation in the brothel homes which made them to submit themselves for sex work (Sakthiprakash, 2005).

The number of women and children in sex work in India is stated to be between 70,000 and 1 million. Of these, 30 per cent are below 20 years of age. Nearly 15 per cent began sex work when they were below 15, and 25 per cent entered between 15 and 18 years (Mukherjee and Das, 1996). A news item published in the Statesman on 12th August 2002 stated that roughly 2 million children are abused and forced into commercial sex every year in India. A rough approximation prepared in 2000 by an NGO, End Children's Prostitution in Asian Tourism, reveals that there are around 2 million prostitutes in India, 20 per cent of them being minors. A study conducted in 1992 estimated that at any given time, 20,000 girls are being transported from one part of the country to another (Gupta, 2003).

A report prepared by CEDPA (1997) revealed that approximately 200 girls and women in India entered to commercial sex every day and 80 per cent were coerced into it (SOS, 2001). There are reportedly 3 lakh to 5 lakh children are in commercial sex work in India (Parkar, Praveen and Preeti, 2001). A UNICEF report on Maharashtra found that at any given time, approximately 40 per cent of the victims of commercial sex exploitation and trafficking are below 18 years of age.

The National Crime Records Bureau (NCRB) statistics for 1999 figured that there were 9,368 cases of trafficked women and children in India. The incidence of trafficking is alarming as it has been a steadily increased since 1997. Reported crimes against women were highest in Tamil Nadu (10.5%). Further more the total number of cases of kidnapping and abduction registered in 1999 was 15,956. Among the women victims, 1960 were reportedly kidnapped or abducted for marriage and9159 persons for commercial sex (ADB, 2002).

Role of Internet

The communication technology industry is spreading its wings across the globe in a greater vigour and power in recent time. Though it is a revolution one side it has its own consequences in the area of sex industry in terms of sex tourism, pornography, cyber sex, networking, etc. It has been understood that the child sex industry is the big money business lot of companies spread their business through internet by hosting a websites and advertisements are given to that effect.

Travel companies on the other side use the internet for their sex tourism business and flourish the business. The nature of the companies are so small that they could easily escape from the law enforcement agencies. Apart from the advent of the internet usage the growth of sex tourism of children can be successfully operated through internet classrooms, message boards, and online organizations not only encourage this form of tourism, but give detailed instructions about how to partake in it. The effect is multifarious when the offenders communicate with others who would travel these countries for this purpose (CACT, 2006).

Enroute to Commercial Sex Work

Trafficking and commercial sex are inseparable if the victim is happened to be a women or girl. Many researchers have identified and reported in their studies on trafficking.

Though there are various laws and amendments to curb commercial sex work they may be classified into three major aspects viz; the Prohibitionist system, the Tolerations system and the legalization system (D'Cunha, 1991). Fortunately or unfortunately Indian laws related to commercial sex are based on the Tolerationist system which does not seek to abolish prostitutes or prostitution per se. Under this system sex workers are supposed to be criminalized by virtue of their work and have more or less the same rights as other citizens. As mentioned, the tolerationist system, which our nation has adopted is reflected in the Suppression of Immoral Traffic in Women and Girls Act (1956). This act came into force in 1958 and was the result of India being the signatory to the United Nations International Convention for the Suppression of Trafficking in Persons and Exploitation of Others passed in New York in 1950. The Suppression of Immoral Trafficking act has now been amended as Immoral traffic in persons prevention Act 1986.

In India most of the women and girls are from Nepal who are recruited for commercial sex work and in Mumbay alone there are approximately 50,000 engaged in the flesh trade. Everyday about 200 girls and women in India enter commercial sex work and 80 per cent of them against their willingness (CEDPA, 2005).

According to the report by the National Commission for Women a growing number of the tribal women and young girls from Jharkhand are being trafficked, lured by promises of employment and marriage to Punjab, Haryana, Delhi, West Bengal and Maharashtra. The girls are given false promises in the name of good jobs by touts but they end up as domestic help, bonded agricultural labourers and brick kiln work.

Women who are brought from different parts of the country are kept in hotels, even go downs and underground places and later smuggled out across the border. These women and girls are sold to organized syndicates or to the gangs. The price is fixed based on the age, beauty, skin colour and virginity (Ranjan, 2005).

Children Destinations

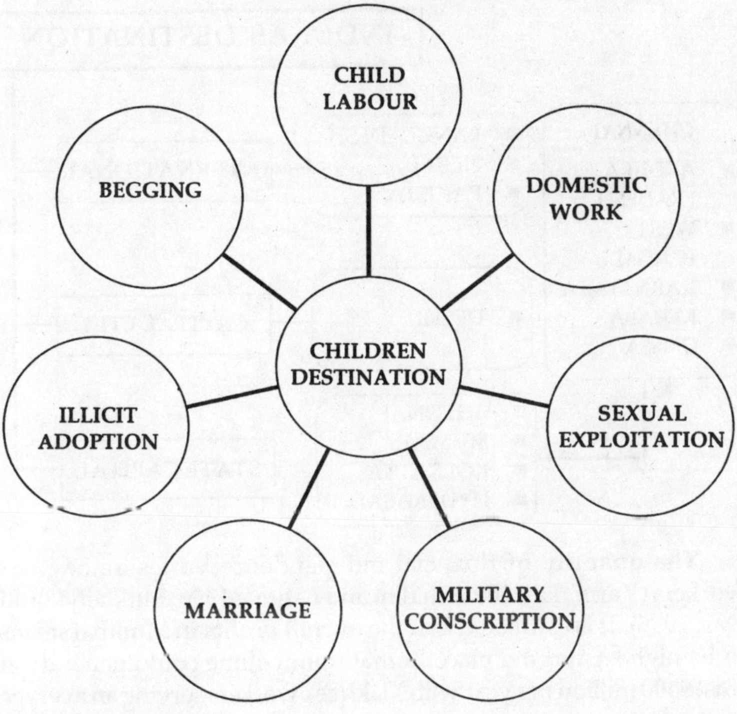

Destination Places

It has been reported by Rozario et al (1988) that the trafficked victims are sold or transferred to various towns and cities through markets (markets are places kept under cover) available in various states. The sale rate is fixed taking into account the age, physical stature, appearance, colour, etc and the amount may vary from a minimum of few hundreds and maximum of thousands nearing a lakh.

Destination Sectors

Trafficked persons are placed in various sectors as the demand is on the increase due to cheap labour, vulnerable nature, easily be exploited, limited or less options, etc. They are in high demand in commercial sex work, pornography, cyber sex and sex tourism, drug peddling, shop lifting, criminal activities, begging, domestic labourers, in unorganized sectors, shops and restaurants, hotels, road side eateries, etc.

Destination

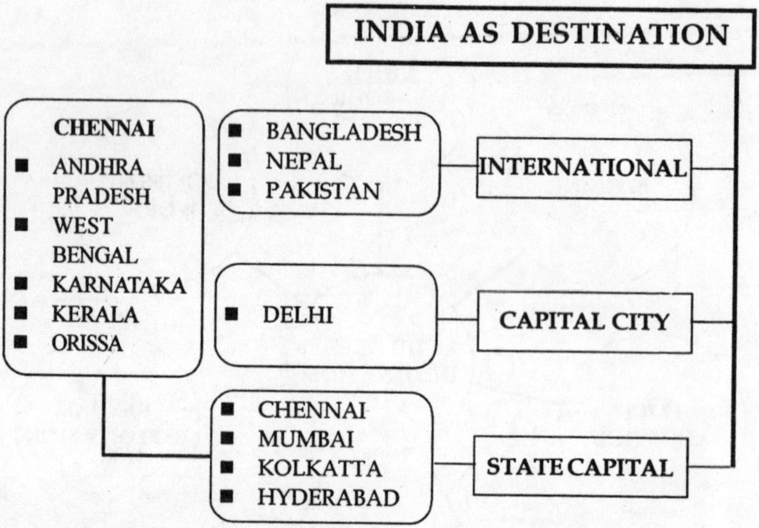

The quantity of financial independence varies among sex workers (Karmakar, 2001; Shalini and Lalitha, 1996; Mukherjee and Das, 1996). It is estimated that the overall profits in Mumbai seems to be highest and the place Kamathipura alone could generate at least $400 million per year with 1 lakh sex workers serving an average of six clients per day.

It is worth mentioning a study by Ganitha (1999) who calculated that transactions in sex trade were worth Rs. 1,85,000,000 in a day and Rs. 37,000 crore per year reflects the enormously high income from this illegal trade. It is also quite alarming that children as young as nine years of age were apparently purchased for Rs. 60,000 at auctions where Arabs bid against Indian men (SOS, 2001). A study of brothels in Delhi reported that 15.4 per cent of the sex workers had no idea of their earnings, as controlling agents cornered all their earnings (Shalini and Lalitha, 1996). The hard earned income by victim women and girls is shared among the various other players and forms an integral part of the sex business. This sharing of income makes the nexus between procurers, pimps, brothel keepers, local rowdies and police so strong that they together promote prostitution (Mukherjee and Das, 1996).

Sex Tourism

Sex trade becomes part and parcel of the tourism industry and hence tourism has also contributed to an enormous extent to the exploitation of children and young girls. Sex tourism or tourism for the purposes for sex has fund its way into the mainstream tourism market (CRG, 2003; DWCD, 1988). Tourism creates conditions which facilitate an easy indulgence. The benefit of anonymity offered by the host country reduces the element of eternal inhibitory factors to the minimum (Nair, 2005).

The growing tourism industry also encourages sex trade resulting in trafficking of women and girls. Same is the case with growing urbanisation and industrialization which contribute to the migration of impoverished women and girls from villages and it facilitates the growth in trafficking of women and girls for sexual exploitation.

Trafficking of women and girls is a world wide problem and it needs diplomatic and effective enforcement of law by the authorities in order to bring to a halt trafficking.

Sex tourism involves various players like travel agencies, tour operators, hotels and others in the tourism industry and some companies even openly advertise the availability of child prostitutes (Nirmala Niketan, 2003)

The consumption of trafficking victims is in the form of commercial sex work, labour, domestic servitude, entertainment and sports, pornography, sex tourism, child marriage, illegal activities like begging, drug peddling and even organ trade. Even the adoption market has a hidden face of trafficking of children. These children range from an age of a few hours to 15-16 years.

Trafficking Economy

Trafficking in human is one of the world's most lucrative businesses after smuggling of arms and drugs. At the advent of globalization, liberalization and privatization the threat to human existence from market forces looms large, with more and more human beings turning into commodities for sale. India is no different and the worst to suffer the brunt of technological boom, consumerism, multi-national culture, loss of traditional sources of livelihood, privatization of basic services, trade agreements, and the path of development India has embarked upon, have been the marginalized and the disadvantaged groups, particularly women and children (CACT, 2006).

The various researchers reported that the trafficking is a high earning venture and it fetches lot of money for all the players in the game. It is astonishing to note the magnitude of money involved in the business as estimated by a study from United Nations that $5 to 7 billion is annual transaction. Richard (2001) observed that profits from trafficking are a major source of income for crime rings. To increase profits, prices are inflated fro various services and documents during cross-border trafficking. The victims are also kept in poor, crowded conditions to cut down costs (Nair, 2005).

Sex Industry

With the advent of erstwhile industrialization and the recent phenomenon of globalization opens the gate of commercial sex trade wider. It is the last decade the sex industry worldwide expanded in velocity and dimension and taken new dimensions and forms. Whether these activities are legal or illegal, a wide range of heap street prostitution, clandestine brothels, nightclubs as well as message parlors, go-go bars, escort and internet services are becoming prevalent. This widening of choice has actively stimulated new consumption habits. From the promoters' perspective, the exploitation of the trafficked girls and women maximize profit and minimize expenses. From the customers perspective the presence of trafficked person allows greater freedom in their behaviour such as sexual intercourse without condoms (Ranjan,2005).

Bonded Labourer and Trafficking

The time immemorial the issue of bonded labours is prevalent in India and the phenomenon has been very well changed due to the enactments and amendments and strict enforcement measures. However; it is to be admitted that it has been reduced and not eradicated. Up to March1999, it has been reported that 2,90,340 bonded labourers had been identified by various state governments (ILO, 2002) Trafficking and bonded labourer are many a time inseparable. It has been reported that there are around 27 million slaves identified in the world of which 15 to 20 million constitute bonded labour in India, Pakisthan, Nepal, Bangladesh. Bonded labourer is widespread in over 20 states in

India. Migrant workers have been found to be working under conditions similar to the bonded labour system in fish processing units in Gujarat, stone quarries in Haryana and brick kilns in Punjab (ILO, 2001).

Easy Money

Trafficking human beings, especially women and children is the easy and quick money earning business. It is considered as the best among the illegal trade. It is even compared as the high money earning source compared to drug, smack and cocaine trafficking.

Nowadays the criminals and gangs have identified trafficking as the flourishing business and entering in it. It is terrible noted that the drug trafficking route is slowly used for trafficking business too.

It is an another estimate by the International Organisation for Migration (IOM) that the global trafficking industry generates up to US $8 billion each year from this trade in human misery.

Traffickers from Thailand have made $8 million profit over six years; by employing women in sweet shops (UN, 2001). Indian estimates of revenues from trafficking are not available and usually, only figures for selling and purchasing girls are mentioned. According to an estimate, girls are sold to brothels for any amount between Rs.15,000 to Rs. 40,000 (HRW, 1995). In India The Commercial sexual exploitation of children accounts for Rs.11,000 crore of the Rs.40,000 crore commercial sex industry (Gupta, 2003).

Consequence of Trafficking

Trafficking created the negative impact on the children at their social, economical, psychological and educational aspects. The parental care and concern is absent for these children first of all. The socialization process is cut off for these victims. The family of orientation is not able to provide adequate orientation because of the absence of the family itself.

This has a serious implication on the lives of the individual in terms of their human and family relationship. At the economical side the children are not produced in terms of their human resource development as they are put it to work at a younger stage makes the maximum development impossible and their productivity is the serious question to be concerned with.

At the psychological level lot of maladjustments, bad habits and serious flow in the personality has taken place which will have an adverse effect on the whole community. Very unfortunately the basic education need to be provided to the children is at stake. The overall impact the trafficking created on the children is a serious subject matter to be probed as it involves the question of the future nation.

The consequence of trafficking on the physical and mental health of the victims has not been properly documented and analysed (Govt. of Sweden, 2001). Reports about the consequences vary, depending on whether the end purpose is included in the adopted definition of trafficking. Thus some, studies may include intakes of human rights violation that occur at the destinations while others may not. Trafficking is understood to have social, economical, educational, health and legal consequences on the victim (Wennerholm, 2002). More over it could also be understood in terms of individual, family and community. The relocation takes children away from their families, communities and support networks, leaving them isolated and utterly vulnerable to exploitation. The face serious problems as they are taken to a new place where they do not understand the local language most of the time and difficult to escape and get help from other source.

Individual—Health

The physical health of the trafficked victims have heavily damaged due to the dreadful experience they undergo. The experience and the ill-treatment are unbearable and unexplainable. The poor nutrition, the bad working and living conditions, less ventilation and light, deplorable and un-conducive atmosphere prevailing in the places where they are housed and working lead them to poor health status.

Though there are no specific studies available to measure the level of health status it is reported by various researchers that the suicidal tendencies, depression and turmoil found among the victims. The mental and emotional state of the children include malevoilence, helplessness, withdrawal, dissociation, self-blame and identification with the aggressor, distraction, foreshortened view of time, normalization and shaping so that the victims convince themselves that their experiences had to happen instead of viewing them as traumatic (Saarthak, 2002).

Consequences of Trafficking in Flow Chart

INDIVIDUAL →	■ ALOOPING FROM FAMILY ■ LACK OF EMOTIONAL SUPPORT ■ HEALTH PROBLEM ■ DRUG ADDICTION ■ SUICIDAL TENDENCY ■ SELF BLAME
FAMILY →	■ DISORGANISATION ■ BROKEN FAMILY ■ DISINTEGRATION ■ UNABLE TO MANAGE ■ FEELING OF HOMELESSNESS
PSYCHIATRIC DISORDERS →	■ POST-TRAUMATIC STRESS DISORDER ■ DEPRESSIVE DISORDER ■ DISSOCIATE DISORDER ■ PSYCHOTIC DISORDER ■ EATING DISORDER
COMMUNITY →	■ LACK OF PARTICIPATION ■ LACK OF SOCIAL SKILL ■ PROBLEM CREATOR ■ BLINKED FUTURE ■ HIV/AIDS ■ SEX TOURISM ■ UNPRODUCTIVENESS ■ CRIME ■ DELINQUENCY

The psychiatric disorders found among the children are post-traumatic stress disorder, depressive disorder; dissociate disorders, psychotic disorders and eating disorders. Women apart from these disorders face an additional stress due to their morality being damaged (ISS, 2003); and also facing moral and legal isolation (Giri, 1999). It is pathetic to note that the trafficked people are vulnerable to HIV/AIDS infections (UNDP, 2002). They are also exposed to drug addiction, high-risk abortion, teenage pregnancies and serious damage to the reproductive health. A study conducted in Daka reported that more than 20 per cent of street children prostitutes die before reaching adulthood; and almost 22 per cent become physically invalid and are fit only for begging (SOS, 2001).

The trafficked victims are left with life-long effects of mental and physical trauma, may also end up with life threatening HIV/AIDS, STD, drug addiction or personality disintegration. It is a denial of right to home and family right to freedom from torture, violence, and cruelty, right to home and family, education and employment, right to health care and right to live with dignity.

Trafficked victims are exposed criminal risks and compelled to lead illegal lives. Illegality taints every dimension of their lives, making them criminals. Their criminalization severely stigmatizes them and intensifies their victimization, and leaves them with no recourse for redress (Sanghera, 2002).

The child domestic workers are victims of varius forms of ill-treatment and abuse such as sexual, emotional, physical which extends equally to both the sexes.

Family

Family is the basic unit of the Indian society. At the family level the impact is serious as the culture pays importance to the family - the intimate relationship, the socialization process, the care and concern for the children and upbringing of children and acts as a cushion during shock. Various consequences listed due to trafficking are disorganization, broken family, disintegration, unable to manage and feeling of homelessness. Absence of children from the family would lead to implication in the character formation and the influence of peer could dominate and lead to serious deterioration in the total personality of the children.

Social

The community has a strong impact due to trafficking which not only involves the violation of a whole gamut of laws and human rights but also threatens the integrity of the community. It becomes a threat to society because traffickers operate across borders with impunity with the growing involvement of organized criminals and by generally undermining the rule of law (Nair, 2005). Trafficking threatens the very fabric of society because it involves not only criminals but also law enforcers. It manifests and perpetuates patriarchal attitudes and behaviour, which undermine efforts to promote gender equality and eradicate discrimination against women and children (ADB, 2002).

The fear over trafficking is evident in social lives of people other countries as it Is illustrated by reports from Albania, which document villages where nine in ten girls over 14 stay away from school because they are afraid of being trafficked, and this fear alters the choices that girls make about their futures (ILO, 2002).

It has been reported that the economic losses to communities and governments are enormous if considered in terms of lost returns on human and social investments. The cost of countering criminal trafficking activities, infrastructure, time investment, personnel etc., puts an additional strain on already limited government resources for law enforcement. A vast amount of potential income from trafficked labour is lost in hidden sectors (ADB, 2002).

More over 'the loss of future productivity and earning power through low educational levels, ill health and potentially premature death is also felt at the country and regional level. Poor nations can ill afford to lose their young people, whole present and future productive capacity is essential to growth. The ravage of disease, including HIV/AIDS, is also an enormous burden on such countries and causes further imbalances between the young and middle-aged potential work force and old people dependent on them (ILO, 2002).

Rights Violation

Trafficking in children is a violation of human rights, including the very right to life, the right to liberty, human dignity and security of person, the right to freedom from torture or cruelty, inhumane or degrading treatment, the right to a home and family, the right to education and proper employment, the right to health care and everything that makes for life with dignity (Mathew, 2005).

There is a long way to go to have a better understanding by all the players in the issue especially the government, non government, research and academic agencies so as to deal adequately this problem. There is also a need to not only create but also readily available current data on the menace with the commitment for updating the knowledge. On the other hand the redressel mechanisms are woefully inadequate and the way the various governmental agencies have dealt with this gross violation of human rights has left much to be desired (Nair, 2005). This dichotomy calls for an in-depth understanding of the dimensions of trafficking in India as also the need for creating an authentic database, which can

Trafficking and Child Rights Violation

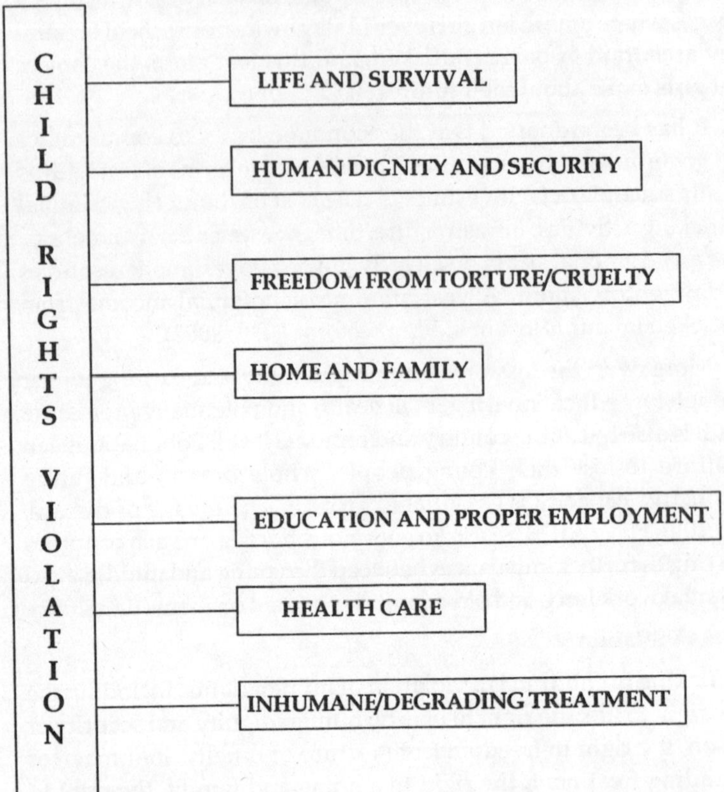

help devise appropriate measures to protect human rights with greater vigor (Mathew, 2005).

Ill-Treatment Experienced

There are lot of ill-treatment's faced by these victims in the form of physical, psychological, and social. The movements and freedom are totally controlled by the traffickers in the form of physical confinement, violence and threat. The torture and turmoil undergone by these victims is intolerable. The trafficking is the tool by which slavery is achieved; the aim of slavery is profit (Bales, 1999). In other words violence is an unavoidable constituent of the trafficking process, either one way or the other the demonstration of violence or control is exercised on the victims. The violence is in the form of initiation, intimidation, punishment and control. Many a time the victims will have literally no control over these types of violence as they are defenseless and susceptible to the situation and not able to do any kind of resistance rather slowly admit, accept and submit themselves to the ill-treatment process.

There were up to eighteen forms of such violence or control has been illustrated by Rozario (1988). They are starving, locked in dark room, beating , brunt, butts, bound forced to drink, strangled, stabbed or killed, physical torture, physical abuse, compelling to use drug and alcohol, etc. Attempts are made to even create a dependency on drugs and alcohol among the victims so that they become more dependent and shall not leave them. There is a psychological pressure experienced by the trafficked children for a period of at least seven to ten days (Nirmala Niketan, 2003). The resulting emotional and physical manipulation of children ensures that the traffickers' activities are kept secret, allowing them to maintain control over the victim.

There is not only psychological dependency created by the traffickers on the children but also social and economic dependency has been created. The victims may not have any money with them and they have no access to finance and they have dependent for food, cloth, cosmetics and other necessities for day to day need to the traffickers. The amount spent on these children starting from purchase, transport, food, cloth, accommodation, etc., are accounted for each individual and the traffickers would always like to earn the investment with profit. Bales (1999) described this phenomenon as 'contract slavery' and which is considered as extremely profitable. Many researchers reported that the victims have even debt bondage with the traffickers (Raymond, 2002; Rozario, 1988; Karmakar, 2001; Mukherjee, 1977; Richard, 1999) show that the magnitude of exploitation on these trafficked people.

Ill-Treatment for Girls

The girls who are trafficked reported that when they are in the brothel house they were frequently subjected to extortion, physical beating or assault and torture, rape and sexual abuse starvation, isolation in dark rooms, injuries, beating with hot iron rods, forced to use drugs and drink, multiple rape, mental torture, forced abortions burning with cigarette butts and terrorized buy gangs and criminals.

Trafficking – Intervention Strategies

United Nations – the top level organization has identified major areas of intervention in trafficking specified in the UN Protocol as **Prevention, Protection** and **Assistance.** The United Nations also laid down the guidelines for action (UNESCAP, 2002).

Most of the studies focused on the interventions and suggestions or guidelines to how to combat the problem. To be specific the two major areas normally covered by various researchers are the criminal justice system and the welfare policies and measures of the government (UN, 2001).

The reasons for poor and inadequate research are attributed to denial of the problem, objectifying the victims and failing to consider their human rights, conflation of trafficking with undocumented migration and improper definitions of the crime (Jordan, 2002).

Contrary to this, the legal and judicial system in India is perceived as formidable by the victims rather than being a deterrent to those who commit offences (SWCD, 1996). It has also to be understood that the procedures and formalities are tedious and time consuming.

Though the rescued children and women are sent back to their original places especially to the parents if available or to the homes; there is hardly any follow up is done on these victims. There is very little action is taken by the police and judiciary against the traffickers and those who are initially responsible for the violation of the rights of these children. It is so happens that the victims become the first witness against the traffickers which made them more vulnerable against the perpetrators and hence the possibility for escaping from the legal net is wider. In cases involving organized crime, they are extremely vulnerable and in fear for their lives (UN, 2001).

Intervention Personnel

The law protectors – the police; is considered as the most important institution in the struggle to eradicate trafficking (UN, 2001). They have greater role and responsibility in preventing and controlling the menace. Very unfortunately the police have close nexus and networking with almost all the players in the trafficking trade since it involves huge amount of money. Studies have indicated that police corruption is prevailing in the trafficking trade and said to be endemic (UN, 2001).

The reports of HRW (1995); DWCD (1996); DWCD (1998) and United Nations (2001) warned that the police have close acquaintance with the brothel owners, being in complicity with traffickers and accordingly the crime of trafficking becomes a low priority.

The conduct and management of rescue operations has also been severely criticized. Most of the reports are critical about the behaviour of the police, how age verification procedures are conducted and the lack of appropriate networking with other concerned agencies like protective homes (STOP, 2002; ADB, 2002; Nirmala Niketan, 2003).

It has to be observed with serious concern that the commercial sex workers prefer to be under the protection of a brothel owners as the latter negotiates with police who are seen as tormentors and are hated in the sex industry (DWCD, 1996).

It has been reported that there are deficiencies found the investigations which result in the acquittal of the accused (STOP, 2002). Though the police are required to play a proactive role, as they have been given preventive responsibility by the legislation; they many a time failed to do that. However they usually limit their involvement to taking reactive measures and addressing the manifestations of the crime, rather than its roots (DWCD, 1996).

However the lack or negative performance of the police could also be understood from their perspectives. Police have a fear of victimization through political involvement as it has evidently observed brothel owners have close links with politicians. The police also find it difficult to send the children to government homes due to lack of facilities and security. There is also lack of communication and awareness on the part of the police personnel and even the judiciary on the availability of appropriate correctional system, the welfare facilities available and the various provisions pertaining to the legislations.

Lack of infrastructure, lack of resources and powerful political and business connections of traffickers are also mentioned as inhibiting the law enforcement machinery (DWCD, 1998). The working and living conditions of police personnel, especially constables, is reported to be dismal (ADB, 2002). There is a lack of per capita time for the constable or sub-inspectors at the grassroots due to other law and order priorities.

Other Factors

Immigration officials and border forces too have close links with the traffickers as there are lots of cross country trafficking taking place through out the world. Trafficked people also come in contact with the officials and some reportedly collaborate with the traffickers. Many trafficked women alleged that immigration officials are involved in the process of their transfer because of a noticeable lack of questioning and examination of their documents (Raymond et al. 2002). The officials may support trafficking by selling visas (GSN, 1997).

Though there are new technologies introduced by various other countries to control trafficking India; is yet to use it. From the point of view of prosecution, developments in the methods of detection and prevention have not kept pace with the creation of new forms of trafficking (Giri, 1999). There are also few researches indicate the need for the sophisticated and innovative investigation techniques are needed to counter the role of organized crime and international syndicates in trafficking (ADB, 2002; Nair, 2002).

Curbing Trafficking

The US State Dept of trafficking in Persons Reported (June, 2005); that the quality and magnitude of the governments' anti-trafficking response, particularly in the law enforcement area, are seriously insufficient relative to India's huge trafficking in persons problem. Only the states like Maharastra and Tamil Nadu have started serious efforts to curb the menace of trafficking through fast courts, which has resulted in an increased number of prosecutions of the traffickers.

Minimum Efforts

But India; as a whole is yet to show more willingness to stop this business or taking steps to minimize the victimization of women and children at the hand of traffickers. The government of India needs to increase the conviction rate of inter-state as well as transnational trafficking crimes. Though there are strong legislations like Immoral Trafficking Prevention Act at the centre and Suppression of Immoral Trafficking Act on women and girls at the state level (in Tamil Nadu) which criminalizes the offenses for selling, procuring and exploiting any person for commercial sex as well as profiting from prostitution but the unwillingness on the part of the law enforcing agencies make the acts futile.

Corruption among the enforcing officials plays a major role in making the government less active in the area of trafficking. For instance, the quest for few hundred rupees by the border guard turns a blind eye to cross border trafficking and police officers take extra step to warn the brothel owners of the impeding raids, in turn, claiming a share in the profit from the brothel a the cost of the enslaved trafficked victim (Ali, 2005).

The report of the US state department on trafficking in persons (June, 2005) need to be comprehensively understand; as it become an annual convention and being published for the last five years. The ultimate mission of the report is to promote awareness on trafficking globally and motivate the countries to trigger their anti-trafficking activities. The report also rates the various nations' programmes through three Ps—Prosecution, Protection and Prevention. Since the report is victim centered as well equal emphasis is given on three Rs as well—Rescue, Rehabilitation and Reintegration.

Anti—Trafficking: 'P' and 'R' Approach

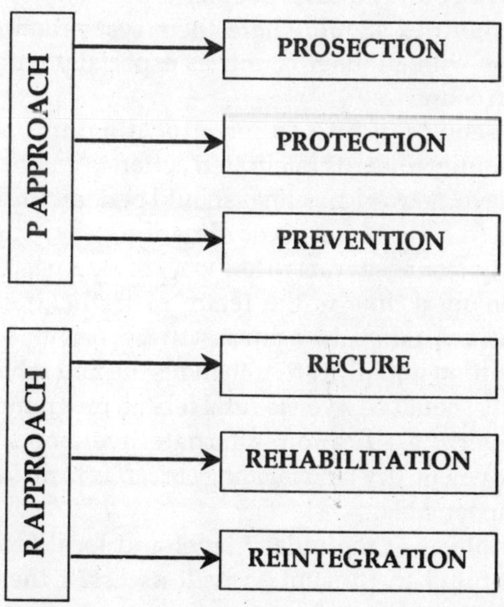

The default countries are graded as Tier III countries. The US government goes one step further in making the other countries to take tangible action against anti-trafficking by compelling them in the form of withholding of non-humanitarian and non-trade related assistance.

Intervention Required

- Awareness programmes by Govt. and NGO targeting risky population and identification of hot spots.
- Mobilizing people locally, nationally and internationally towards this cause.
- Creating employment opportunities especially during off seasons or hard seasons.
- Identifying alternative livelihoods will make them not to leave the habitat and fall a fry with the traffickers.
- There is a proper awareness programme about the pros and cons and of trafficking among general masses and specifically the victims.
- Trafficking legislations should be enacted making trafficking women ad children a felony instead of a misdemeanor.
- Public sharing of information in various forums such as conferences, workshops and seminars could be organized to sensitize and educate people.
- The countries should share their best practices to assist victims with all other countries especially with the traffic driven countries.
- Involvement of NGO's for educating and piloting the community towards integrated action to combat the issue.
- State level network meetings should periodically be arranged to have a higher level of coordination.
- Poverty, lack of education, low wages forces people to migrate and many a time in the realm of trafficking and hence initiatives taken to address these issues basically as prevention initially rather than rescue and rehabilitation.
- Priority should be given to rural related programmes in terms of poverty eradication, alternate livelihood, additional employment, dry land farming etc., so as to make the habitat self sustainable.
- Committees at the village level and local level could be constituted to prevent as well as assist the vulnerable population.
- Effective gender sensitization for women should be made more effective and strong.
- The intervention personnel should be given sensitization training periodically and made compulsory before given charge.

- Multifaceted approach like health care, counseling, education, training and social integration shall be done with integral approach.
- The enforcement officials both at the centre and the state shall be trained and equipped with the objective of protecting the vulnerable group in to the web of trafficking.
- Specific legislation is the need of the hour to promote anti-trafficking activities and to enforce specific measures.
- The rescue and rehabilitation measures shall be qualitatively improved so as to better reintegration of the victims shall be ensured.

Enforcing Legal Provisions

Traffickers must be put into task strictly using the legal provisions. The enforcement directorate must activate ànd book the culprits under any or all the laws applicable such as criminal laws, laws against slavery, sexual exploitation, illicit adoption, sex tourism, involuntary servitude, forced or compulsory labour, forced conscription into armed conflict debt bondage, forced marriage, forced abortion, forced pregnancy torture, cruel, inhuman degrading treatment, rape and sexual assault, body injury, kidnapping, unlawful imprisonment, labour exploitation, withholding of identity papers and corruption (Siwal, 2005).

Participation of Children

The child rights related issues are to be made known to the children who are supposed to be the stakeholders. Awareness programmes in what so ever manner shall be given to the children in general and to children in distress in particular. They need to know the channels in which they can represent their case by themselves or with child rights activists or with local people who have interest on children. The participation may ensure less likely to expose them to risk and danger.

Enhancing Capacity of the Communities

In case of children trafficking for labour activities the communities need to be educated. The various stakeholders of the community in terms of trafficking such as the ward members, presidents, influential persons, elders, women and youth groups need to be sensitized by providing knowledge, skill and authority to respond to child right problems.

MAJOR ANTI-TRAFFICKING INTERVENTIONS – National and International

The overall contribution of various countries in combating trafficking could be summarized as follows :

- The problem of trafficking has been projected into a high profile and high priority issue.
- Increased awareness on trafficking by various stakeholders and at all levels.
- Drafting of the SAARC Convention on Trafficking.
- increased allocation of financial and other resources by governments, the UN System, and international donors.
- High level of advocacy in reviewing policies and legislation related to trafficking issues.
- amplified information and data on the routes, forms, processes, and methods employed.
- Identification of the countries of origin, transit and destination in the circuit of trafficking within the South Asian region as well as outside.
- Identification of key causes of trafficking as well as the vulnerable and marginalized groups whose members are more likely to be trafficked.
- Better understanding of the consequences and impact of trafficking on the victims, their families and communities.
- Better understanding of the social, economic and cultural impediments to prevention of trafficking, and recovery, repatriation and reintegration of women and children affected by trafficking.
- Increased facilities and support to victims of trafficking in terms of shelters, halfway homes, medical care, counseling, training programmes, and outreach initiatives to potentially affected groups.
- Increases networking, dialogue and partnership among the various stake holders.

Major Anti-Trafficking Interventions

An assessment of the anti-trafficking interventions and initiatives in the selected countries of this study entails an evaluation of both the strengths and weaknesses of the various practices. As is evident from the above list of achievements, there is certainly little doubt that. particularly over the past decade, the various stake holders involved as key players in the anti-trafficking movement have made some remarkable gains. The following major, successful interventions and practices may be identified as highlights of anti-trafficking work:

Interventions by Self -organised Groups

In attempting to grapple with the problem of trafficking, an overwhelmingly disproportionate degree of energy, effort, and, activities of NGOs have focussed on the trafficking of women and girls into the prostitution industry. However, up until recently, little or feeble effort was made by NGOs to either form partnerships with sex workers organisations wherever these existed, or in mobilising and challenging sex workers to take up the issue of trafficking and forced prostitution, and the commercial sexual abuse of minors in the sex industry.

In the past four-to five years the movement for the self organistion of sex workers has emerged and gained strength, particularly in India and Bangladesh. Durbar Mahila Samanvyaya Committee (DMSC) and the Usha Collective of Sex Workers in Calcutta, SANGRAM and VAMP in Sangli Maharashtra, the Sex Workers Collective in Trichi, Durjoy in Dhaka, Shakti project of floating sex workers in Dhaka, and the Tangail sex workers organisation are some of the up-coming self organisations of sex workers which have recently begun to include interventions to reduce the forced entry of women and voluntary/forced entry of minors into the sex industry.

In addition to these organisations which have explicitly placed trafficking on their agenda along side the promotion of sex workers' human rights, some other organisations working with sex workers in major cities of India (Mumbai, Pune, Calcutta, Delhi, Chennai) have gradually but surely begun to dialogue with sex workers on issues of trafficking and assistance to trafficked women and girls in their ambit of activities. Prerna (Mumbai) and Sanlaap (Calcutta) for instance, in addition to providing services like child care, training, shelter, health care, education and legal assistance to children of sex workers and recovered victims, have also begun to initiate the necessary albeit difficult conversation with sex workers to undertake the challenge of arresting the influx of minors into prostitution.

The programmes undertaken by DMSC, SANGRAM and Durjoy are impressive indeed in their mass scale mobilisation of sex workers to organise for their rights, for better working and living conditions and for freedom from abuse, coercion, violence and stigmatisation. Activities to address trafficking of women and girls figure prominently in their mandates. Members of DMSC and Durjoy have both made a formal commitment to stop the forced entry of women and the trafficking of all minors into the sex industry. DMSC monitors this trend via its newly formed Slf Regulatory Boards.

It was extremely heartening to discover that in the three red light areas of Calcutta where Self-regulatory Boards are functional, not a single minor girl was visible in the brothels. These self organisations of sex workers acknowledge that combating trafficking is an enormously challenging task on account of the vested interests of highly powered persons, the immense rate of profits involved, and the and the intensely criminalized and hierarchized power structure of the sex industry. However, a commitment and concrete interventions to reduce trafficking are visible on the part of these sex workers' organisations in this regard.

This development cannot be overlooked or underestimated. If trafficking within the sex industry is to be combated then there is no option but to mobilize the support and active participation of sex workers and possibly other players in the red light areas. These players and sex workers are the 'insiders' who have full knowledge of processes and methods whereby trafficking occurs as well as the identity and location of the victims.

These 'insiders' may either be colluders who benefit from the trade of trafficking in varying degrees or they may be passive and indifferent observers. Through self organisation of sex workers in the above groups, an extremely significant project is underway to polarize or neutralize the colluders through intensive awareness and lobbying activities, and to win over the passive watchers and other players as allies.

Since these attempts are not only recent but novel and path breaking as no previous examples or guidelines exist, they do occasionally falter. However, what is worth noting is that for the first time in the arena of prostitution and trafficking, extremely vital, challenging and path breaking models are being explored and tested to actively involve sex workers and their communities in combating the very difficult problem of trafficking.

Support to Returnees

This example of successful and laudable intervention to provide assistance to returnees from brothels was not envisaged or designed as a conscious anti-trafficking intervention. However, on account of an emergency situation the manner in which several NGOs rallied to support the returnees and undertook the challenge of housing and reintegrating them can be held up as an exemplary initiative in anti-trafficking work.

In February 1996 the authorities in Mumbai raided brothels in the Kamathipura red light area of the city and 'rescued' more than 400 women and girls describes by them as 'victims' of forced prostitution. Of these over 200 were young women and girls from Nepal. Having rescued them, the authorities did not know what to do with the 'victims'. The Nepali women and girls, it was decided by the authorities, should be repatriated to Nepal. However the government of Nepal was not willing to take charge of them or bear any responsibility.

This emergency situation was given immediate attention by several NGOs in Nepal who united and successfully housed and provided assistance to the returnees from Mumbai. This particular case is a prime example of the callousness and lack of planning or preparedness on the part of the authorities to deal with so-called victims of trafficking once they have been rescued. On the other hand, this is a remarkable example of the commitment and to the issue and readiness to bear the responsibility of assisting victims of trafficking despite limited resources on the part of NGOs in Nepal. This case becomes an example of exemplary intervention in handling an emergency situation from the NGO sector. At the same time it raises some important questions in terms of examining and grasping the response particularly of the governments by highlighting the query: What lessons have been learnt by the authorities and the other stake holders from this experience? What new and alternate steps have been taken by the state to address such eventualities and emergency situations?

Peer Mobilisation

The above experience provided an opportunity for another interesting and noteworthy development. Several of the returnees from Mumbai who were sheltered by various organisations engaged in anti-trafficking work organised themselves to form a group called

Shakti-Samuh and decided to develop activities for doing outreach work in the affected and catchment areas from which 'victims' of trafficking are routinely drawn in Nepal.

Thus, affected districts in the countryside of Nepal, carpet factories and other industrial sites as well as street children have been targeted by members of Shakti-Samuh for outreach, awareness raising and social mobilisation. While, as an organisation Shakti-Samuh could do with considerable support in terms of financial and human resources, and certainly leaves much to be desired for in terms of overall strength, yet as a model of self organisation and mobilisation of 'returnees' who are active in designing and implementing activities to combat trafficking it is laudable. This initiative has not received the attention or support it should from the rest of the stake holders, nor has its potentialities been explored.

Interception and Repatriation

Several NGOs in Bangladesh, Nepal, and India have been active in intercepting, recovering and repatriating women and children affected by trafficking. An extremely important intervention was made by the Bangladesh National Women Lawyers Association (BNWLA) when it intercepted a groups of little boys who were in the process of being trafficked to the Middle East for camel jockeying. Similarly, many a victim of trafficking has been rescued and repatriated under extremely difficult and challenging circumstances by the NGO sector.

These organisations provide shelter, medical care, counseling, education, training and other forms of support to the victims, and try their best to reintegrate them into their communities. Maiti-Nepal, ABC Nepal, Worec, CWIN, Saathi, BNWLA, CWCS, Aino-Sailesh Kendra, Sanlaap, Joint Women's Programme are some of the many organisations which are active in organising recovery and reintegration of women and children affected by trafficking. They continue to learn from their ongoing experience in the field, and as a result often engage in active cooperation and partnership with each other. The recent growth of networks, both national and cross border are an outcome of this cooperation. However, limited resources, limited mutual cooperation, and sometimes inadequate grasp of the situation at the conceptual and ground level act as constraints. Some of these organisations have begun to organise effective outreach into affected communities in the countryside. This is a very positive step and needs to be supported and expanded. In summation, it remains to be said that the terrain of rescue and reintegration is a very challenging and complex one. Yet, despite the fact that many NGOs are engaged in rescue, repatriation and rehabilitation, the issue of recovery and reintegration has not received the concerted and joint attention which it deserves from the anti-trafficking movement either at the conceptual or at the operational levels.

Policies and Programmes of Government

At the central level Department of Women and Child Development is dealing with the protection and assistance policies to combat trafficking among women and children. At the state level each state has its own infrastructure either in the name of Department / Directorate of Social Welfare or Social defense.

National Plan

It was DWCD in the year 1988 which initiated a national level action plan to combat trafficking and commercial sex among women (DWCD, 1988). This elaborate plan covered a range of aspects, such as prevention, awareness raising, economic empowerment, rescue and rehabilitation. Coomarasamy noted that the plan was incorporated to cover innovative ideas, with the social welfare component being dealt with in detail – from rescue and rehabilitation to the education of the children of commercial sex workers and their housing and shelter (UN, 2001).

Though the national plan had been appreciated by people on the one hand it has also been criticized for lack of an integrated perspectives on intelligence relating to trafficking- rescue-rehabilitation- reintegration (SAP, 2001). The uncovered areas of the study are funding details, child pornography, implementation bottlenecks and violation of right to family for the children of commercial sex workers and no focus on the policies and strategies relating to finding and punishing traffickers (UN, 2001)

Prevention

The country report by ADB (2002) explains the an assortment of poverty alleviation and pro-women programmes launched by different departments to prevent defenseless sections from being trafficked. The report acknowledges that effective source area programming needs a holistic viewpoint. Government initiatives comprise the Integrated Child Development Scheme (ICDS) and

Swarna Jayanthi Swa Rozgar Yojana on the eve of the Golden Jubilee Celebrations of our nations freedom. The Swadhar scheme which was launched in December, 2001 targeted towards women in complicated circumstances including rescued trafficking victims (DWCD, 2001).

The DWCD is also plans to devise a national media strategy with the state level initiates being handled by its state counterparts. The Jabali scheme in Madhya Pradesh exclusively address the Bhedia, Bhancadara and Sansui tribes by bringing a holistic approach to rehabilitation and prevention plans for the children of trafficking victims.

Rehabilitation

The prime purpose of rehabilitation is the rejuvenation or reintegration of the children to their original parents. The institutional placement is considered only if the family environment is not conducive for the welfare and development of the children. There may be number of reasons for that viz., broken family, absence of father or mother or either parents, second marriage by either one of the parents, extra-marital relationship of parents, bad habits of father, quarrelsome nature of the parents, economic reasons, psychological reasons, etc., may tender the children to be placed in other institutions.

The institutional placement involves at the first instance government run homes, regular schools, vocational training schools, care homes of NGO's, transit points, etc. Very unfortunately the government run homes have been criticized for lot of fit palls such as corruption, poor infrastructure, meager budgets, inadequate provisions for psychological care, ineffective skill building, etc. (DWCD, 1996). Most of the women end up doing nothing for long periods in these homes, while those who do not wish to be rescued, view the home as a prison. The UN's view is that protective custody as practiced in South Asia is a serious violation of women's rights and it is important that the governments for the region re-examine this concept as well as the conditions in the government homes where women are kept (UN, 2001).

The availability of short stay homes or homes for the minor girls is missing in few places. The short stay homes and the juvenile homes are to be established under the Juvenile Justice Act (Care and Protection) 2000. For instance states like Haryana has not provided short stay homes for the minor girls (Tribune, 5th July 2003). Though all the required states are to provide such homes, only a few states have done it. The homes that have been set up are overcrowded and are not sufficiently equipped to address inmates' primary needs. The Juvenile Welfare Board (presently it is Child Welfare Committee) has also been criticized for functioning in isolation (Nirmala Niketan, 2003).

The process of rejuvenation is not that easy and it involves various stakeholder and it is a complex process altogether. In support of this view it has been reported in India today (28th July, 2003) that a minor girls who was pregnant refused to have an abortion after being rescued. In cases where the parents are considered unfit or unreliable, children need to be institutionalized. In the absence of a special court to take up the issue the charge of the child is relinquished to the parents. This is problematic as the child is likely to be re-trafficked (Nirmala Niketan, 2003).

Reintegration

It is the greater responsibility of the government machinery and the agencies involved in the rehabilitation to successfully do the reintegration programme for each children. It is a serious and lengthy process as lot of resources, personnel, time investment is required. Finding suitable rejuvenation package requires expertise in the field. The researchers in the field observed that there are not enough models of recovery, repatriation and reintegration that prioritize the preference and interests of trafficked women and children (Sanghera, 1999; ADB, 2002).

There is also a dearth of holistic rehabilitation programmes and support mechanisms (Nair, 2005).

Agencies Involved

There are both Government and Non Government organizations, Research and Academic institutions involved in prevention, rescue, rehabilitation, punishment, follow-up programmes to combat trafficking. At the central level Ministry of Home Affairs, Ministry of Social Justice and Empowerment, Department of Women and child Development, National commission for children, National Commission for Women, National Human Rights Commission, National Aids Control Organization, etc. are directly involve in the issue.

In the political front, National politicians and public health officials seem to be in a state of denial about the seriousness of the problem (Nirmala Niketan, 2003).

The UN's Response to Trafficking

The response of the UN System (UNS) to the trafficking of women and children in a coordinated manner and at a regional level is of recent origin. The various country offices of the diverse UN agencies have been active on the issue of trafficking in varying degrees for a considerable length of time. However, it is only in the very recent past, in the current year to be more precise, that UN interagency initiatives at the country level as well as at the regional level have been seriously envisaged and developed to address the issue of trafficking of women and children.

The year 1999 as such marks a watershed in the anti-trafficking movement as far as joint UN initiatives at the country and regional level are concerned. Most of these interventions are still in the planning stage and hence it is not possible to assess their impact. However the initiation of such a coordinated move is certainly noteworthy.

It needs to be noted as well that the UN agencies are in a unique position of having the expertise, credibility with governments and networks, including both GOs and NGOs, to address the multi-faceted factors connected with the issue of trafficking, and as such, offer the possibility for an effective and coordinated response to the problem of trafficking in the region. The UN System offers the following comparative advantages:

- The UN's universality; access to global resources and expertise for a wide-range of activities in the prevention, protection, recovery and reintegration of victims of trafficking.
- The UN's political and sectoral neutrality.
- The UN's ability for capacity building of institutions.
- The UN's capacity and credibility for working in close cooperation with governments and NGOs.
- The UN's ability to support governments in implementing and monitoring ratified international conventions and in promoting the ratification of crucial conventions.

A UN Task Force on Trafficking in Nepal was set up following an interagency consultation on trafficking of women and girls which was convened by UNDP in September 1998. The UN Task Force in Nepal was coordinated by the UNDP, and a UN Mission consisting of three consultants was mandated to prepare a project proposal to combat trafficking of women and girls in Nepal. This proposal, which was submitted in August has been worked into a project document which is in the process of being finalised currently. It is expected that the document will be signed at a ceremony attended by the Prime Minister and other key government representatives by the end of November, 1999.

A UN Task Force in Bangladesh has been formed as well to develop a country level project proposal for combating the trafficking of women and children. This interagency Task Force which is coordinated by UNESCO and steered by UNAIDS, has recently hired a national consultant to put together a project document to combat trafficking of Bangladeshi women and children. It is hoped that the project will become effective in the early part of the year 2000.These proposals aim to foster ownership of the various project activities by the relevant governments, NGOs and other concerned stakeholders, create partnerships amongst the various stakeholders, and develop coordinated activities amongst the various UN agencies to combat trafficking in the respective countries.

In addition to the above two Task Forces at the country level, the Office of the High Commissioner for Human Rights (OHCHR) has recently become actively involved in the issue of trafficking of persons with a special focus on trafficking in women and children. The High Commissioner has made public her decision to give high priority to the issue of trafficking. Concrete steps, including the allocation of additional human and financial resources, have already been taken to implement this decision.

The OHCHR Trafficking Programme was established in March 1999. Its objective is to work towards the integration of human rights into the international, regional and national anti-trafficking initiatives, and the emphasis is on legal and policy development. The programme does not plan to undertake large-scale projects or to otherwise duplicate the activities which are already being implemented, but to act as a catalyst and a support to the existing programmes and initiatives. The OHCHR organised two workshops in Nepal in March 1999, and is currently working on developing some pilot projects on trafficking in Nepal in cooperation with the UN Task Force. The High Commissioner is also currently examining the SAARC Convention on Trafficking from the standpoint of human rights.

At a recent UNAIDS Regional meeting held in Kathmandu Nepal, October 1999, it was decided to form a Regional Task Force on Trafficking and HIV/AIDS in order to develop and facilitate the implementation of regional interventions on the issue in Southwest and South Asia; the Regional UNDP office has been assigned the role of coordinating activities under this recent initiative. This present proposal is rooted therefore, in this recent development at the UN level as well.

While it is not possible to provide a complete inventory of the activities and interventions undertaken by the various UN agencies on trafficking and related issues in the past decade, some of the major activities are highlighted below.

UNDP country as well as regional offices have prioritized trafficking and its connection with HIV/AIDS in a major way within the region. Under its South and Southwest Asia Project on HIV & Development trafficking of women and girls and related issues of migration, advocacy and legal and ethical concerns have been identified by UNDP as key areas of focus. As mentioned earlier, The UNDP country office in Nepal sponsored and coordinated the UN Task Force on Trafficking of women and Girls in Nepal. The UN Mission established under this Task Force prepared a proposal for interagency cooperation to combat trafficking which is in the process of being operationalized. Similarly, the UNDP country office in Bangladesh is part of a UN Task Force on Trafficking in Bangladesh. The regional UNDP office envisages the key role of coordination for all its country offices within the region in the implementation of the activities at the regional level.

Role of International Agencies

UNICEF has played a key role in advocacy and awareness raising on the issue within the region. Its various country offices have also developed and conducted training workshops with law enforcement agencies especially the police on sensitization, investigation and establishment of women's cells. Plans are afoot, especially in Nepal to develop community policing and assist in the reintegration of exploited children. UNICEF had also sponsored research for situation analyses on trafficking in the various countries, as well as supported skills training, protection and reintegration for children at risk, survivors of trafficking, and children of sex workers.

Community surveillance and legal training too have been sponsored by UNICEF particularly in Nepal, alongside training women on legal issues, setting up paralegal committees at the ward, VDC and DDC levels. Support has also been provided by UNICEF for drafting a revised anti-trafficking Act in Nepal. The UNICEF country office in Bangladesh too has been active in supporting and promoting anti-trafficking interventions by encouraging research, advocacy, and training.

The Rights Cluster of this office in particular has undertaken some remarkable documentation and activities particularly in relation to the trafficking of children and adolescents, and their increased vulnerability. The India country office overseas a vast ambit of activity and has supported both the government and NGOs in developing and implementing various kinds of activities and programmes on trafficking.

It works closely with the Department of Women and Child Development and in 1996, jointly-sponsored six major meetings in different parts of the country to formulate policy guidelines and a programme document to support future programmes and strategies and develop a data base on trafficking of children and their commercial sexual abuse. In addition UNICEF has sponsored cross border police workshops on the issue of trafficking.

UNIFEM provides technical assistance to the Ministries concerned with women and children in the respective countries. As its mandate, UNIFEM has undertaken advocacy as well as sponsoring action-research on the issue of trafficking in the region. UNIFEM has been playing a leading role in supporting advocacy on the part of NGOs on the SAARC Convention on trafficking. UNIFEM also provides technical assistance to the various women's ministries and departments in developing databases and collating information on non-traditional employment opportunities for women.

ILO-IPEC supports NGO prevention programmes, awareness raising, rescue and rehabilitation. Assistance is provided to projects to develop training packages to sensitize primary school teachers in human rights, child rights, and to establish prevention camps in trafficking prone areas. ILO-IPEC also supports workshops for legal experts and prosecutors on enforcement and legislation regarding trafficking. ILO conducts intensive advocacy on issues of child rights and child labour and works closely with the ministries of labour and social welfare in the concerned countries.

International Organisation of Migration (IOM) has placed trafficking on its regional agenda and is particularly concerned with understanding and operationalizing the distinctions between migration and trafficking. The IOM focuses primarily on cross border trafficking seeks to strengthen organisations and programmes which provide support to survivors of trafficking.

In addition to the UN agencies mentioned above, many others including UNFPA, WHO and UNAIDS are committed to addressing the issue of trafficking through their principal mandates

Role of International NGO's

There are number of international NGOs have incorporated women and child specific programmes related specifically to addressing issues of trafficking in their activities. Most of these organisations focus on socially and economically marginalised groups. Their activities in the main focus on income generation, community development, health, literacy, and developing local leadership. These organisations have also played a key role in effecting policy and legislative change.

Save the Children Alliance

The various chapters of save the children alliance and allied members works at the level of child rights, focussing on the empowerment of the girl child, and combating abuse and violence against girls at the local level. This organisation has prioritized trafficking as one of its main activities and is in the process of conducting research on trafficking of girls with a view to finding effective strategies for prevention, as well as for the protection and reintegration of those affected by trafficking. The Alliance is focussing increasingly on partnerships with local organisations and engaging in capacity building.

The Asia Foundation is collaborating with a number of NGOs in Nepal through its various programs including the Rights, Responsibilities and Advocacy program in 21 districts and its Family Planning and Reproductive Health Programme in 10 districts.

Plan International works through partners for the recovery and rehabiliation of victims of trafficking from Brothels. Phased out shelter facilities, counseling and training to affected women and girls are part of the services provided by this organisation.

Action Aid is working on women's rights, property rights, and violence against women, including trafficking. This organisation works with affected communities in trafficking prone areas.

Red Barna/Red Barnet Support NGOs working in the field of children, and has chosen, as part of its mandate, to support anti-trafficking programmes. In Bangladesh, Red Barnet plays a very active role in ATSEC (Alliance Against Trafficking and Sexual Abuse of Children). This organisation focuses on advocacy, building capacity of organisations, supporting research, and funding support services to survivors and potential victims of trafficking.

In addition to the above, some major INGOs and donor organisations such as CIDA, DANIDA, SIDA, OXFAM, CEDPA, Horizons/Population Council, to name a few, are all either directly or indirectly active in supporting activities and interventions to address the issue of trafficking in the region. USAID too has been extremely active on the issue of trafficking of women and girls, and has developed a special programme for South Asia to support national and regional anti-trafficking initiatives. A sizable amount of financial resources have been allocated for these activities.

There are host of NGOs and community organisations in India working either directly or indirectly on the issue of trafficking, and it is not possible to describe their work in a report of this nature. However, almost the entire range of activities subsumed under anti-trafficking work and related aspects are covered by these organisations. As such, the range of activities covered by these organisations include:

- Research and documentation
- Advocacy at various levels
- Awareness and social mobilisation
- Prevention
- Recovery, repatriation and reintegration
- Housing and shelter
- Medical care and counseling
- Education and child care
- Skills training

- Alternative income generation and economic empowerment
- Policy and legislative reform
- Media and communication

A few NGO networks have recently emerged in the region. These are mostly country based but do include cross border interventions and perspectives on their agendas.

The National Network Against Girl Trafficking (NNAGT) was established in 1990. It brings together representatives from NGOs, government institutions, advocate, political leaders, media persons and concerned individuals to address the issue of trafficking of Nepali girls. The network is represented by district and village based organisations across Nepal. NNAGT's principal activities are focussed on advocacy, promoting interaction and partnerships between network members, establishing a resource centre for information and documentation, training and technical support to members, mapping of vulnerable areas of intervention, and monitoring. This network is committed to supporting the coordinated national agenda and Action Plan to address the problem of trafficking.

The Alliance Against Trafficking of Women and Children in Nepal (AATWIN) draws its members from all regions of the country. It focuses on prevention, advocacy, technical and lobbying training, media campaigns, and research and documentation. This network undertakes an integrated approach to combat the problem of trafficking. Increasingly, it is focussing on the linkages between migration and trafficking. AATWIN has been an active advocate on the SAARC Convention on Trafficking and is engaged in lobbying for recommended changes to this Convention.

Traffic Watch Bangladesh (TWB) is reportedly a recently formed network which works in tandem with Traffic Watch Bangladesh-Youth Network (TWB-YN), and Traffick Watch South Asia (TWSA). The secretariat for all these networks is at the Centre for Women and Children Studies. Traffic Watch Bangladesh engages in awareness raising campaigns, conducts dialogues and trainings with the police and journalists, undertakes research and documentation, as well as advocacy on the issue of trafficking of women and children.

Bangladesh Shishu Adhikar Forum is a network of children workers' and child rights organisations in Bangladesh. This network initiates advocacy programmes on the issue of child labour and trafficking, produces and distributes information and education material, underatkes awareness raising, supports skills training for minors and youth, and engages in policy and legislative review.

Action Against Trafficking and Sexual Exploitation of Children (ATSEC) is a network which has two chapters, one in Bangladesh and the other in West Bengal. ATSEC was formed in June 1998 after a one-day workshop on "Working Strategies to Combat Child Trafficking and Child Prostitution". This workshop was organised by Red Barnet Partner's Coordination Body, and currently Red Barnet acts as a facilitator for ATSEC Bangladesh for financial management and in preparing projects. For two of its projects, ATSEC has entered into agreements with UNICEF Bangladesh and USAID. The ATSEC West Bengal chapter is coordinated by Socio-Legal Aid Research and Training Centre (SLATRC). ATSEC engages in cross border activities to facilitate advocacy, research, social mobilisation, technical assistance and programme support at the national and regional levels. It also aims to develop capacity of GO-NGOs and other development groups to plan and implement advocacy programmes.

As mentioned earlier, a majority of these networks, particularly on trafficking, are of very recent origin. With the exception of the Bangladesh Shishu Adhikar Kendra whose direct focus is on child workers and child rights, the rest of the networks which focus on trafficking do not have many substantial successes or achievements to boast of. This could be due to the fact that they have been recently constituted. Most of their activity currently is centred on organising workshops and conferences to raise awareness and engage in advocacy on the issue of trafficking. While these networks have a broad based membership and claim to engage in a wide range of anti-trafficking activities, their effectiveness in addressing trafficking of women and children remains to be proven.

Sanghera (1999) has observed that there are lots of gap in anti-trafficking initiatives include the absence of reliable data, inadequate advocacy efforts, little or no analysis of laws, an insufficient understanding of the human rights framework, very few interventions for prevention and the lack of standards for the treatment of victims.

Outcome

Trafficking studies help in creating better understanding of trafficking in the country. It should also help in pinpointing vulnerabilities, the strategies that have worked in strengthening the vulnerable and in creating proper programmes and policies to tackle the issue (Nair, 2005).

Legislation

There are various legislations in India enacted to control trafficking. To start with Article 23 of the Indian Constitution prohibits all forms of trafficking. The suppression of Immoral Trafficking Act 1956, Immoral Traffic (Prevention) Act 1986, etc., have not created any tangible results in combating the menace and no mass awareness or action against trafficking in the country (D'Cunha, 1998).

There are number of laws, rules and regulations enacted in India to combat trafficking. Unfortunately the law and legal system in many countries especially in South Asia dis-empowers trafficked persons through an erosion of their constitutional and human rights while ostensibly attempting to protect them from harm and abuse—an impact that is contrary to the aims of anti-trafficking measures (Sanghera, 1999). Moreover the laws speak about the rehabilitation of the children mostly and not about the women who are rescued from the trafficking bondage.

Globally enacting law and amending to earlier provisions is a continuous and concrete step witnessed in the realm of any criminal offence and trafficking is no exception. Curbing the menace through law is a welcome feature to start with and to get standardized legal guidelines so as to implement the anti-trafficking strategies.

The strategic intervention the National and International institutions shall encourage and sponsor research programmes related to trafficking would promote better understanding of the phenomenon by the various stakeholders.

International Law Relating to Trafficking

It is the Herculean task to mention all the legislations enacted in various countries to curb the menace. To mention few is the worthy note:

Labour Perspectives

It is to be noted that there are hardly any study completely focusing on the child labour perspectives in trafficking phenomenon. There are also studies in the perspectives of migration and trafficking. Though lot of studies available on trafficking; most of them equated

- Bangkok Declaration by Representatives of Asian Countries on irregular Migration, 1999.
- Bihar Witchcraft Prevention Act, 2000.
- Bonded Labour System (Abolition) Act, 1976.
- Constitution of India, The preamble, Articles 14, 15, 19(1) (G), 21, 23(1), 39(A), 39(F), 46, 49.
- Convention on the Prostitution and Immediate Action for the Elimination of the Worst Form of Child Labour, 1988.
- Convention on the Rights of the Child, 1989.
- Immoral Trafficking (Prevention) Act, 1956 (Amended in 1986).
- International Convention on Civil and Political Rights 1966 (came into force in 1976).
- Indecent Representation of Women (Prohibition) Act, 1986.
- Maharashtra Protection of Commercial Sex Workers Act, 1994.
- SAARC Convention on Preventions and combating Trafficking of Women and Children into Prostitution 2002.
- Universal Declaration of Human Rights, 10 December 1948.

trafficking as commercial sex business or sex industry. Most of the reports on trafficking for commercial sex work and there have been no studies that have dealt exclusively the issue of trafficking for labour exploitation (Nair, 2005).

The child labour is generally divided into four major sectors such as Cultivators, Agricultural labourers, manufacturing, household industries and others. At the national level most of the child labour involved in an unorganized sectors where these children are losing their childhood. The match and fire works in Sivakasi Tamilnadu, the carpet industry in Palamau, Varanasi and Mirzapur, Powerloom industry in Bhiwandi, Maharastra, lock manufacturing in Aligarh, Gem polishing in Jaipur, Rajasthan, pottery work in Khurja and Glass factories in Firozabad in Utter Pradesh, Shellac industry in Bihar and Madhya Pradesh and the beedi manufacturing, brick kilns, plantation, tea shops and domestic work all over the country are apparent examples where the exploitation of children takes place.

Trafficking of children for labour too needs urgent attention as it is closely linked to migration that is directly a result of development policies and cannot be prevented unless there is a global pressure for another world where people's human rights are recognized, respected, promoted and protected.

To have a better understanding on forced or compulsory labour it is explained as work or service which is extracted from any person under the menace of any penalty and for which the said person has not offered himself voluntarily (Jordan, 2002).

It is obvious to note that from the report of HRW published in 1999 that there are 15 million children were working as 'virtual slaves' and most of such children found in carpet industries. It is pathetic to observe that children are also in bondage as bonded labourers in various organized and unorganized sectors such domestic work, silk work, beedi work, footwear, sporting wears, silver jewelry, synthetic and precious gemstones, hand-woven wool carpets and in service industries such as tea shops, restaurants, truck shops, brick industry, match industry, cracker industry, etc. Illegal-activities is the another dangerous sector where these Children are placed as forced labour who are found in prostitution, begging, drug selling and petty crime.

Labour Exploitation

There are various forms and levels of labour exploitation in India. It is highly prevalent in unorganized sector and illegal trade like this is indirectly encouraging labour exploitation since it cannot be claimed before the court of law. The Supreme Court has defined labour exploitation as all those who are paid less than the stipulate minimum wages fall within the category of bonded labourers.

There is an interesting statistics which says that at present there are 350 million workers in the unorganized sector who are not paid the prescribed minimum wages. Besides, there are 120 million children between the age of 6 and 14 years who are not going to schools, Thus million 470 people, a little less than half of the population of India, are in the state of bondage (Iyer, 2003).

On the other hand it is calculated that in India the child labour ranges from 60 million to 115 million. A recent study conducted by ILO in Napel found that the children were trafficked for the purpose of domestic work, work in hotels and restaurants, carpet and weaving industry (Subedi, 2002). Children trafficked for labour exploration may also be subjected to sexual abuse and exploitation. Employers prefer to hire children because they cost less, are easier to

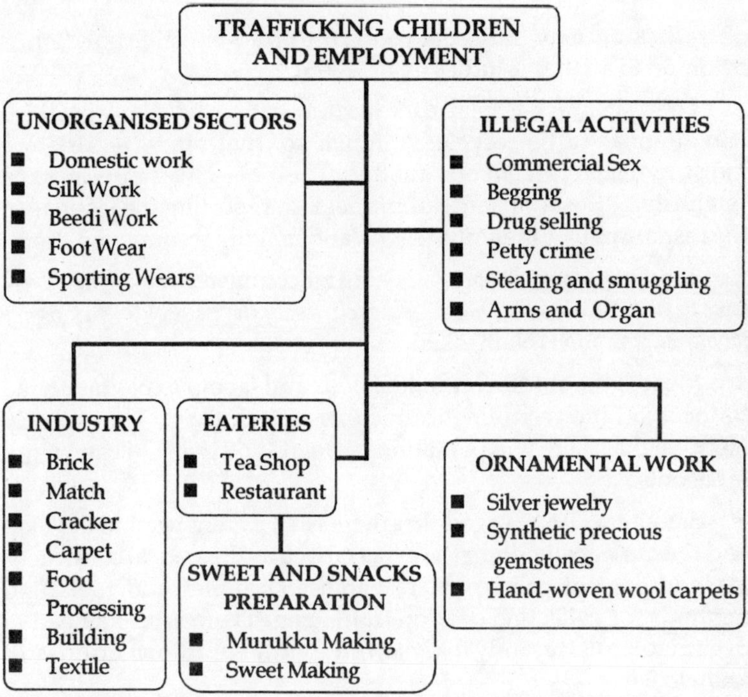

cheat, exploit and intimidate and are hard-working (Nirmala Niketan, 2003, ISS, 2003).

More over the children are exploited in the small scale industry, agricultural sector, construction work, industrial work, eateries, sweet stalls, etc. Children are also trafficked for illegal activities such as drug peddling, organ trading, forced marriages, stealing, begging, etc. Trafficking is also done for entertainment and sports activities such as camel race, dancing, work in circus, etc. have been reported by various authors and researchers. In South Asia, trafficking forms part of the immense child labour problem in the subcontinent, often related to debt bondage, whereby a child is in effect sold to pay off a debt, frequently a debt deliberately imposed by the exploiter with this in mind (CACT, 2006).

Gaps in Literature

Considering the hidden and criminal nature of the problem the data presented by most reports is valuable because of this very scarcity, while the definitions, perspectives and approaches to the problem of trafficking may vary, the concern to find effective solution is common to all these studies (Nair, 2005).

The content and format of the majority of the studies are repetitive and appear to be recycle, so much so, that often, reports are indistinguishable from one another. Their objectives appear to be establishing the occurrence of trafficking, reporting the lacunae in the responses by different agencies and making recommendations.

Most of the reports on trafficking for commercial sex work. *There have been no studies that have dealt exclusively the issue of trafficking for labour exploitation* (Nair, 2005).

Most of the studies on child labour and labour exploitation fail to focus on the recruitment practices of traffickers. They merely mention that there is exploitation by dalals and their children work for agents.

Sanghera (1999) urged that there is an urgent need to develop and fine tune methodological aspects such as theoretical constructs, methodological principles, research techniques and tools and methods for collecting data on trafficking. There is also a need to organize, collate and analyse the available information and knowledge.

As Child Labour

Trafficking among children for labourer is recognized as the serious concern by International Labour Organization and it expressed greater apprehension as recognized the imperative need to address it at the national, regional and multilateral cooperation to combat it. Within ILO's mandate, trafficking in persons for purposes of labour exploitation, in particular forced and compulsory labour and other slavery like practices, is covered by number of ILO Conventions. The important one to be worth mentioned here is to curb trafficking in children and women in 'Worst Form of Child Labour Convention, 1999', (No.182).

The issue of trafficking over the past decade has reached epidemic proportions and no country in the world is untouched by this evil phenomenon (Ali, 2005).

It has been reported that in South Asia, the worst form of trafficking relate to the illegal movement of women and children for the purposes of exploitation in sectors such as commercial sex work and child labour of all forms and of course the low status of women increase their vulnerability as targets for traffickers and limits their options as survivors seeking new life (Skeldon, 2001).

The increasing child labour and bonded labourer create a climate in which the trafficking of children for prostitution and hasardus work. The trafficked children are reported to be engaged in carpet weaving, Beedi rolling, and silk weaving; embroidery, wage labour, hotel work, etc., (Human Rights watch, 1996; NOREC, 2002).

A research study reported that 17 per cent of the domestic workers were less than 15 years old and also reported that girls aged 12 to 15 were the preferred choice of 90 per cent of employing households (UNICEF, 1997). In an another study conducted by ILO estimated that at least 1.3 lakh children are employed in India's hand knitted carpet industry (US Department of labour, 1997).

Legal and Child Labour

In India among the many laws enacted the Child Labour Act passed in 1986 becomes prominent as it has vital and adequate provisions for the freeing and rehabilitation of children found in forced labour conditions. On the contrary it failed to carry strong criminal proceedings against the traffickers as it has provision for only to the maximum of three years of imprisonment for the culprits. It is the impression given by much legislation is that the laws against trafficking for labour purposes the provisions are not sufficient in imposing criminal penalties for those who are responsible for the forced or bonded labourer, child labour and domestic servitude until recently.

It is from 10th October 2006 the children under 14 years old are banned from working in eateries and homes in occupations like domestic servants, workers in dhabas, restaurants, hotels, motels, teashops, resorts, spas and other recreational centres. The child labour (Prohibition and Regulation) Act was enacted in 1986 is now amended in 2006. The important provisions of the act shall be:

- The child is defined as person below the age of 14 years
- The act regulates the condition of employment in all occupations and processes not prohibited under the Act
- The act prohibits employment of children in 13 occupations and 57 processes contained in part A and B of the schedule to Act
- Any person who employs any child in contravention of the provisions of section 13 of the act is liable for punishment

with imprisonment for a term which shall not be less than three months but which may extend to one year or with fine which shall not be less than Rs. 10,000 but may extend to Rs. 20,000 or both.

It is in 1985 the issue of child labour in India attracted public attention and debate, it has become the focus of major consideration after the advent of globalization.

It is the sorry state of affairs that the US State Dept. on Trafficking in Persons, June, 2005 has placed India under the Tier 2 Watch list for a second consecutive year. It is high time that the Government of India should realize the evils of human trafficking and takes concrete steps to preserve the dignity of women and children.

Prominent Gaps

Notwithstanding the commendable gains made by the anti-trafficking movement in the region over the past years, some major gaps remain (Sanghera, 1991). The salient areas which need to be urgently addressed are:

1. Conceptual and Operational Issues

- the definition of trafficking
- conflation of trafficking with prostitution
- conflation of trafficking with legal and illegal migration, and smuggling
- conflation of trafficking of adult women with minors and children
- little or no intervention in trafficking for other purposes besides prostitution

2. Research

- methodology of research on trafficking of women and children
- lack of statistical and quantifiable data
- reliability of data
- paucity of trained researchers
- strong ideological and moralistic biases in research

3. Advocacy

- inadequate advocacy at the SAARC level to influence the SAARC Convention on Trafficking
- limited advocacy for cross border cooperation and collaboration at the multi-lateral and bilateral levels

- insufficient lobbying with government representatives and organisations at the national level
- absence of a media advocacy strategy as well as a code of conduct for the media

4. *Legislation and Law Enforcement*

- lack of sound analysis of relevant laws and the various legal regimes
- insufficient grasp and hence operationalization of the human rights framework
- uncritical and skewed enforcement of the ITPA and the 1949 Anti-Trafficking Convention
- lack of gender and rights sensitisation in law enforcement
- inadequate and slanted law enforcement as well as corruption in the legal structure

5. *Prevention*

- very limited intervention for prevention at source
- extremely limited programmes and schemes for viable, alternate economic empowerment
- near absence of effective involvement, participation and ownership of affected communities and groups in prevention initiatives

6. *Recovery, Repatriation and Reintegration*

- near absence of models of recovery, repatriation and reintegration which prioritize the preference, interest and rights of women and children affected by trafficking
- absence of recognition of the women's right to have say in determining their own future with respect to repatriation, residence and livelihood
- absence of humanitarian standards for the treatment of trafficked women and children
- further victimization and criminalization of trafficked victims by their treatment as illegal migrants due to absence of legal status and citizenship rights

Critical Evaluation of the Major Gaps

Further the various research gaps are critically evaluated by Sanghera, Jyoti, (1991) in her report to the United Nations.

The Trafficking Definition

The definiton of trafficking continues to be the subject of debate, and there is no conclusive or even commonly agreed upon definition globally, regionally or even nationally. This in itself is indicative of the degree of ideological contention which marks the discourse on trafficking and related issues.

Absence of consensus of the definition of trafficking has crucial implications on strategic planning and programme development since some of the definitions of trafficking which inform concrete practice may be contradictory to each other. However, there are some basic elements of trafficking that are widely agreed upon, such as, violence, deception, coercion, deprivations of freedom of movement, abuse of authority, debt bondage, forced labour and slavery-like practices, and other forms of exploitation or use of force.

The above elements are largely and commonly agreed upon, and trafficking is considered to be a violation of the basic rights of women and girls. The issue however, gets mired in controversy and confusion when prostitution too is considered as a violation of the basic human rights of both adult women and minors, and equal to sexual exploitation per se. From this stand point then, trafficking and prostitution become conflated with each other.

This conflation is also historically grounded. It is important to remember that the historical understanding of trafficking in international law has been focussed primarily on the movement of women and girls across borders for the purpose of prostitution. This is indeed the key citation of the 1949 Convention on the Suppression of Traffic in Person and the Exploitation of Others which declares that the very entry of a woman into prostitution with or without her consent, and third party involvement is an offence. This Convention forms the basis of legislation which governs all laws on prostitution and trafficking in most countries of the South Asian region.

Hence, after years of defining trafficking as the problem of "sex trafficking in women" it is highly problematic for governments and many NGOs to shift their analysis and make a distinction between trafficking on the one hand which by definition is tantamount to abuse and a violation of human rights, and prostitution on the other which does indeed entail elements of consensual activity and coercion if it is forced prostitution.

On account of the historical conflation of trafficking and prostitution both legally and in popular understanding, an overwhelming degree of effort and interventions of anti-trafficking groups are concentrated on trafficking into prostitution. As such, the Draft SAARC Convention, as well as all the programmes of the governments of Bangladesh, Nepal and India focus on trafficking for the purpose of prostitution.

The conflation of trafficking with prostitution per se and not with forced prostitution results in some crucial problems:

1. A disproportionate degree of attention, efforts, resources and interventions are focussed exclusively on trafficking for the purpose of prostitution. Trafficking for other purposes such as domestic labour, forced marriage, to other unregulated industrial and agricultural sites, etc., remain comparatively, largely neglected by anti-trafficking groups.
2. When both trafficking and prostitution are considered to be equally abusive, exploitative and violative of the human rights, then all persons involved in prostitution become victims of trafficking needing to be rescued. This conclusion is slightly off kilter and not supported by the reality on the ground. Not all women working in prostitution are trafficked, and not all victims of trafficking are confined to prostitution alone.
3. A natural corollary flowing from the above conclusion is the conflation of women with children and minors. When there is no recognition of the fact that not all women in prostitution are held in force and that some enter it voluntarily, then the autonomy of women and their agency to make choices, however limited these may be, is denied. When adult women are denied agency then they are infantalized, i.e., they are treated as equal to minors and children who, it is more or less universally agreed, may not enter commercial sex work since it is extremely hazardous for children and as such violates their rights as children. Such a conflation of women with children deprives women of their adult status, and their right to mobility, sexual autonomy, agency and work.

The Impact of Migration on Trafficking

Trafficking cannot be seen outside of the context of migration in today's world. In fact increasingly, the two elements have become inextricably linked like a tightly bound couplet in the equation 'migrant trafficking'. This has led to a growing fuzziness of boundaries particularly between illegal migration, smuggling of persons, and trafficking. Increasingly, a greater number of cases and instances are reportedly those which fall on the borderline of illegal migration, smuggling and trafficking, and on account of overlapping elements, it is difficult to distinguish one from the other.

The common factor between each one of these is that the subject or the person who is in the process of being transported whether illegally or through smuggling or trafficking is invariably a 'willing' traveler during the process of transportation. In the course of this study there were hardly any cases of forcible abduction or kidnapping reported.

Furthermore, in instances of even suspected or proven trafficking, the 'victim' during the process of recruitment and transportation accompanies the agent 'willingly' for a variety of reasons, mostly under deception or false promise of a well-paying job. As such, almost all cases of trafficking today by definition are only instances of illegal migration and/or smuggling during the first phase of the journey, i.e., recruitment and transportation. Therefore, during this first phase it is extremely difficult to establish trafficking since up until after this phase the crime of trafficking has not actually happened.

Trafficking Process

In a majority of the cases studied and discussed in the context of South Asia, the crime of trafficking is actually evidenced in phase two of the journey, i.e. when the willing migrant and unsuspecting victim is actually delivered to a site of work which may either be a far cry from the promised 'well-paying' job, or may subjugate the 'victim' under conditions of work of which she had no prior knowledge, and therefore did not consent to.

These conditions are invariably such that they blatantly violate the person's human rights and range from an oppressive and exploitative living and working environment to forced labour and slavery-like practices. Concretely, these include sale of the victim to an 'owner', debt bondage, physical and psychological violence, restriction of mobility and association, appropriation of legal identity such as passport or other travel documents, and other forms of abuse and control. The agent or the broker profits from the sale and exploitation of the 'victim' often on an ongoing basis and is one among a chain of profiteers who benefit from the act of trafficking.

It is therefore crucial to bear in mind that the process of trafficking occurs in at least two-phases namely, recruitment and transportation, and confinement to the site of work. Since the duped victim colludes with the agent in her own transportation, it is only in phase two that she discovers that she has been deceived or that her fundamental rights have severely compromised. By then invariably, it is too late for her to escape and/or for NGOs or other stake holders to access her since she is confined to an underground or invisible site of work where her movements are watched and controlled.

The rapidly changing socio-economic profile of countries within the South Asian region, and particularly the causes mentioned above have provided the bases for outmigration of marginalized populations. As such, large numbers of human beings—women, men and children—migrate either voluntarily from and within these countries in search of means to eke out a living, or are trafficked by means of deception or direct coercion. *While migration and trafficking are distinct and separate they are at the same time integrally connected. The pressing need to migrate in search of work creates a fertile ground for traffickers and unscrupulous agents to exploit this need and profit from it.* As such, trafficking is increasingly an outcome of the need to migrate, and the complexity of this equation needs to be fully grasped.

The complexity of trafficking lies in that, on account of the way in which the trade is presently conducted within the region, it can only be established post facto, i.e. after it has happened. This makes it very difficult to intercept victims because they are confined in invisible and underground sites. There is an urgent need engage in a serious discussion on this problem and to develop tools, criteria, indicators and a methodology whereby victims of trafficking may be identified prior to them being finally trafficked.

Research Measures

Since the inception of anti-trafficking work in the region, research on the issue has been a crucial activity undertaken by NGOs, research institutes, and independent researchers. Over the past years an immense amount of relevant data has been gathered and presented in regards to the magnitude and mechanisms of trafficking. However, a few gaps may be identified in the research activity, these relate to

- methodology of research
- conceptual depth and clarity
- quality of data
- problem with statistics
- analytical approaches

This is largely due to the fact that no methodologically sound statistical data collection or analysis has been done to date. Similarly, statistical information for India and Bangladesh is often recycled without any hint of the methodological possibility of verifiability. The lack of distinction between trafficking and migration is partly responsible for difficulty in securing reliable statistical data on women and girls affected by trafficking. And yet, there appears to be a pressing need to procure some figures for the numbers of victims of trafficking in order to assess the magnitude of the problem.

In addition, there are no clearly defined methodological principles which inform many of the research projects. Theoretical constructs, research methods, research techniques and methodological rigour are often compromised. And most importantly, the approach taken to analyse the phenomenon of trafficking in many studies is one which casts social reality in bleak and mutually exclusive categories of black and white. Such an approach does not reflect reality as it is experienced and lived, and needs to be critically rethought.

There is an urgent need to develop and fine tune the methodological aspects such as, theoretical constructs, methodological principles, research techniques, research tools and methods for researching the issue of trafficking.

The Rights Approach

Governments in particular have tended to take those steps which are easiest to carry out without having to address fundamental structures of economic, social and gender inequality. As such, punitive law enforcement rather than protection of human rights of women and children affected by trafficking has been the main focus of state response. Instead of focusing on the manner in which the rights of victims could be protected and enhanced, government response has been further curtailment of some of these rights in the name of protection.

For much of the recent past, the issue of trafficking in South Asia was being framed exclusively within the context of the following perspectives: violence against women; abuse and exploitation of children; child labour or a sociological framework. Recently however, trafficking of women and minors is being framed within a human rights perspective, and trafficking is being defined as a fundamental violation of human rights. While this approach offers a far greater advantage in the arena of advocacy, the human rights framework is not always adequately understood and translated, particularly at the operational level.

Legal Regime and Law Enforcement

Most government action rarely addresses the corrupt practices enabling traffickers to thrive. Organised crime syndicates as well as smaller brokers operate in the region within and across borders in the region. It has been reported that often they receive active support and collusion from government and state representatives. The latter in turn, receive benefits and remuneration for their support and services. Ironically hence, often those who are enjoined with the task of 'busting' the trafficking network are the very same people who may have a vested interest in sustaining it.

This constitutes one of the key obstacles in the elimination of trafficking. Therefore, it is important that any initiative or dialogue on trafficking includes both, the representatives of the state (law enforcers and policy makers) on the one hand, and community and NGO activists on the other. This is critical for establishing responsibility, accountability and ownership, as well as a meaningful partnership in anti-trafficking action.

Many recommendations on trafficking across the region advocate more stringent laws for the traffickers and greater protection for the victims. There is no question that the entire terrain of legislation and its enforcement leaves much to be desired for. However, more stringent and punitive laws may not be of particular help when the already existing laws (several of which do address many dimensions of trafficking) are either not enforced or only half-heartedly enforced. If it is recognised that in many instances, the very agents of the state who are responsible for enforcing laws are themselves engaged in a flagrant abuse of the legal structure, then placing greater punitive power in their hands is often tantamount to intensifying the victimisation of the victims. And hence, the demand for more border surveillance posts manned by security guards as a measure to combat cross-border trafficking needs to be rethought carefully.

Demanding greater stringency in laws may often act as a deterrent in registering cases against the perpetrators of a crime. In the border district of Jessore in Bangladesh wherefrom a bulk of the trafficking of children and women occurs into India, not a single case of trafficking has been registered in the district court in the past two years. Ever since trafficking has been declared a non-bailable offence more than two years ago, it has become much more difficult for a complainant to supply hard and 'conclusive' evidence to convict an offender.

The Media: Representation and Advocacy

In the arena of the media a focused strategy or code of conduct have yet been devised for the region. It is commonly observed that the media represents the issue as well as the victims of trafficking in stark and mutually exclusive categories of good and evil, black and white. As such, all women and girls who have been trafficked are pure victims with no possibility of exercising their agency, and all the brothel keepers, employers and agents on the other hand are evil, slave drivers.

Such an approach does not reflect reality and may end up creating a moral panic with a negative and counterproductive fall-out. The following example may serve to illustrate this point. Upon the intensification of an anti-trafficking campaign in the certain villages of Bangladesh via the mass media which warned all parents of young girls to be wary of strangers, it was reported that many girls were withdrawn from the village schools. At the same time, two roving salesman were lynched to death in two villages on suspicion of being traffickers.

There is a strong and regrettable tendency within the visual media, in particular the visual media, to sensationalise the issue of trafficking today. This trend needs to be seriously critiqued and arrested as it may end up doing more damage to the cause of anti-trafficking work by creating and projecting stereotypes which eventually hamper understanding of the issue, its causes and consequence.

Strategic Interventions Required

- Make the legal and law enforcement institutions more responsive to the needs of victims of trafficking.
- Promote advocacy and develop linkages at the international level.

- Develop and Fine-tune models and mechanisms at regional and national level.
- Minimum Human Rights Standards for the Treatment of Trafficked Persons.
- Strategies for designing and implementing anti-trafficking work.
- Initiate and intensify work to reach agreement and deeper understanding.
- Initiate rights protective strategies for designing and implementing anti-trafficking work.

Limitation

Difficulties in Studying Trafficking

The clandestine and complex nature of the phenomenon, anonymous clientele, low visibility, fear of police, fear of brokers, pimps, brothel owners, traffickers, fear of exploitation and after math effects made the researchers find it difficult to arrive at an accurate conclusion. The first and foremost difficulty is the lack of relative data on various issues and problems of trafficking from any source. It is also difficult to rely on one single source as the information and figures drastically differs form one source to another. Hence the researchers find it difficult to locate sources and face non-cooperation from those involved (Phinney, 2001; Blanchet, 2002; Pandey, Jena and Mohanty, 2002; SECD, 1988). This probably explains why a majority of the studies have very small sample sizes.

On an all India basis a study conducted by Rozario in 1988 in the field is the only available source to have a national perspective. Similarly a study conducted Institute of Social Sciences New Delhi (2005) on all India basis focusing the Human rights perspectives is an another document available for the scholars. There are also most of the studies they use case studies with few individuals, news paper clippings, stories of victims, studies conducted at controlled circumstances and data collected in the presence of other players in the business make researches to arrive at concrete conclusions. This opinion has very well been supported by Blancher (2002) that studies conducted at rehabilitation homes do not adequately represent the life path of most of the trafficked victims.

More over the complexity of the cases makes it difficult to apply standard definitions to specific instances and trafficking stories are difficult to squeeze into little boxes (Blancher, 2002). In the context of slavery Bales (1999) argues that people are inventive and flexible and the permutations of human violence and exploitation are infinite.

It has been observed by various researchers that the lack of validated data and information is one of the major limitations for developing sustainable and inclusive strategies to fight trafficking. The continued collaboration and co-operation of the various agencies such as government, NGO, research institutions, media and civil society organizations should be ensured in a bigger way to tackle this menace.

Chapter 3

Designing Trafficking Study: Methodology

The design of the study is exploratory in nature as it explores labour perspectives. The study discovers the economic details of the family, working condition they had underwent, modus operandi, ill-treatment experienced, Psychosocial problems the children due to trafficking and the future prospects and plans of the victim children.

Source of Data

The primary source of data collection has been done from the children who are trafficked and returned at the time of the study using the structured interview schedule. More over information is also collected through observation, Discussion with children, family and NGO personnel, Government and Non Government material sources.

Pilot Visit

Pilot visit was made along with the investigators selected for the purpose. The purpose of the visit was to identify the rampant villages and trafficking in Usilampatty taluk of Madurai district. The strategy adopted were to approach the Village Presidents, ward members, self-help group representatives, youth members through their associations, NGO representatives and prominent persons in the villages.

Initially it was difficult to gather information about the children those who have gone on trafficking to various other states for labour. Later after explaining to them that it is only for research purpose the researcher could collect details of children who had gone and returned fresh and who are at present. The already went and returned children were the source of information at the later stage and who gave us valuable information.

Tool for Data Collection

A structured interview schedule was constructed taking into account the objectives of the study. The main areas covered are personal profile of the children, family background, economic details, expenditure pattern, working condition, time of work, conditions of work spot, wage and salary, modus operandi, ill-treatment, Psychosocial aspects, bad habits and future prospects.

Pre-Tested

The tool is pre-tested for correction and modification and logical sequence. It was felt that the name of the trafficked children need not be asked at the initial stage and kept as optional; since it involves legal complications as perceived by the respondents and hence it was kept as optional and deleted from the tool. Expert consultancy was also sought to standardize the tool

Duration of Data Collection

The primary data collection was done for more than 6 months starting from 15th June 2006. The data collection was suspended for a month during December 2007 due to panchayat elections. The investigators are given orientation for this purpose as to how to establish rapport, winning their confidence and collect data. With the close supervision of the researcher in the field the investigators collected data from the respondents for each respondent it took more than 3 hours to complete. For quite a few respondents second visit was also made.

During data collection the parents, siblings or relatives or friends were also present and hence it is advantageous in certain respect and disadvantageous when details about their psychosocial aspects probed, as influence of others in the response is unavoidable. Discussion with NGO's working in the field, village representatives the local elders and self help group members were initiated to get their opinion and to have an in depth understanding.

Details About the Study Area

The study area comprises of both Chellampatty and Usilampatty Panchayat Unions. The profile of these two panchayat unions are given below in this table for a better understanding.

Usilampatty Taluk Details
(Chellampatty and Usilampatty Panchayat Unions)

Category	*Usilampatty P.U.*	*Chellampatty P.U.*
Village panchayat	18	29
Hemlet	139	206
PHC Sub centres	20	21
Social Assistance Coverage		
Usilampatty taluk 2002-03	6190	--
Nutritional meals centres	133	165
Beneficiairies	1485	3560
District HQ Hospital	1	nil
Library	1	nil
Primary Agri coop Bank	5	17
Commercial Bank	9	4
No of Milk coops.	56	56
Veterinary Hosptial & sub	1 + 6	0 + 2
Wells for irrigation	3923	5006
Mulbery cultivation	22.5 acres	nil

Source: Maduria Diary, 2004.

General Profile of Usilampatty Taluk

The total area of the taluk is 565 Sq. Km with the total population of 1.78 lakhs and among them 19 thousands are children. The taluk's literacy level is 1.09 lakhs. The rural population comprises 83 per cent. The rainfall in this area is calculated as 0.99 Cm. The taluk headquarters Usilampatty has a Head quarters hospital, a regulated market and a judicial court. The taluk has been divided into five Revenue Inspector headquarters. There are 112 fair price shops covering 65,353 Ration Cardholders.

General Features

- People are very traditional thinking and outlook as far as culture and civilization is concerned
- Still backward socially, economically and educationally
- Major area under cultivation is dry farming.

Social

- The social composition : The taluk is predominantly covered by Primalai Kallar Community. They are attached with caste consciousness and traditional religious sentiments. There also other backward community people and Scheduled caste people live

- Caste consciousness is both stronger—for the unity; and Weaker—for the dominance and atrocities on SC;
- The level of education is low
- Women and girl children are not given due share in education, rights, social participation, etc.
- Dowry is rampant and accepted custom
- Marriage remarriage and divorce are very common—distinguishing feature of the Kallar community and it is a social custom. Divorce and remarriage are easy
- Female infanticide—the area is popularly known for this phenomenon
- Cash gift or presentation in cash for occasions like marriage, house warming, puberty, etc. is an extra-ordinary affair in the sense that it involves huge amount of money which is normally an unaffordable amount
- Child labour and child trafficking is rampant
- Migration in search of job or business is a common feature

Political

- Caste based political parties are stronger
- Influence of caste based politician's play a dominant role
- Though there is no apparent communal conflict noted or reported in the press there exist the caste divide.

NGO's Working

There are number of NGO's working for social development with range from targeting children to elderly. The primary programmes of these organizations are Self-Help groups, children's education, child labour, dropouts, female infanticide, trafficking issues, rural development etc.

To mention few such organizations who also work in the filed of trafficking are: Wed Trust, SIRD, SJSSS, SISU, ORD, WORLD VISION, SACRED, ICCW, ASSEFA, PREED, SHEPHERD, GOOD HOPE, MASW, PACHE TRUST, etc.

Universe and Sampling Frame

The trafficked children under the age of 18 in the villages of Usilampatty taluk of Madruai district form the universe of the study.

It has been found after the pilot visit that snowball sampling is the ideal method to select respondents. The children are taken as groups in trafficking process to other states and hence in each village if one child is identified then it is easy to locate other children. The villages are selected during the pilot visit based on the criteria that where the trafficking is rampant or known for trafficking as observed by NGO, local leader and self group members. In total there are 119 children are interviewed and the data is collected.

Name of the Village	*Frequency*
A. Ramanathapuram	3
Allikundam	2
Annyyoor	2
Anyyoor	3
Arriyapatti	3
Boothipuram	2
Doddapanaickanoor	7
Duraisamypuram pudur	8
E. Kottaipatti	2
Jothilnayakanoor	2
Kanavaipatti	2
Kanniyampatti	3
Karampatty	9
Kattakaruppanpatti	2
Keeripatty	5
Koppilipatti	2
Kuppanampatti	3
Kuravakudi	7
Lingappanayakanoor	6
Manuthu	2
Maruthampatty	4
Meenatchipuram	1
Mekkilarpatti	3
Melapatti	1

(Contd.)

Name of the Village	*Frequency*
Nalluthevanpatti	2
Pannaipatti	2
Poduvarpatty	3
Poliyampatti	5
Pothampatti	4
Potulapatti	2
Potulpatti	2
Rajakkapatti	2
Sempatti	2
Sikkampatti	2
Thimmanatham	4
Vadugapatti	3
Vadugapatti colony	3
Villani	2
Villani perumalpatti	2
Total	119

Analysis of Data

The collected data and information is codified and a data base is created in SPSS package. For better presentation and comparison tabulation and cross tabulation are done. Wherever required diagrams and figures and flow charts are used to present the report in an attractive manner.

Scope of The Study

As the study focused on the economic status, working condition, modus operandi, ill-treatment faced at the work spot and their future plans in the dimension of trafficked children as child labourers; the results of the study can be generalized to the whole of India where the children are trafficked only for the purpose of the child labour in various type of work. The study can be applied to both male and female children if they are recruited only for certain type of work, which involves their hard labour.

STUDY AREA USILAMPATTI TALUK

MADURAI DISTRICT

Chapter 4

Trafficking in Children–Labour Perspectives and Unconscious Phenomenon: An Analysis

This chapter deals with the analysis and interpretation of the data collected through interview schedule in the field-Usilampatty Taluk. The personal profile, family background in terms of economic aspects, cause, the contact person or the recruiter, trafficking destinations, type of industry, type of work, working conditions, ill-treatments, exploitation, psychological problems, bad habits developed and the future plan of the respondents are analysed in detail. The data is presented in simple tables, cross tables and diagrams.

Personal Profile

Figure – 1
Age Distribution

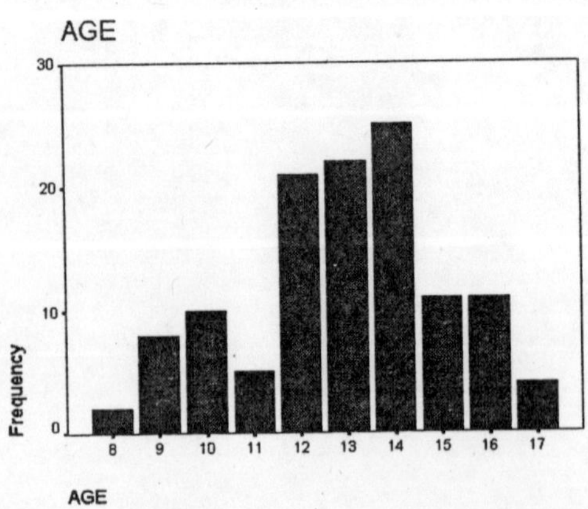

Age Distribution

The most preferred age for trafficking in Usilampatty taluk for Murukku making to other States is 12, 13 and 14; is very well portrayed in the bar chart with the mean age of 12.94. This is the tender age group after their primary schooling considered as ideal group to start with for the labour work as they are newly recruited they become cheap and could be bend to the size and shape they want. The age and the physical appearance are the two important determinants in selecting children for work in these areas. The murukku making company run by native people in rural areas of various States in India; recruit children for their enterprises for a period of one year contract. As the area Usilampatty Taluk is considered as backward area in terms of education and economics it could supply lot of such children to these States.

There are children recruited in the age group of 15, 16 and above if the above categories are not found for their requirement. It is observed that when the age increases the amount paid to the children is also increases. There are also children needed for them in these age group for marketing their product and go for collection of money from the retail vendors.

There are also children trafficked at the age group of 10 and below represent their vulnerability in terms of social and economical aspects of the family. Though the government is extending lot of welfare programmes in terms of free education, nurtritional food, free text books, free transport, egg to the meals thrice a week, separate board of education of Primalai Kallar community as Kallar Reclamation Board to look into the educational needs of these community children and lot of developmental initiatives by Development departments of the Government and Non Governmental Agencies – become futile when children are not sent to schools but trafficked at these tender ages is a miserable state of affairs needs immediate intervention.

Sex of the Respondents

There are 68.9 per cent of the respondents are male children and 31.1 per cent are female children in the study. In this area only male members are preferred as the work requires very hard labour in terms of manual work. More over the enterprises are located in far off places especially in other states and hence the employers select only male children.

Table-1
Sex of the Respondents

Sex of the Respondents	*Frequency*	*Percentage*
Male	82	68.9
Female	37	31.1
TOTAL	**119**	**100.0**

Among the 37 girl children 30 children (25.2%) are employed in the cotton mill. It is the trend in Tamilnadu that most of the cotton mills now opened their gate wide to unmarried young girls preferable in the age group of 14 to 19. Almost all the cotton mills sent off their permanent employees and these girls are recruited through various agents in almost all the parts of the state especially backward districts like viruthunagar, sivaganga, Ramnad, Madurai, Tirunelveli, etc.

Educational Status

It is observed that more than fifty percent of the trafficked children are drop outs after the primary schooling. There are 25.2 per cent not even gone to the stage of primary education. There are also few illiterate respondents found among the sample. There is a greater amount of constraint found among either before primary school or after the primary school in this area. The attitude of the parents and the economic status of the family are the crucial factors found for trafficking of these children either before primary or after primary education. It is to understand that the children are considered by their family of orientation as earning member or the supporter than as the future generation who need nurturing and care. It is also to be taken note that the parents hardly spend money for education of these children as it is taken care by the government.

Table-2
Educational Status

Educational Status	*Frequency*	*Percentage*
Upto 3rd	30	25.2
Primary	69	58.0
Middle	12	10.1
9th and above	8	6.7
TOTAL	**119**	**100.0**

Figure – 2
Details of Caste

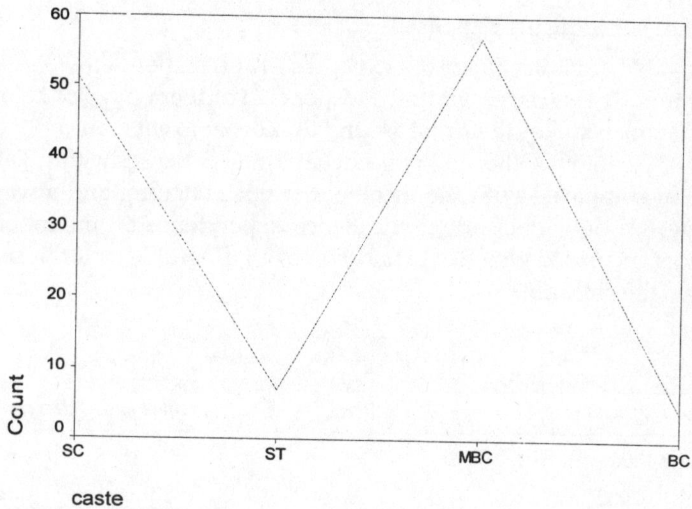

Details of Caste

Caste: Almost equal amount of representation for both Scheduled caste and the most backward caste has been portrayed very well implies that there is no discrimination for the trafficking evil spirit. Though the most backward caste here represents solely by the Primalai Kallar community the dominant caste found among the study area – Usilamapatty taluk which, has fully susceptible to child trafficking.

II. Details of Family of Orientation

Income and Size of The Family

The mean income and the size of the family are calculated to understand the family background the respondents at the first instance. The mean income is calculated as Rs. 1290 per month implies the occupational status of the family members. Most of the family members are engaged in unorganized sector and hence the income is not regular and sufficient and hence it is difficult to feed the family members with the mean size of the 5.81. The size of the family also indicates that the two family norms are not adequately adopted. With this low income it is very hard to feed the total family hence the children become the substitute for earning some more money for the family. In other words the burden of the parents is shared by these children at the cost of their childhood.

Details of Monthly Expenses

The table explains about the expenses of the respondents' family per month. It is observed that 63.9 per cent of them pay out below 1000 which makes them just around the corner to get loan and they become debtors. Other 15.1 per cent have their expenses within 3000. When compared with the income it is not matching and always there is a deficient budget and hence dependence on the money lender increased which in turn becomes a vulnerable factor posted upon the children.

Table-3
Details of Monthly Expenses

Total Expenses	*Frequency*	*Percentage*
Below 1000	76	63.9
1001 to 2000	13	10.9
2001 to 3000	18	15.1
Above 3000	12	10.1
TOTAL	**119**	**100.0**

Details of Having Wetland

Possession of land is not only an asset but also the status symbols whether dry land or wetland. Wetland in the study area means area irrigated by way of canal irrigation, well irrigation and tank irrigation. More than 25 per cent of the respondents' family has wet land and among them 20 per cent having the area ranging from 1 to

Table-4
Details of Having Wetland

Wetland	*Frequency*	*Percentage*
1 to 3 Acres	24	20.2
4 to 6	5	4.2
7 and Above	2	1.7
TOTAL	31	26.1
No Land	88	73.9
TOTAL	**119**	**100.0**

3 acres represents the economic status. It is to be understood that the economic status is not low as reported by many research studies that low economic status is one of the major causes for in the field of trafficking. It is to be differently understood that there could also be various other reasons for these respondents to get caught in the trafficking chain. There are five respondents having wetland in the range of 4 to 6 acres shows the stronger economic position.

Details of Dry Land

There are also 10 per cent of the respondents' family is having the dry land ranges from 1 to 3 acres. Though there is status as to have land; these dry lands have no economical and money value and hence cannot bring greater consideration for assessing their economical position. Contrarily these lands could also be considered as assets by the respondents when there are emergency situations such as the pressures from the local money lenders are concerned.

Table-5
Details of Dry Land

Dry Land	*Frequency*	*Percentage*
1 Acre	2	1.7
2 Acres	6	5.0
3 Acres	4	3.4
TOTAL	12	10.1
No Dry Land	107	89.9
TOTAL	**119**	**100.0**

Figure—3
Details of House

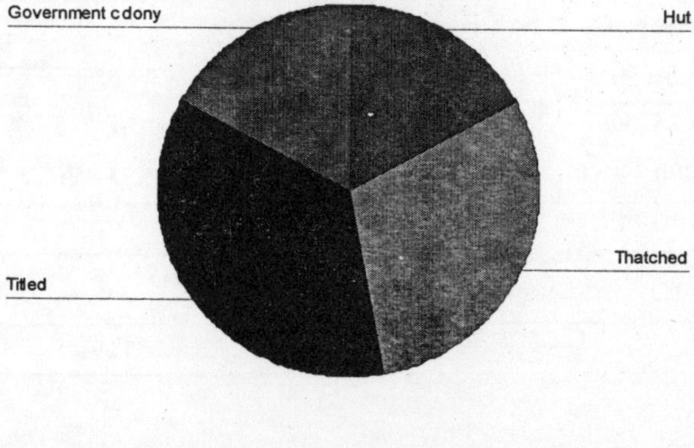

Details of House

House details: Housing is to provide facilities to the residents added with the social status. Majority of the respondents have thatched (30.3%), and Tiled (36.1%) houses shows the social and economic status of the respondents. The respondents living in Hut and Government colony houses represent 32 per cent make one to understand the low economic and social status of the respondents. It is to be understood that the Government colony residents are the selected beneficiaries of the government from the scheduled caste category and hence they are economically deprived group and living below poverty line. Though there is benefit received the government it could not help the respondents' family to escape from the clutches of trafficking. Unfortunately the ultimate benefit or impact that could be created by the government schemes and projects is in one way not fulfilled.

Habit and Amount of Savings

It is interesting to note that there are 33 respondents family have the habit of saving. The saving amount ranges from below 10,000 to more than 1 lakh and even one of the respondents' families could save more than Rs. 2.0 lakh. It is to be understood that these amounts are the family income and speak for the status of the family in terms of economic position. This saving amount and mode of saving suggests us that the causes for the trafficking issue are not necessarily due to poverty alone. There could also be other reasons such as want to start their own business, earn more money and wrong model already set by the ex-trafficking victims makes one to think that the

Table–6
Habit and Amount of Savings

Amount of Savings	*Frequency*	*Percentage*
Below 10000	5	4.2
11000 to 50000	20	16.8
51000 to 1 Lakh	7	5.9
2 Lakh and above	1	.8
TOTAL	33	27.7
No Savings	86	72.3
TOTAL	**119**	**100.0**

intervention should also include these important factors and a different approach is required.

Figure—4
Mode of Savings

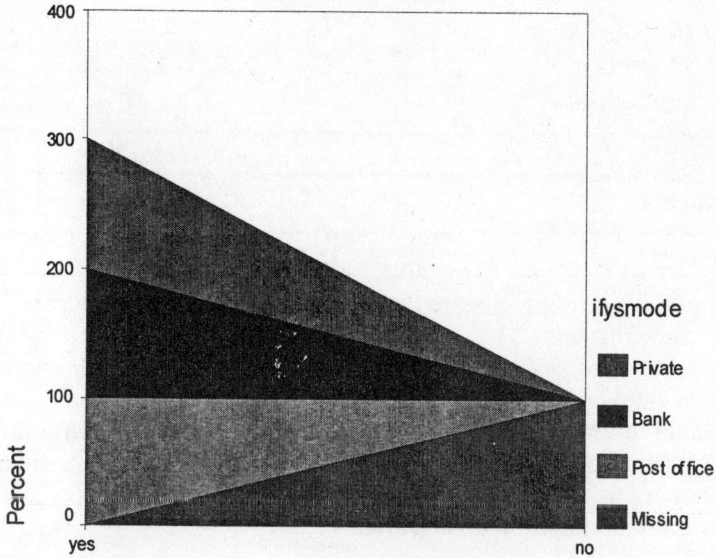

Mode of Savings

Habit of Savings : It is interesting to note that there is a saving habit found among the respondents' family (27.7%) and the saving is done in both formal and informal agencies such as bank and post office and one in private with local people. Surprisingly a considerable number have saved Rs. 11,000 to Rs. 50,000 is a welcome feature. These habits must be encouraged and should be taken note of while planning for any rehabilitation programme to curb the menace of trafficking.

Amount of Debt

The amount of debt is also quite alarming as more than 44 per cent among the debtors borrowed an amount ranges from Rs. 11,000 to Rs. 50,000 implies the burden lies on the family. There are also respondents' family borrowed money to the tune of one lakh and above raises serious danger signal. The private money lenders are high in number in number as far as Usilampatty Taluk is concerned

Table-7
Amount of Debt

Amount of Debt	*Frequency*	*Percentage*
Below 10000	15	12.6
11000 to 50000	53	44.5
51000 to 1 Lakh	5	4.2
1 Lakh and above	8	6.7
TOTAL	**81**	**68.1**
No Debt	38	31.9
TOTAL	**119**	**100.0**

and it is a status symbol to declare openly that they are involved in financial business. They use all sorts of methods starting from torture, threat to live, oral and physical abuse, etc to get it repaid. There is also another important peculiar feature found among the Primalai Kallar community is that offering CASH GIFTS (moie or seimurai in Tamil) for occasions - normally an amount unmanageable to the status of the presenters. This has been reported in various documents and researches done in this area.

Figure—5
The Source of Debt

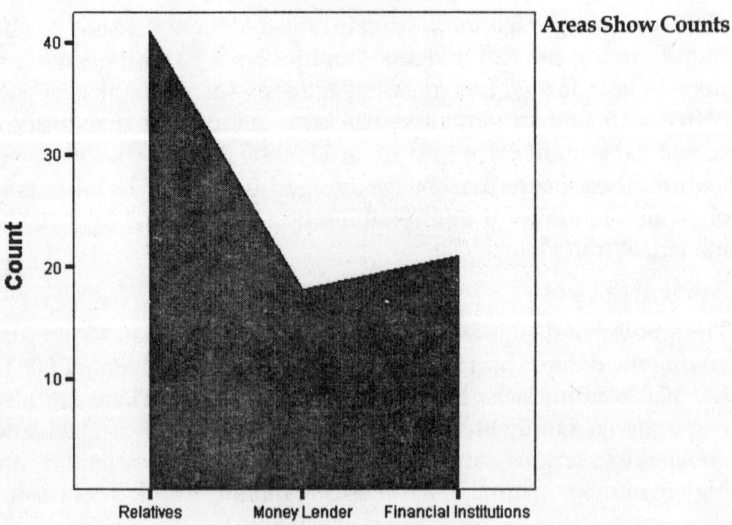

The Source of Debt

Most of the borrowings took place with the relatives other wise relatives turned money lenders as they also charge interest like any other local money lender. Only a considerable family admitted that they got money from the money lenders. While borrowing they are the relatives and while start repaying or unable to pay they become the enemies. The nature of the lending business in this area is such that the interest rate is so alarming and the type of interest such as auto interest, run interest, meter interest, etc. (local interest models practiced by the money lenders) makes the borrower; the everlasting debtor.

Table-8
Rate of Interest

Rate of Interest (%)	*Frequency*	*Percentage*
12.00	9	7.6
24.00	20	16.8
36.00	46	38.7
48.00	4	3.4
60.00	2	1.7
TOTAL	81	68.1
No Loan	38	31.9
TOTAL	119	100.0

The Rate of Interest

The interest rate is more than 100 per cent or 200 per cent or even up to 300 per cent if the systematic and scientific calculations are made with the amount and the repayment. It is crystal clear to understand the respondents' family sent their wards merely to repay the old debts. The main source of debt is their relatives. It is seen that majority 36.1 per cent of the respondents' family get loan for marriage expenses and 21 per cent of them get to repay their old debts. It is also to be understood that they have to pay more than twice and thrice of this original amount so that their debts can be cleared.

Purpose of Loan

Debt: This is a serious matter to be dealt with as far as the study area is concerned. There are lots of complications and implications witnesses everyday among the debt victims. It could be another

Table-9
Purpose of Loan

Purpose of Loan	*Frequency*	*Percentage*
Education	8	6.7
Marriage	43	36.1
Repay Old Loans	27	22.7
Others	3	2.5
TOTAL	81	68.1
No Loan	38	31.9
TOTAL	119	100.0

serious area of study. The rate of interest, the nomenclature given to the debt, the mode of recovery and the ill-treatment by the money lenders are quite dangerous and looked into seriously. The recent enactment to prevent and curb such private money lenders has only little to do with these blood sucking lenders and it has hardly any impact in these villages. The trafficking family is a prey to these money lenders and they can not easily escape from the clutches of the lenders.

Whenever there is a torture and turmoil from the lenders they try to find various means to escape from the money lender for the time being and one such way is to put their children in trafficking and get an advance amount to pay the lender.

It could be observed from the field through the local representatives and NGO personnel through their self help group women that the money lenders and the traffickers or the agents have close nexus with each other. In many cases the agents approach the money lenders to target families so that their vulnerability is exploited and they become the easy target to the agents.

It is to be remembered that in various other studies it has been reported that the enforcement personnel, police, local administration and the pimps and agents had close nexus in the trafficking field. As far as this study is concerned the agents and the traffickers use money lenders also as an important source to gain access to the vulnerable families and it become an easy target.

Causes/Reasons for Traffickings

Though poverty is the predominant perceived cause expressed; the land holdings and income of the family shows a different picture. It is assumed that there are other reasons such as earn quick money, to meet the immediate needs, to get away from the clutches of greedy debtors are the factors hiding behind the cause poverty. It can also be predicted that 'poverty' is the big banner where in these people can conceal themselves behind so that the actual reasons need not be revealed. Nevertheless poverty can also be a dominant reason for a considerate population to send their wards to traffickers.

Table–10
Causes/Reasons for Traffickings

Cause	*Frequency*	*Percentage*
Poverty	105	88.2
Ignorance	5	4.2
Earn More Money	9	7.6
TOTAL	**119**	**100.0**

Traffickers or Recruiters

It is this table which is the representative sample of the title of this study. The unconsciousness of the parents, village leaders and elders has approached the children to be trafficked for such work. It is also observed that the parents are approached by the brokers or elders or influential persons or the money lenders. Moreover the parents are directly compelled by the PUSH and PULL factors which made up their mind and approach their own wards to put them in the trafficking chain. The parents are looking only at the immediate

Table–11
Traffickings or Recruiters

Person Contacted for Work	*Frequency*	*Percentage*
Broker	15	12.6
Elder	29	24.4
Village Leader	3	2.5
Parents	72	60.5
TOTAL	**119**	**100.0**

need or the crisis rather than the future prospects of their own future generation. In 60.5 per cent of the respondents the parents themselves approached the children and encouraged to get locked with the trafficking chain. The brokers or the agents play a lesser role though they have network among themselves with the individual entrepreneurs the unawareness and unconsciousness of the parents and community makes the business easy for such recruiters.

Figure – 6
Accompanying Persons Destination

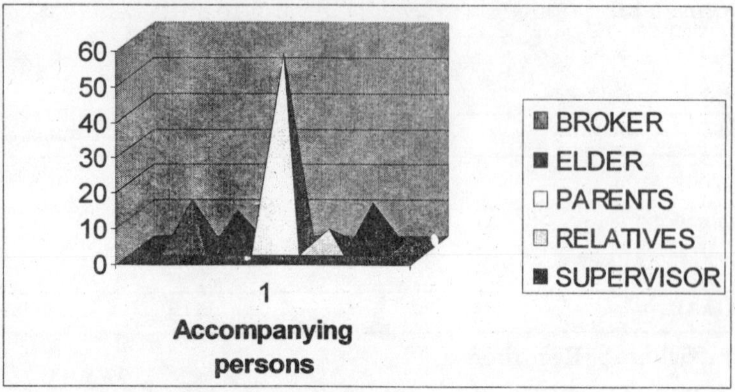

Accompanying Persons Destination

Here again the parents play a vital role in accompanying the children to the respected destination. It is apparent that nearly 55 per cent of the parents associate with the children. Then comes the brokers (14.3%). With the full knowledge of the parents the respondents are taken to work.

Table-12
Prior Knowledge About the Destination

Prior Knowledge	*Frequency*	*Percentage*
Know the Destination	53	44.5
Unaware the Destination	66	55.5
TOTAL	**119**	**100.0**

This table shows the awareness of the respondents with regard to the destination. The 55.5 per cent of those have gone to work without knowledge. The parents have also not given any prior information regarding the destination to their children. It shows the pathetic situation of the respondents. They have gone into without knowing that they are to be in cages.

Intra and Inter State Trafficking—The Route

When analysed the places where these children are taken is quite interesting as these rural children who may not know even the nearby town or the district head quarters are taken to far off places ranging to southern, northern and even north eastern states. Among the States Tamil Nadu, the home state has the major portion of having one third of the respondents (33.6%) and the nature of the work within Tamil Nadu is cotton mills (all girl respondents), hosiery industry in Tiruppur, and hotel industry in various other parts. In the other state Karnataka tops the list in having (16.0%) of the respondents followed by Andhra Pradesh (12.6%), Madhya Pradesh (11.8%), Maharastra (10.9%), Uttar Pradesh (6.7%) and Kerala, Kolatta and Assam 6, 3 and one respondent respectively. The mobilization to other state is mostly for Murukku making business. The destination to states like M.P., U.P., Maharastra, even to West Bangal and Assam—makes the children more vulnerable in their mere location that it is a strange place, a different culture, an unknown language, etc., adds the misery to the children and they cannot do anything except head to the wimps and fancy of the employer.

Table-13
Intra and Inter State Trafficking

State	*Frequency*	*Percentage*
Tamil Nadu	40	33.6
Karnataka	19	16.0
Andhra Pradesh	15	12.6
Madhya Pradesh	14	11.8
Maharashtra	13	10.9
Uttar Pradesh	8	6.7
Kerala	6	5.0
Kolkatta	3	2.5
Assam	1	.8
TOTAL	**119**	**100.0**

Mode of Travel

The mode of travel is observed as both train and bus. For many of the children traveling in a bus is an greater enjoyment and traveling in a train takes them high as they have no access to train travel. This is another factor of motivation to the children they could travel in train and that too for two three days makes them accept the offer without knowing the reality. Nowadays the traveling in train along with group of children found to be rather risky as reported by the agents and parents since there are lots of constraints by the enforcement officials especially the Railway police who could easily locate and catch and place them before the Child Welfare Committee for rejuvenation. The local representatives and the NGO's working in the field acknowledged the fact and hence now traveling in bus even to far off places otherwise avoiding traveling in train is the trend while taking children in groups to these types of clandestine activities.

Figure – 7
Mode of Travel

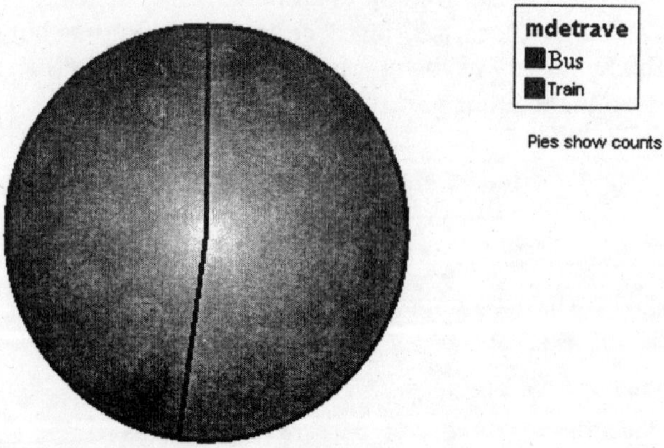

The Contract Amount

Details of Advanced Paid from The Contract Amount

Majority of the respondents (64.7%) knew that the advance amount paid for their contract. It is for the 35.3 per cent of the respondents the knowledge of whether the advance amount paid or not, it is inferred that children are kept away from the dealing with the traffickers. Many occasions the deal is completed with the recruiter

Table-14
Details of Advanced Paid

Advance	*Frequency*	*Percentage*
Advanced Paid	77	64.7
No Advance	42	35.3
Total	**119**	**100.0**

and with the parents. It is also observed that it few occasions where the elder brother of the children engages in the dealings without any consultation or reference given to the children.

Table-15
Advanced Amount Paid

Amount	*Frequency*	*Percentage*
500	6	5.0
550	2	1.7
600	1	.8
650	1	.8
700	16	13.4
800	10	8.4
850	1	.8
900	1	8
1000	8	6.7
1100	1	.8
1200	1	.8
1300	1	.8
1500	1	.8
2000	3	2.5
2500	15	12.6
3000	9	7.6
TOTAL	**77**	**64.7**
No Advance	42	35.3
TOTAL	**119**	**100.0**

The advance amount paid to the parents is ranging from Rs.500 to Rs. 3000 with a Mean amount paid Rs. 1427. It could be observed that children are taken to far off places just paying a meager amount like Rs. 500, Rs. 600, and Rs. 700. This table is presented as actual without arranging it in the class interval with a view to have a clear picture and accurate details about it.

There are 26 respondents who are paid Rs. 700 and Rs. 800 implies the low grading and low value to the children. On theother hand how the labour become so cheap to the employers who could earn enormous amount through the labour of this children. There are also 15 respondents who are paid an advance amount of Rs. 2,500 implies that the year contract could be few years than the normal contract of one year.

Total Contact Amount and the Year of Contract

Table-16
Total Contact Amount and the Year of Contract

Amount	*Contract Years*								*Total*
	1.00	2.00	3.00	4.00	5.00	6.00	8.00	10.00	2
5000.00	2								2
6000.00	5								5
7000.00	5		1						6
8000.00	8		2						10
9000.00	1								1
9600.00			1						1
10000.00	2		15		2				19
12000.00		1			3			1	5
13200.00					1				1
15000.00				1			1		2
18000.00					2				2
20000.00			1		1				2
24000.00			1	1		1			3
30000.00			6	3	6	1			16
36000.00				1	6				7
TOTAL	23	1	27	6	21	2	1	1	82
Not Known									37
TOTAL									119

When the total amount of contract and the year of contract crossed it could be portrayed that concentration of respondents more in one year, three year and five year contract. The odd number of year of contract is the preferable year as it goes with the sentiment of the people.

This observation is in contraction with the views expressed by the NGO personnel that the normal period of contract is one year. When discussed with the NGO staff again with this findings it is opinioned that the business is so flourishing that the traffickers and recruiters now going for more years of contract so that they need not loose the experienced hands and search for new children is minimized.

The amount of contract ranges from a minimum of Rs. 1000 per year to the maximum of Rs. 12,000. It is also understood that sometimes it is fixed per year basis and few cases it is lump sum.

When analysed contract period there are also a child under 10 years contract and majority of the children are below 5 years contract. When the years of contract is compared with the age one can easily understand that the employers are traffickers are very much careful enough in establishing the contract as they reach adult stage by 18 years or so they will be relieved from the work. This implies that the employers are in the advantage side of keeping only children with them so that they can be easily exploited. Once they become adult they may claim for more salary and other rights. The preferred year of recruitment is 13, 14 and 15 is an important factor in determining the contract and fixing the contract amount.

Type of Industry

Murukku Company is nothing but preparing sweets, snacks and other eatable items in bulk and supply to the retailers and even directly to the customers. The people in the study area migrated to various other states such as, Andhra Pradesh, Karnataka, Kerala, Maharastra, Orissa, and to other far off places either alone or along with their families to do the murukku making business. As the business is flourishing more and more men and women fly to other states for this business.

Having Murukku Company is a money earning business as the local people, NGO and local representatives perceive. It is true as those who engage in such work proved by increasing their economic status in their own villages. It is a positive note as observed by the researcher and reported by the NGO and local representatives that

Table–17
Type of Industry

Type of Industry	*Frequency*	*Percentage*
Cotton Mill	30	25.2
Murukku Company*	50	42.0
Hotel	18	15.1
Hosiery Company	12	10.1
Cement Industry	6	5.0
Appalam Company**	2	1.7
Biscuit Company	1	.8
TOTAL	**119**	**100.0**

* : Murukku company means preparing snacks and sweets on whole sale basis.

** : Appalam company implies making of pappad used as a side dish to south Indian food.

the money earned in other states through this business are invested in local area or village in land, house and in other properties. This could also bring some employment opportunities to the local laborers as most of them invest in the lands and start doing agriculture in absentia.

On the other hand these business people find the children of their own local area as money earning machines as they are the cheap and hard working labour. Their property in terms of house, land, jewellery is the resultant factor of the hard bitter labour of these children.

Type of Work

Nearly half of the respondents put into the production work means they are not directly involved in the production but help the other

Table–18
Type of Work

Type of Work	*Frequency*	*Percentage*
Production	48	40.3
Sales	27	22.7
Packing	13	10.9
Marketing	5	4.2
Menial Work	6	5.0
Helper	20	16.8
Total	**119**	**100.0**

experienced and adult workers in the production area. The production here means making or preparing sweet and murukku (snacks) as most of the respondents are selected for this purpose. The murukku making working is popular among the people in the study area as it fetches lot of income to the entrepreneur. The children are put into various other works such as sales, packing, marketing, coolie work or helper. The coolie work implies any type of menial job assigned to the children then and there and there is no fixed work. They can be placed normally at the lower strata among the trafficked victims.

The children are placed in various categories of work according to their age, experience, physical nature and skills and talents. The experienced persons are placed in the marketing and sales especially in murukku making business.

Type of Work and Type of Industry

The above table depicts about the type of work the respondents undergo in each and every industry. It is observed that 25.2 per cent

Table-19
Type of Work and Type of Industry

Type of Industry	*Type of Work*												*Total*	
	Production		*Sales*		*Packing*		*Mar-keting*		*Coolie*		*Helper*			
	N	%	N	%	N	%	N	%	N	%	N	%	N	%
Murukku Company	16	13.4	20	16.8	11	9.2	1	.8	1	.8	1	.8	50	42.0
Cotton Mill	30	25.2											30	25.2
Hotel											18	15.1	18	15.1
Hosiery Company	1	.8	7	5.9			4	3.4					12	10.1
Cement Industry									5	4.2	1	.8	6	5.0
Appalam Company	1	.8			1	.8							2	1.7
Biscuit Company					1	.8							1	.8
Total	**48**	**40.3**	**27**	**22.7**	**13**	**10.9**	**5**	**4.2**	**6**	**5.0**	**20**	**16.8**	**119**	**100.0**

of the respondents work in the production area of cotton mill represent that the children are put to work in the power loom frame and it is also to be remembered here that all the respondents are girls. With regard to murukku company there is a higher representation in the production (16.8%) area followed in the sales area (13.4%). Normally children in the sales section are taken in a vehicle along with the produce to help the salesmen (the salesmen is either an adult men–the driver cum owner or the experienced trafficked children. Moreover the children in the hotel industry all of them (15.1%) work as helpers who do the work such as dish wash, servers, and cleaning work.

Children are asked to various jobs and responsibilities as that of any organized sector with line and staff function such as production, sales, marketing, coolie and helper and the various categories of children are placed. Based on the age, experience, talent, physical structure or strength these children are assigned various jobs. It is understood that it is immaterial where the children is placed by every children should undergo the huge task of hard and over work.

Type of Industry and Age

Table–20
Type of Industry and Age

Type of Industry	*Age Categories*				Total
	Upto 10	*11-12*	*13-14*	*15 & Above*	
Cotton Mill	6 5.1%	4 3.4%	14 12.0%	6 5.1%	30 25.6%
Murukku Company	7 6.0%	12 10.3%	20 17.1%	11 9.4%	50 42%
Hotel	3 2.6%	2 1.7%	6 5.1%	7 6.0%	18 15.4%
Hosiery Company	1 .9%	5 4.3%	4 3.4%	2 1.7%	12 10.3%
Cement Industry	1 .9%	1 .9%	3 2.6%	1 .9%	6 5.1%
Appalam Company		2 1.7%			2 1.7%
Biscuit Company				1 .9%	1 .9%
TOTAL	**18** **15.4%**	**26** **22.2%**	**47** **40.2%**	**28** **23.9%**	**119** **100.0%**

For the purpose of the study the samples are grouped into four categories. More than forty per cent (40.2%) of the samples belong to the age category of 13 and 14 is the most wanted category among the recruiters. As the labour involves hard work and manual labour; the children are selected based on the age and physical structure. The contract amount is fixed on these two criteria mainly apart from their experience in similar type of work or already been trafficked for similar work. The distribution of the age group to various industry indicates that there is no trend as to what age group is most preferred to type of the industry rather every children is in need of every work. Depend upon their age the type of work is available from helper, menial work, production, sales, etc., and hence these industries can accommodate any age group of children even the below 10 years category is a very danger signal.

Figure—8
Type of Industry and Sex

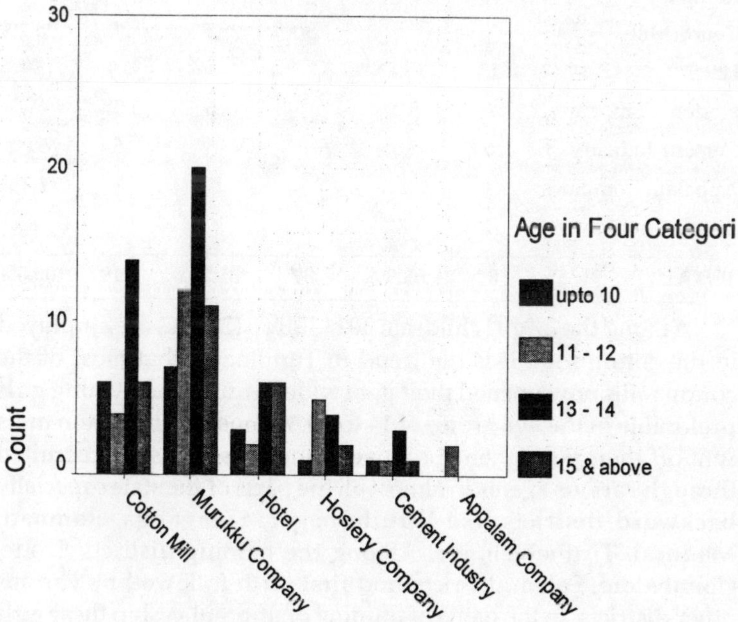

Type of Industry and Sex

It has been observed that there are 68.9 per cent of the respondents are male children and 31.1 per cent are female children and among the industry; Murukky company prefers only male members as it requires very hard labour in terms of manual work. More over the enterprises are located in far off places especially in other states and hence the employers select only male children. In the similar way Hotel business employed 18 children which constitute 15.1 per cent of the total sample.

Table–21
Type of Industry and Sex

Type of Industry	*SEX*					
	Male		*Female*		*Total*	
	N	*%*	*N*	*%*	*N*	*%*
Murukku Company	50	42.0%			50	42.0%
Cotton Mill			30	25.2%	30	25.2%
Hotel	18	15.1%			18	15.1%
Hosiery Company	6	5.0%		6	5.0%	
Cement Industry	6	5.0%			6	5.0%
Appalam Company	1	.8%	1	.8%	1	1.7%
Biscuit Company	1	.8%			1	.8%
TOTAL	**82**	**68.9%**	**37**	**31.1%**	**119**	**100.0%**

Among the 37 girl children; 30 children (25.2%) are employed in the cotton mill. It is the trend in Tamilnadu that most of the cotton mills now opened their gate wide to unmarried young girls preferable in the age group of 14 to 19. Almost all the cotton mills sent off their permanent employees and these girls are recruited through various agents in almost all the parts of the state especially backward districts like Viruthunagar, Sivaganga, Ramnad, Madurai, Tirunelveli, etc. Among the gaining districts Erode, Coimbatore, Salem districts find first birth followed by various other districts. In the name of training or apprenticeship these girls are recruited for a period of three years contract (normally) attracted with various schemes; placed them in the mill premises itself provided boarding and lodging – extract a work profit equivalent to many times than their payment (training stipend) It is an another trend to be probed into seriously.

Age and Type of Work

The age group in the production work is more or less equally distributed and no one age group is preferred or not preferred in the production work makes one to infer that the trend is not the one age group but every children. What ever be the age group of children there is bar as far as the trafficking phenomena for labour as far as this region is concerned.

This table once again confirms the observation in tune with the earlier table on age and type of industry. However in the sales section more than half of the respondents' belong to the below 12 years category is observed in the table is worth mentioning as these children are helpers taken in a vehicle along with the produce by a driver cum salesman cum owner. Helper is found to be another category where little less than one fourth (23.1%) belong to the more

Figure – 9
Age and Type of Work

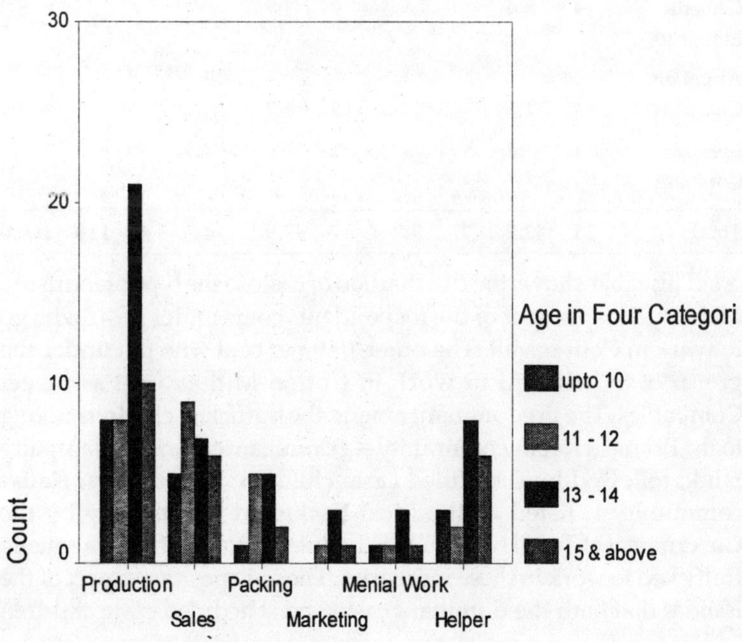

than 15 years category is understood that these children are with less skill and talent in other type of work and hence placed in the helper category. The helper category is one who are assigned specific work (in any type of work) and placed where ever they wanted.

Caste Distribution and The Type of Industry

Table-22
Caste Distribution and the Type of Industry

Type of Industry	*Caste*								*Total*	
	SC		*ST*		*MBC*		*BC*			
	N	*%*	*N*	*%*	*N*	*%*	*N*	*%*	*N*	*%*
Murukku Company	19	16.0	4	3.4	25	20.9	2	1.7	50	42.0
Cotton Mill	13	10.9			17	14.3			30	25.2
Hotel	9	7.6			8	6.7	1	.8	18	15.1
Hosiery Company	6	5.0	3	2.5	2	1.7	1	.8	12	10.1
Cement Industry	4	3.4			2	1.7			6	5.0
Appalam Company	2	1.7			2	1.7				
Biscuit Company	1	.8			1	.8				
Total	**51**	**42.9**	**7**	**5.9**	**57**	**47.9**	**4**	**3.4**	**119**	**100.0**

This table shows the distribution of caste to the type of industry. Majority 14.3 per cent of the respondents come under MBC who go to work in Cotton Mill. The other 10.9 per cent who fall under the group of SC also go to work in Cotton Mill as well as Sweet Companies. The predominant among the trafficked children belong to the Primalai Kallar community – a dominant caste in Usilampatty taluk; followed by scheduled caste children. The Primalai Kallar community is listed as the Most Backward Community by the Government of Tamil Nadu. The Scheduled caste children are equally trafficked to work in these industries. The only positive aspect of the issue is that both the dominant caste and scheduled caste children are stay together, work together, eat together and live together in their trafficked destinations.

First Contact Person/Recruiter and Type of Industry

It is strange to observe that for 72 respondents the parents are the first contact person who motivated the children to take it work in these industries. In this study the researcher wanted to know the modus operandi of the trafficking phenomena and formulated as one of the objectives. It is strange to understand that the parents are very much convinced in sending their wards to work or put them in the trafficking chain. In other words this shows the unconsciousness on the part of the parents about the consequences or the impact of trafficking on the future life of the children. Though parents are motivated through various sources such as relatives, neighbours, friends, local entrepreneur who has established units especially the Murukku company, etc., their attitude has been positive towards the trafficking business.

Table–23

First Contact Person/Recruiter and Type of Industry

Type of Industries	*First contact person / recruiter*				*Total*
	Broker	*Elder*	*Village leader*	*Parents*	
Cotton Mill	1 6.7%			29 40.3%	30 25.2%
Murukku Company	5 33.3%	22 75.9%	2 66.7%	21 29.2%	50 42.0%
Hotel				18 25.0%	18 15.1%
Hosiery Company	7 46.7%	3 10.3%	1 33.3%	1 1.4%	12 10.1%
Biscuit Company		1 3.4%			1 .8%
Cement Industry	2 13.3%	2 6.9%		2 2.8%	6 5.0%
Appalam Company		1 3.4%		1 1.4%	2 1.7%
Total	**15** **100.0%**	**29** **100.0%**	**3** **100.0%**	**72** **100.0%**	**119** **100.0%**

Sending children to Murukku Company is the trend recently been set in the study area Usilampatty Taluk and it is not considered as a negative phenomenon rather it is found as a boon during distress. Similarly there are 25 per cent of the parents' who contact their want or motivated them to join in the hotel industry. Though the broker or agent contacted only 15 respondents in the study it should be understood that they have greater role in motivating or instigating or pressuring the parents in admitting their wards in the trafficking chain. The other contact persons are elders (29 respondents) and village leaders (3 respondents) suggest that it become community activity and all the sections of the population involve in one way or the other. The participation of the community is essential to curb the menace become evidently observed.

Schooling and Type of Industry

The schooling years and the type of the industry is crossed in the above table. It has been observed that the schooling has nothing to do with the type of industry they were working. For instance in murukku company there are 53.3 per cent of the respondents belong to up to 3rd standard followed by middle schooling (41.7%), Primary schooling (39.1%) and 9th standard and above (25.0%). In the cotton mill the primary school category constitute 34.8 per cent followed by middle school (25%). It is to be understood these children are taken to work for manual and physical nature the education is not a consideration.

Table-24
Schooling and Type of Industry

Type of Industries	*Schooling Categories*				*Total*
	Upto 3	*Primary*	*Middle*	*9th & above*	
Cotton Mill	10.0%	34.8%	25.0%		25.2%
Murukku Company	53.3%	39.1%	41.7%	25.0%	42.0%
Hotel	20.0%	15.9%	8.3%		15.1%
Hosiery Company	6.7%	5.8%	16.7%	50.0%	10.1%
Biscuit Company	3.3%				.8%
Cement Industry	3.3%	2.9%	8.3%	25.0%	5.0%
Appalam Company	3.3%	1.4%			1.7%
Total	**100.0%**	**100.0%**	**100.0%**	**100.0%**	**100.0%**

Schooling and Type of Work

When crossed the type of work with schooling of the respondents it has been found that among the primary educated (69) most of them found a place in production (53.6%); among the up to 3rd standard category (30) most of them found in sales (33.3%); among the middle school group majority placed in production followed by sales and helper category.

It is to be inferred that schooling has no relevance with the type of the work as though the categories of work are classified as production, sales, packing etc., their actual work is to assist them in the area of operation with the adult worker. It is also understood from the respondents during the data collection that because of the experience and skill developed during their work for number of years they would be allowed to do it independently. This status would take a minimum of 3 years to a maximum of 6 years depends upon the age, physical structure and the interest.

Table–25

Schooling and Type of Work

Type of Work	*Schooling Categories*				*Total*
	Upto 3	*Primary*	*Middle*	*9th & above*	
Production	6 20.0%	37 53.6%	4 33.3%	1 12.5%	48 40.3%
Sales	10 33.3%	12 17.4%	3 25.0%	2 25.0%	27 22.7%
Packing	5 16.7%	5 7.2%	1 8.3%	2 25.0%	13 10.9%
Marketing	1 3.3%	2 2.9%	1 8.3%	1 12.5%	5 4.2%
Menial Work	2 6.7%	2 2.9%		2 25.0%	6 5.0%
Helper	6 20.0%	11 15.9%	3 25.0%		20 16.8%
Total	**30** **100.0%**	**69** **100.0%**	**12** **100.0%**	**8** **100.0%**	**119** **100.0%**

Causes and the Type of Industry

This table shows the major Industries the respondents go to work based on the causes. It is noted that 24.4 per cent of the respondents work in Cotton Mill and 18.5 per cent of the respondents go to Murukku Company and 12.6 per cent of them go equally to sweet company and to hotel due to poverty. The 2.5 per cent go to work in Murukku Company due to Ignorance.

Though poverty is the predominant perceived cause expressed; the land holdings and income of the family shows a different picture. It is assumed that there are other reasons such as earn quick money, to meet the immediate needs, to get away from the clutches of greedy debtors are the factors hiding behind the cause poverty. It can also be predicted that 'poverty' is the big banner where in these people can conceal themselves behind so that the actual reasons need not be revealed. Nevertheless poverty can also be a dominant reason for a considerate population to send their wards to traffickers.

Table–26

Causes and the Type of Industry

	Cotton Mill		*Murukku Company*		*Hotel*		*Hosiery Company*		*Cement Company*		*Appalam Industry*		*Biscuit Company*		*Total*	
Causes	N	%	N	%	N	%	N	%	N	%	N	%	N	%	N	%
Poverty	29	24.4	43	36.1	15	12.6	11	9.2	5	4.2	1	.8	1	.8	105	88.2
Ignorance	1	.8	3	2.5					1	.8					5	4.2
Earn more money	4	3.4	3	2.5	1	.8			1	.8			9	7.6		
Total	30	25.2	50	42.0	18	15.1	12	10.1	6	5.0	2	1.7	1	.8	119	1000

Duration of Work

Majority of the respondents (63%) are compelled to work from 11 to 15 hours per day with a mean hour of 12.30 hours; implies how these children are tasked. This over work would definitely lead to deterioration in the physical, mental and social development of the individual. There are also children who are working for 16 hours per day (7respondents) makes one to think that the greedy nature of the employer on one hand and the exploitation and vulnerability of the children on the other. There are 31.1 per cent of the children are put to work below 10 hours. Taking away their childhood is a curse and giving them such hours of work would doubly burden the children.

Figure—10

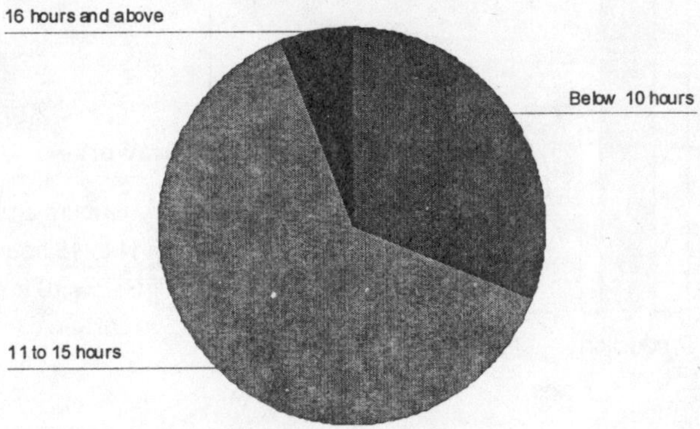

Type and Duration of Work

The bar chart shows the distribution based on the duration of work in each type of work. It is seen that 21.8 per cent of the respondents work for 11 to 15 hours at an average everyday in production and sales area. The duration of work falls between 11 to 15 hours for 10 percent of those who work in packing section which is a serious issue to be considered. Due to this the respondents are defenseless both physically and psychologically. Studies have shown that these types of people can have direct consequences on the child's development, both physical and mental. It shall be remembered that even for adult employees the working hours are regulated as eight hours. The pathetic condition of the children are that they are compelled to work on an average of 15 hours per day in most of the cases could really hamper their physical, mental and social development. It would definitely have its repercussions in their future life.

Production area mentioned in the table is nothing but the sweet making or mixture making and they are the helpers in the preparation of it. It is an odd job because the 'production' here means making children work through out the day starting at an early time of four or

Figure – 11
Type and Duration of Work

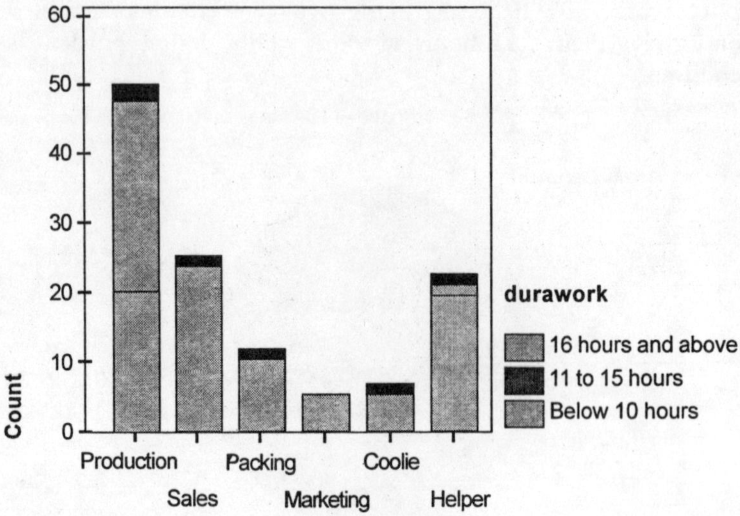

five O' clock in the morning and closing around 11 or 12 at midnight make the children miserable and they are expected to work on par with the adult workers.

Rest Time During Work

Table-27
Rest Time During Work

Rest Time During Work	*Frequency*	*Percentage*
Morning and Evening	43	36.1
Evening and Night	1	.8
Morning to Night	2	1.7
Morning	30	25.2
Evening	36	30.3
Night	3	2.5
TOTAL	115	96.6
Not Rest	4	3.4
TOTAL	**119**	**100.0**

This table discloses the timings of rest the respondents obtain. It is seen that the mainstream of the respondents get time off only in the mornings. Their functioning hours commence from evening 4 to morning 2 by which they become free only in the morning.

It is to be understood that hardly any rest is given to these children since they are under a period of contract and in most of the cases for a year. It should also to be remembered that working hours ranges from 11 to 15 hours per day. Apart from the sleeping hours, time for food and everyday needs they get hardly any rest in between the working hours. The rest time for the respondents means the time for break fast, lunch and dinner and not in between work.

Rest Timings and the Type of Industry

Data provided in table discloses the timings of rest the respondents obtain in every industry they work. It is seen that the mainstream of the respondents get time off only in the mornings, predominantly

Table–28
Rest Timings and the Type of Industry

	Timings of Rest													
	Morning and Evening		*Evening and Night*		*Morning to Night*		*Mor-ning*		*Evening*		*Night*		*Total*	
	N	*%*	*N*	*%*	*N*	*%*	*N*	*%*	*N*	*%*	*N*	*%*	*N*	*%*
Murukku Company	22	19.1			2	1.7	6	5.2	16	13.8	2	1.7	48	41.7
Cotton Mill	9	7.8					7	6.1	14	12.2			30	26.1
Hotel	1	.9					15	13.0	1	.9			17	14.8
Hosiery Company	10	8.7							2	1.7			12	10.4
Cement Industry			1	.9			1	.9	3	2.6			5	4.3
Appalam Company							1	.9			1	.9	2	1.7
Biscuit Company	1	.9											1	.9
Total	43	37.4	1	.9	2	1.7	30	26.1	36	31.3	3	2.6	115	100.0

those who work in Hotels (13%). Their functioning hours commence from evening 4 to morning 2 by which they become free only in the morning. The 12 per cent of those who work in Cotton Mill get rest in the evenings.

It is to be understood that hardly any rest is given to these children since they are under a period of contract and in most of the cases for a year. It should also to be remembered that working hours ranges from 11 to 15 hours per day. Apart from the sleeping hours, time for food and everyday needs they get hardly any rest in between the working hours. The rest time for the respondents means the time for break fast, lunch and dinner and not in between work.

Nature of Work, Manageability and Exposure to Extreme Climate

Table-29

Nature of Work, Manageability and Exposure to Extreme Climate

		Frequency	*Percentage*
Nature of Work	Manual Work	77	64.7
	Hard Work	42	35.3
	TOTAL	**119**	**100.0**
Manage to Work	Unmanageable	93	78.2
	Manageable	26	21.8
	TOTAL	**119**	**100.0**
Exposure to Extreme Climate	HOT CLIMATE	74	62.2
	COLD CLIMATE	45	37.8
	TOTAL	**119**	**100.0**

Work Difficulties

It is observed from the table that the children experienced lot of difficulties in the work field as perceived as manual and hard work and difficulties expressed by almost all the children. It is really a hard task loaded and over burdened with the tender children. It is inferred that lot of pressure and strain added with the work since it involves huge amount of labour and the resultant factor is fatigue which will make them more tiredness and stunned growth.

Majority of the children are unable to manage their work (78.2%). This may be due to the manual work (64.7%) they have to do. The children are exposed to various other factors like extreme hot climatic conditions (62.2%) and cold climates (37.8%) which make them unmanageable and tedious. Due to these deplorable conditions their health becomes worse gradually.

Details of Nature of Floor

It is apparent that the nature of flooring of the work spot for 23 per cent of the respondents is dangerous. They work in a very hazardous location which may cause serious injuries for the children. But all these are not considered by the supervisors or the owners. The floor is made up of cement which is not more serious. This is opting for those who work in murukku companies, cement industries. But for those who work in platform hotels the floor is muddy.

Table-30
Details of Nature of Floor

Floor	*Frequency*	*Percentage*
Dangerous	23	19.3
Slippery	94	79.0
None	2	1.7
TOTAL	119	100.0

Ventilation and Lighting at the Work Spot

Fundamentally every work spot should have proper ventilation and lighting facilities. It is more vital for those who work. But here it is

Table-31
Ventilation and Lighting at the Work Spot

		Frequency	*Percentage*
Ventilation Required	Ventilation Need at the Work Spot	102	85.7
	Ventilation is Enough	17	14.3
	TOTAL	**119**	**100.0**
Lighting Required	Lighting Needed at the Work Spot	106	89.1
	Lighting Not Needed	13	10.9
	TOTAL	**119**	**100.0**

wretched to see that nearly 85 per cent of the work spots do not have proper ventilation facilities. Also it is to be noted that 89.1 per cent of the respondents are in need of lighting facilities to their work spot. This shows a clear picture about the tribulations; the respondents face.

Dangers in Work

It is alarming to note that majority of more than 88 per cent of the respondents experienced the dangers due to the trafficking they have undergone. The various dangers experienced are accidents, fire accidents, heavy work, injury, skin problem, and the like. Putting children is itself is dangerous to their life and personality and serious deterioration to the nation. Added to that exposing them to dangerous situations mentioned above apart from their child labour status make the condition more miserable and these children may go beyond repair if such situation continues.

Table-32
Dangers in Work

Dangers in Work	*Frequency*	*Percentage*
Accident	22	18.5
Fire Accident	21	17.6
Heavy Work	17	14.3
Over Heat	17	14.3
Sudden Injury	8	6.7
Sking Problem	6	5.0
Pouring of Oil	5	4.2
Over Luggage	4	3.4
Eye Problem	3	2.5
Skill Problem	2	1.7
TOTAL	**105**	**88.2**
NO DANGER	14	11.8
TOTAL	**119**	**100.0**

Dangers Faced and the Type of Industry

The list of dangers the respondents face in each and every type of industry is exposed in this table. It is perceived that more number of accidents crop up in every industry especially in Hosiery companies

(5.7%), Cotton Mill (3.8%) and in Murukku companies (3.8%). Mostly respondents are sent to work in these types of industries and they do not have any security in their life. The next form of hazard they face is fire accidents. It is high in Sweet companies (11.4%) and in Murukku companies (6.7%). They are also open to the elements of over heat in Hotels (12.4%). It shows a lucid picture about the type of surrounding they work.

Table-33
Dangers Faced and the Type of Industry

	Cotton Mill	*Murukku Company*	*Hotel Company*	*Hosiery Industry*	*Cement*	*Total*
Pouring of oil	3.8%				9%	5.7%
Accident	4%	4.89%		6.0%	3%	4.82%
Over Luggage	3.8%	8.64%		5.7%	2.9%	21.04%
Fire Accident		3.92%				3.82%
Eye problem	2%	20.0%				20.03%
Over heat	1.91%	1.03%	13%			2.91%
Skill problem	1.0%	2.9%	12.4%	2%		16.2%
Sudden injury	1%	7%	2%	1.9%		1.98%
Total	1.012%	4.84%	1.91%	8%	5%	7.65%
Skin problem	11.42%	45.7%	14.3%	7.6%	5.72%	100.0%

Other Difficulties During Work

Table-34
Other Difficulties During Work

Other Difficulties	*Frequency*	*Percentage*
Sleep Late at Night	63	53.0
Wake Up Early	18	15.2
No Rest	8	6.7
Over heat	4	3.3
TOTAL	**93**	**78.2**
No Difficulties	26	21.8
TOTAL	**119**	**100.0**

The children also experienced other difficulties such as heavy work, sleep at late night, wake up too early and exposed to heavy heat and cold could cause serious damage to the children's health. It has been observed that more than 75 per cent of the respondents experienced such intricacies in the work spot. Heavy work given to the children may deteriorate their health and it would have its consequences in the future life of the individual. Sometimes they may susceptible to serious health illness. Sleeping at late night (20.2%) and wake up early (15.1%) could cause sleeping problems and other complications to the children. It is to be understood that all the above mentioned factors are highly detrimental to the concept of childhood.

Other Difficulties Faced and the Type of Industry

From the table, the difficulties faced by the respondents in the industry they work are illustrated. It is clear to see that nearly 17 percent of those who work in hotels suffer by sleeping late at nights. They have to work up to midnight and some go to work in the morning. They get drained due to lack of sleep. Some of those who work in Murukku Companies (11.8%) and Cotton mill (9.7%) have heavy work. They get totally exhausted in person. They are made as non stop machines.

Table-35

Other Difficulties Faced and the Type of Industry

	Other Difficulties							
	Heavy work	*Sleep late at night*	*Wake up early*	*No rest*	*Skin problem*	*Ill treat-ment*	*Over heat*	*Total*
Murukku Company	20 21.5%	5 5.5%	16 17.2%	4 4.4%	1		1 1.1%	23 24.7%
Cotton Mill	9 9.7%	2 2.2	1 1.1%	2 2.2%		1 1.1%		15 16.1%
Hotel	1 1.1%	16 17.2%	1 1.1%					18 19.4%
Hosiery Company	7 7.5%							7 7.5%
Cement Industry	2 2.2%	1 1.1%		1 1.1%	2 2.2%			6 6.5%
Total	**39** **41.9%**	**24** **25.8%**	**18** **19.4%**	**8** **8.6%**	**2** **2.2%**	**1** **1.1%**	**1** **1.1%**	**93** **100.0%**

As children coping up with the hard and continuous labour in hazardous working conditions aggravates their difficulties and put them in turmoil. The difficulties faced and the nature of the job they were doing is analysed to depict a concrete picture. Heavy work, sleep at late night, wake up early, no rest and over heat are reported by the respondents.

Met Accident and Wound/Scar Acquired

It has been reported that there are 23 respondents (19.3%) met with an accident in their work spot or in the course of employment and developed wound or scar (17.6%). The wound or the scar they have developed not only physically and also psychologically as depicted in the forth coming pages while analyzing the psychological problems of these children. This is a serious factor taken into account how the care and protection of the children are at stake. It also speaks about the safety of the children and highly dangerous as to question of life is a serious matter to be considered immediately. It is worth noted that 21 per cent of the respondents have got any scar or wound during their work. They are more at peril of getting any such thing. The nature of work decides all those.

Table-36
Met Accident and Wound/Scar Acquired

		Frequency	*Percentage*
Met Accident	Met with Accident	23	19.3
	No Accident	96	80.7
	TOTAL	**119**	**100.0**
WOUND/SCAR	Had Wound/Scar	21	17.6
	No Wound/Scar	98	82.4
	TOTAL	**119**	**100.0**

Occupational Diseases

The respondents are out in the open to work related diseases. Almost 12.6 per cent of the children have got occupational diseases and it is existed for 5 years for 1.7 per cent of the respondents. Other 5.9 of them have got it for 1 year. Due to the hot and cold conditions of the work spot they are at the risk of obtaining to various occupational diseases.

Types of Ill-Treatment Faced

The employers wanted most of the time from these children a high return by making them hard and continuous labour and wanted to extract the maximum essence out of them; hence the ill-treatment becomes predictable. The respondents underwent various types of ill-treatment such as oral, physical torture abuse and caste discrimination. It has been analysed in terms of their employment. The ill-treatment is the maximum in murukku making company followed by cotton mills.

Table-37
Types of Ill-Treatment Faced

Types of Illtreatment	*Frequency*	*Percentage*
Oral	84	70.6
Physical Torture	7	5.9
Abuse	9	7.6
Case Discrimination	7	5.9
None	12	10.1
TOTAL	119	100.0

It should be understood that there are both and scheduled caste children are trafficked and put to work in the same place; but the Primalai Kallar caste is the dominant caste against the scheduled caste in their place of residence. The various reasons reported for such ill-treatments are being playful during work, Careless mistakes, Inability to work, not punctual, Requesting for REST, Sleeping due to over work, talking during work and Working slowly. These reasons seem to be baseless as these are the characteristics feature of the childhood and manifestations of the inability to ascertain their childhood features. These evident behaviours pressurize the community to take steps to curb the menace as it indicates the seriousness of the problem.

Person Who Ill Treat

The respondents faced lot of ill-treatment. It is obviously seen that 47.1 per cent of the respondents are treated ill by the employers. It is due to the commitment of small mistakes, sleeping during work, talking during work, and working slowly. Some are severely punished by beating, increasing the work load, pouring cold or at

Table–38
Person Who Ill Treat

Person Who ill Treat	*Frequency*	*Percentage*
Employer	56	47.1
Supervisor	35	29.4
Others	20	16.8
TOTAL	**111**	**93.3**
NO Illtreatment	8	6.7
TOTAL	**119**	**100.0**

times hot water on them. At times they provide no food. It is obvious to commit mistakes especially children, but the employers and supervisors doesn't consider and the respondents are severely ill treated which shows the cruelty of the employers.

Ill-Treatment and the Type of Industry

Table–39
Ill-Treatment and the Type of Industry

Type of Industry	*Ill-Treatment*									
	Oral		*Physical torture*		*Abuse*		*Caste Discrimination*		*Total*	
	N	%	N	%	N	%	N	%	N	%
Murukku Company	32	27.7	4	3.3	2	1.7	5	4.2	44	36.8
Cotton Mill	25	21.0					2	1.7	27	22.6
Hotel	16	13.4	1	.8					17	14.2
Hosiery Company	5	4.2	1	.8	5	4.2			11	9.2
Cement Industry	3	2.5	1	.8	2	1.7			6	5.0
Appalam Company	1	.8							1	.8
Biscuit Company	1	.8							1	.8
Total	**84**	**70.6**	**7**	**5.9**	**9**	**7.6**	**7**	**5.9**	**119**	**100.0**

Ill-treatment is inevitable and unavoidable in the trafficking issue and it becomes part and parcel of the victims as depicted in the table. All the children in one way or the other faced ill-treatments in range of oral abuse, torture, abuse and caste discrimination. The murukku company children are the worst affected by the ill-treatment as more than one third of the respondents experienced the ill-treatment. It is to be understood that the respondents faced multiple ill-treatments or a combination of ill-treatment. With each children the predominant ill-treatment experienced are taken for the study and compared with the type of work they underwent.

The employers wanted most of the time from these children a high return by making them hard and continuous labour and wanted to extract the maximum essence out of them; hence the ill-treatment becomes predictable. The respondents underwent various types of ill-treatment such as oral, physical torture abuse and caste discrimination. It has been analysed in terms of their employment. The ill-treatment is the maximum in murukku making company followed by cotton mills. It should be understood that there are both and scheduled caste children are trafficked and put to work in the same place; but the Primalai Kallar caste is the dominant caste against the scheduled caste in their place of residence.

Psychological Problems

The mental health is also very important for a person. This table shows the seriousness of the mental health of the respondents. Of this nearly 31 per cent of them are under severe depression. It may be due to the work over load, ill treatment of the supervisors, and separation from their family members. Every thing has gone

Table-40
Psychological Problems

Psychological Problems	*Frequency**	*Percentage*
Felt Depressed	38	31.9
Felt Under Privileged	16	13.4
Felt Neglected	18	15.1
Lost Hope	9	7.6
No Self Confidence	8	6.7

*: Multiple response

mechanical, in the sense that they have got no one to share their feelings. This is understood in the table that majority 15.1 per cent of the respondents have got the feeling of neglection where as 13 per cent of the respondents have felt under privileged.

Psychological Problems and the Type of Industry

Among the psychological problems it has been perceived by the respondents that they have feeling of depression (31.9%), feeling of under-privileged (13.4%), feeling of neglect (15.1%), hopelessness (7.6%) and having no self confidence (6.7%). Over loading of work, ill-treatment, bad habits and desperate future have contributed the feeling of depression among the children which is found predominant among all the psychological troubles. These psychological issues may get aggravated if the children are not properly and appropriately rejuvenated.

Table–41

Psychological Problems and the Type of Industry

Psychological concerns	*Cotton Mill*	*Murukku company*	*Hotel*	*Hosiery Company*	*Cement Industry*	*Appalam Company*	*Biscuit Company*	*Total*
	%	%	%	%	%	%	%	%
Depressed	7.6	13.4	3.4	4.2	2.5	.8		31.9
Not Depressed	17.6	26.9	5.9	4.2	.8	.8	.8	68.1
Felt Underprivileged	2.5	5.9	.8	2.5	1.7			13.4
Not Felt Underprivileged	22.7	36.6	14.3	7.6	3.4	1.7		
Felt Neglected	2.5	7.5		3.4	.8	.8		15.1
Not Felt Neglected	22.7	34.5	15.1	6.7	4.2	.8	.8	84.9
Hopeful	22.7	39.5	15.1	10.1	3.4	.8	.8	92.4
Hopelessness	2.5	2.5			1.7	.8		7.6
Self Confident	24.4	39.4	14.3	9.2	3.4	1.7	.8	93.3
No Self Confidence	.8	2.5	.8	.8	1.7			6.7

Bad Habits Acquired Because of Trafficking

The respondents have acquired many bad habits due to trafficking. Some habits they have are smoking, drinking, tobacco, panparak, and drug habits. Since they are not monitored by any one, they easily attain all these habits. It seen that majority 68.1 per cent of the respondents have the habit of smoking and 34.5 per cent have drug habit.

Table–42
Bad Habits Acquired Because of Trafficking

Bad Habits	*Frequency**	*Percentage*
Smoking	81	68.1
Drinking	36	30.3
Tobacco Sewing	39	32.8
Panparak Usage	41	34.5
Drug Habit	21	17.6

*: Multiple response

Reasons for Bad Habits

The reason for the bad habits is shown in the above table. Some reasons are categorized such as work pressure, ill treatment, feeling of loneliness, availability and enjoyment. It is obviously seen that nearly 35 per cent of the respondents get into bad habits due to the availability. They are easily exposed to these types of habits and due to this their physical as well as mental health goes worse.

Table–43
Reasons for Bad Habits

Reasons for Bad Habits	*Frequency*	*Percentage*
Work Pressure	12	10.1
Ill Treatment	2	1.7
Lonely	5	4.2
Availability	42	35.3
Enjoyment	10	8.4
TOTAL	**71**	**59.7**
No Bad Habits	48	40.3
TOTAL	**119**	**100.0**

Bab Habits Acquired and the Type of Industry

The type of work and the bad habits are compared and it reveals that most of the respondents have the habit of smoking with no variation

Table-44
Bab Habits Acquired and the Type of Industry

Bad Habits	*Cotton Mill*	*Murukku company*	*Hotel*	*Hosiery Company*	*Cement Industry*	*App-alam Com-pany*	*Bis-cuit Com-pany*	*Total*
	%	%	%	%	%	%	%	%
SMOKING								
YES	17.6	29.5	8.4	8.4	2.5	.8	.8	68.1
NO	7.6	12.6	6.7	1.7	2.5	.8		31.9
DRINKING								
YES	8.4	15.1	1.7	5.0				30.3
NO	16.8	26.8	13.4	5.0	5.0	1.7	.8	69.7
TOBACCO								
YES	10.1	12.6	4.2	3.4	2.5			32.8
NO	15.1	29.3	10.9	6.7	2.5	1.7	.8	67.2
DRUG								
YES	4.2	10.9	1.7	.8				17.6
NO	21.0	31.1	13.4	10.1	5.0	.8	.8	82.4
PANPARAK								
YES	7.6	18.5	3.4	2.5	1.7		.8	34.5
NO	17.6	23.5	11.8	7.6	3.4	1.7		65.5

in the type of industry they work. It is obviously seen that more than 29 percent of the respondents who work in Murukku Company 17 percent of the respondents who work in cotton mill and have the habit of smoking which shows that the respondents are easily in peril to grasp to various bad habits. The various other bad habits such as drinking, tobacco, drug use and panparak (a new substance used to keep it in the mouth for a longer period of time to give a soothing effect and this habit has been identified as the prelude for cancer) The reasons are due to work over load, away from the parental care, influence of peer and ill-treatment of the employers; would make them indulge in such vices.

Reasons for Bad Habits and Type of Work

The reason for bad habits and the type of work is crossed in the chart. It exemplifies that majority 21.6 per cent of the respondents

Figure—12
Reasons for Bad Habits and Type of Work

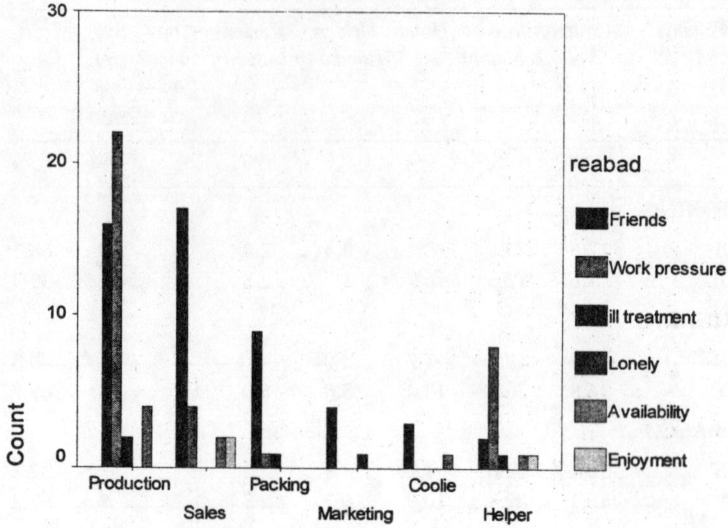

who work in the production section get in to bad habits due to work pressure. The timings of work is in an average of 11 to 15 hours and they have heavy work which may be one of the grounds to get in to these habits. They are hard-pressed. Friends are also one of the influencing factors for 16.7 per cent of those who work in sales section.

The peer or friend's influence is the predominant factor attributed by the respondents as the dominant factor for their bad habit. The peer influence is dominant as they stay, work and live along with them in a new environment where they are away from their parental care. The neglected and depressed feeling could be an underlying factor for the high peer influence.

Work pressure is identified as an important factor that attributed for bad habits acquired by these children. The hard labour, ill-treatment, torture, no rest, hazardous working conditions, lack of proper ventilation and light and deplorable working condition are the contributory causes to aggravate the work pressure and in turn the children indulge in bad habits. It not only affects the physical and mental status but also the total personality of the children.

Future Plan

While asking about the future plan of the respondents' greater part of them have planned to get a good employment opportunity. It may be that they might have not got good amount of money. Some have planned to get into business. Other part of the respondent's wished to go for vocational education. The major portion of the respondents opting for employment is a dangerous signal that there are greater chances for re-trafficked. This could also be an indicator of vulnerability that they once again fall prey to the traffickers.

Figure – 13
Future Plan

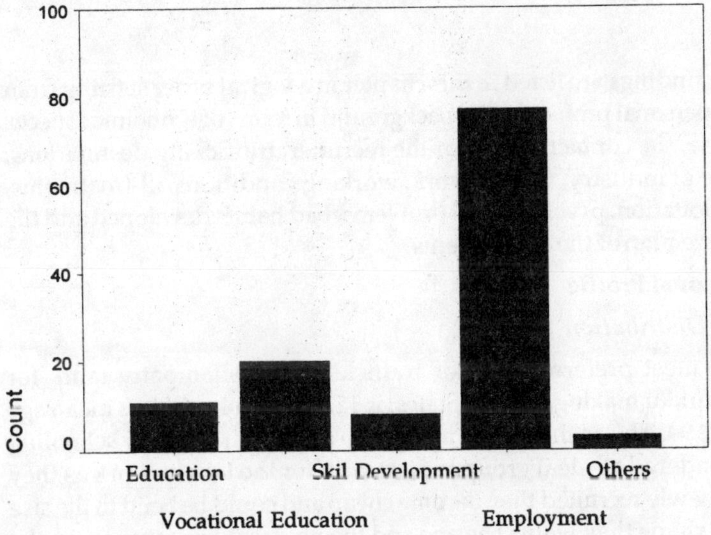

Chapter 5

Findings and Suggestive Intervention

The findings are listed in this chapter in a logical order starting from the personal profile, family background in terms of economic aspects, cause, the contact person or the recruiter, trafficking destinations, type of industry, type of work, working conditions, ill-treatments, exploitation, psychologicai problems, bad habits developed and the future plan of the respondents.

Personal Profile

Age Distribution

The most preferred age for trafficking in Usilampatty taluk for Murukku making to other States; is 12, 13 and 14; with the mean age of 12.94. This is the tender age group after their primary schooling considered as ideal group to start with for the labour work as they are newly recruited they become cheap and could be bend to the size and shape they want. The age and the physical appearance are the two important determinants in selecting children for work in these areas.

There are children recruited in the age group of 15, 16 and above if the above preferred categories are not found for their requirement. It is observed that when the age increases the amount paid to the children is also increases. There are also children needed for them in these age group for marketing their product and go for collection of money from the retail vendors.

There are also children trafficked at the age group of 10 and below represent their vulnerability in terms of social and economical aspects of the family.

Educational Status

It is observed that more than fifty percent of the trafficked children are drop outs after the primary schooling. There are 25.2 per cent not even gone to the stage of primary education. There are also few illiterate respondents found among the sample. There is a greater amount of constraint found among either before primary school or after the primary school in these area. The attitude of the parents and the economic status of the family are the crucial factors found for trafficking of these children either before primary or after primary education. It is to understood that the children are considered by their family of orientation as earning member or the supporter than as the future generation who need nurturing and care. It is also to be taken note that the parents hardly spend money for education of these children as it is taken care by the government.

Sex of The Respondents

There are 68.9 per cent of the respondents are male children and 31.1 per cent are female children in the study. In this area only male members are preferred as the work requires very hard labour in terms of manual work. More over the enterprises are located in far off places especially in other states and hence the employers select only male children.

Among the 37 girl children 30 children (25.2%) are employed in the cotton mill. It is the trend in Tamilnadu that most of the cotton mills now opened their gate wide to unmarried young girls preferable in the age group of 14 to 19. Almost all the cotton mills sent off their permanent employees and these girls are recruited through various agents in almost all the parts of the state especially backward districts like viruthunagar, sivaganga, Ramnad, Madurai, Tirunelveli, etc.

Details of Caste

Caste

Almost equal amount of representation for both Scheduled caste and the Most backward caste implies that there is no discrimination for the trafficking evil spirit. Though the most backward caste here represents solely by the Primalai kallar community the dominant caste found among the study area – Usilamapatty taluk which, has fully susceptible to child trafficking.

II. DETAILS OF FAMILY OF ORIENTATION

Income and Size of the Family

The mean income and the size of the family are calculated to understand the family background the respondents at the first instance. The mean income is calculated as Rs.1290 per month implies the occupational status of the family members. Most of the family members are engaged in unorganized sector and hence the income is not regular and sufficient and hence it is difficult to feed the family members with the mean size of the 5.81. The size of the family also indicates that the two family norms are not adequately adopted. With this low income it is very hard to feed the total family hence the children become the substitute for earning some more money for the family. In other words the burden of the parents is shared by these children at the cost of their childhood.

Details of Monthly Expenses

Regarding the monthly expenses of the respondents' family; it is observed that 63.9 per cent of them pay out below Rs. 1000 which makes them just around the corner to get loan and they become debtors. Other 15.1 per cent have their expenses within Rs.3000. When compared with the income it is not matching and always there is a deficient budget and hence dependence on the money lender increased which in turn becomes a vulnerable factor posted upon the children.

Details of Having Wet Land

Possession of land is not only an asset but also the status symbols whether dry land or wetland. Wetland in the study area means area irrigated by way of canal irrigation, well irrigation and tank irrigation. More than 25 per cent of the respondents' family has wet land and among them 20 per cent having the area ranging from 1 to 3 acres represents the economic status. It is to be understood that the economic status is not low as reported by many research studies that low economic status is one of the major causes for in the field of trafficking. It is to be differently understood that there could also be various other reasons for these respondents to get caught in the trafficking chain. There are five respondents having wetland in the range of 4 to 6 acres shows the stronger economic position.

Details of Dry Land

There are also 10 per cent of the respondents' family is having the dry land ranges from 1 to 3 acres. Though there is status as to have land; these dry lands have no economical and money value and hence cannot bring greater consideration for assessing their economical position. Contrarily these lands could also be considered as assets by the respondents when there are emergency situations such as the pressures from the local money lenders are concerned.

Details of House

Housing is to provide facilities to the residents added with the social status. Majority of the respondents have thatched (30.3%), and Titled (36.1%) houses shows the social and economic status of the respondents. The respondents living in Hut and Government colony houses represent 32 per cent make one to understand the low economic and social status of the respondents. It is to be understood that the Government colony residents are the selected beneficiaries of the government from the scheduled caste category and hence they are economically deprived group and living below poverty line.

Habit and Amount of Savings

It is interesting to note that there are 33 respondents family have the habit of saving. The saving amount ranges from below 10, 000 to more than 1 lakh and even one of the respondents' family could save more than Rs.2.0 lakh. It is to be understood that these amounts are the family income and speak for the status of the family in terms of economic position. This saving amount and mode of saving suggests us that the causes for the trafficking issue are not necessarily due to poverty alone. There could also be other reasons such as want to start their own business, earn more money and wrong model already set by the ex-trafficking victims makes one to think that the intervention should also include these important factors and a different approach is required.

Mode of Savings

It is interesting to note that there is a saving habit found among the respondents' family (27.7%) and the saving is done in both formal and informal agencies such as bank and post office and one in private with local people. Surprisingly a considerable number have saved Rs. 11,000 to Rs. 50,000 is a welcome feature. These habits must be encouraged and should be taken note of while planning for any rehabilitation programme to curb the menace of trafficking.

Amount of Debt

The amount of debt is also quite alarming as more than 44 per cent among the debtors borrowed an amount ranges from Rs. 11,000 to Rs. 50,000 implies the burden lies on the family. There are also respondents' family borrowed money to the tune of one lakh and above raises serious danger signal. The private money lenders are high in number as far as Usilampatty Taluk is concerned and it is a status symbol to declare openly that they are involved in financial business. They use all sorts of methods starting from torture, threat to live, oral and physical abuse, etc to get it repaid. There is also another important peculiar feature found among the Primalai Kallar community is that offering CASH GIFTS (moie or seimurai in Tamil) for occasions – normally an amount unmanageable to the status of the presenters. This has been reported in various documents and researches done in this area.

Source of Debt

Most of the borrowings took place with the relatives other wise relatives turned money lenders as they also charge interest like any other local money lender. Only a considerable family admitted that they got money from the money lenders. While borrowing they are the relatives and while start repaying or unable to pay they become the enemies. The nature of the lending business in this area is such that the interest rate is so alarming and the type of interest such as auto interest, run interest, meter interest, etc., (local interest models practiced by the money lenders) makes the borrower; the everlasting debtor.

Rate of Interest

The interest rate is more than 100 per cent or 200 per cent or even up to 300 per cent if the systematic and scientific calculations are made with the amount and the repayment. It is crystal clear to understand the respondents' family sent their wards merely to repay the old debts. The main source of debt is their relatives. It is seen that majority 36.1 per cent of the respondents' family get loan for marriage expenses and 21 per cent of them get to repay their old debts. It is also to be understood that they have to pay more than twice and thrice of this original amount so that their debts can be cleared.

Purpose of Loan

Debt

There are lots of complications and implications witnesses everyday among the debt victims. The rate of interest, the nomenclature given to the debt, the mode of recovery and the ill-treatment by the money lenders are quite dangerous and looked into seriously. The recent enactment to prevent and curb such private money lenders has only little to do with these blood sucking lenders and it has hardly any impact in these villages. The trafficking family is a prey to these money lenders and they can not easily escape from the clutches of the lenders.

Whenever there is a torture and turmoil from the lenders they try to find various means to escape from the money lender for the time being and one such way is to put their children in trafficking and get an advance amount to pay the lender.

It could be observed from the field through the local representatives and NGO personnel through their self help group women that the money lenders and the traffickers or the agents have close nexus with each other. In many cases the agents approach the money lenders to target families so that their vulnerability is exploited and they become the easy target to the agents.

Causes/Reasons for Trafficking

Though poverty is the predominant perceived cause expressed; the land holdings and income of the family shows a different picture. It is assumed that there are other reasons such as earn quick money, to meet the immediate needs, to get away from the clutches of greedy debtors are the factors hiding behind the cause poverty. It can also be predicted that 'poverty' is the big banner where in these people can conceal themselves behind so that the actual reasons need not be revealed. Nevertheless poverty can also be a dominant reason for a considerate population to send their wards to traffickers.

Modus Operandi

The actual in depth picture of the modus operandi was observed through the NGO personnel, self help group members and the youth group members through formal and informal discussion. The modus operandi as observed was very interesting. The entrepreneurs approach through parents as far as the Murukku Company is concerned. These owners are small business man engages in Candy and Murukku Making /Eatable Making. For the cotton mills the girls are contacted by the agents or brokers or the local elders directly. The girl children are taken for Textile work in Tamilnadu itself to Erode and Coimbatore Districts.

The other important way of approaching is the small entrepreneurs or agents approach through the moneylenders who could either provide details about the families who are in the burden of debt and in which family the preferable age group children are available. Some times the moneylenders themselves instigate or pressurize the parents to sent their wards to labour and repay the debt.

The agents also posing as friend and convincing families by giving false hopes in the form of advance amount or salaries; misleading the parents and children that they would acquire new skills start their own business is future, and also by given assurance that they will give loan during festivals, ceremonious and occasions etc.

Traffickers of Recuiters

This finding is the representative sample of the title of this study. The unconsciousness of the parents, village leaders and elders has approached the children to be trafficked for such work. It is also observed that the parents are approached by the brokers or elders or influential persons or the money lenders. Moreover the parents are directly compelled by the PUSH and PULL factors which made up their mind and approach their own wards to put them in the trafficking chain.

The parents are looking only at the immediate need or the crisis rather than the future prospects of their own future generation. In 60.5 per cent of the respondents the parents themselves approached the children and encouraged to get locked with the trafficking chain. The brokers or the agents play a lesser role though they have network among themselves with the individual entrepreneurs the unawareness and unconsciousness of the parents and community makes the business easy for such recruiters.

Accompanying Persons to Destination

It is the parents who again play a vital role in accompanying the children to the respected destination. It is apparent that nearly 55 per cent of the parents associate with the children. Then comes the brokers (14.3%). With the full knowledge of the parents the respondents are taken to work.

Prior Konowledge About the Destination

The awareness of the respondents with regard to the destination is found that there are 55.5 per cent of the respondents have gone to work without any prior knowledge. The parents have also not given any prior information regarding the destination to their children. It shows the pathetic situation of the respondents. They have gone into without knowing that they are to be in cages.

Intra and Inter State Trafficking

When analysed the places where these children are taken is quite interesting as these rural children who may not know even the nearby town or the district head quarters are taken to far off places ranging to southern, northern and even north eastern states. Among the States Tamilnadu, the home state has the major portion of having one third of the respondents (33.6%) and the nature of the work within Tamil Nadu is cotton mills (all girl respondents), hosiery industry in Tiruppur, and hotel industry in various other parts.

In the other state Karnataka tops the list in having (16.0%) of the respondents followed by Andhra Pradesh (12.6%), Madhya Pradesh (11.8%), Maharastra (10.9%), Uttar Pradesh (6.7%) and Kerala, Kolatta and Assam 6, 3 and one respondent respectively. The mobilization to other state is mostly for Murukku making business. The destination to states like M.P., U.P., Maharastra, even to West Bangal and Assam- makes the children more vulnerable in their mere location that it is a strange place, a different culture, an unknown language, etc., adds the misery to the children and they cannot do anything except head to the wimps and fancy of the employer.

Mode of Travel

The mode of travel is observed as both train and bus. For many of the children traveling in a bus is a greater enjoyment and traveling in a train takes them high as they have no access to train travel. This is another factor of motivation to the children they could travel in train and that too for two three days makes them accept the offer without knowing the reality. Nowadays the traveling in train along with group of children found to be rather risky as reported by the agents and parents since there is lot of constraints by the enforcement officials especially the Railway police who could easily locate and catch and place them before the Child Welfare Committee for rejuvenation. The local representatives and the NGO's working in the field acknowledged the fact and hence now traveling in bus even to far off places otherwise avoiding traveling in train is the trend while taking children in groups to these types of clandestine activities.

Details of Advance Paid From the Contract Amount

Majority of the respondents (64.7%) knew that the advance amount paid for their contract. It is for the 35.3 per cent of the respondents the knowledge of whether the advance amount paid or not, it is inferred that children are kept away from the dealing with the traffickers.

In most of the occasions the deal is completed with the recruiter and with the parents. It is also observed that it few occasions where the elder brother of the children engages in the dealings without any consultation or reference given to the children.

The advance amount paid to the parents is ranging from Rs. 500 to Rs. 3000 with a Mean amount of Rs. 1427. It could be observed that children are taken to far off places just paying a meager amount like Rs. 500, Rs. 600, Rs. 700.

There are 26 respondents who are paid Rs. 700 and Rs. 800 implies the low grading and low value to the children. On the other hand how the labour become so cheap to the employers who could earn enormous amount through the labour of this children. There are also 15 respondents who are paid an advance amount of Rs. 2,500 implies that the year contract could be few years than the normal contract of one year.

Total Amount and Period of Contract

The amount of contract ranges from a minimum of Rs. 1000 per year to the maximum of Rs. 12,000. It is also understood that sometimes it is fixed per year basis and few cases it is lump sum.

When analysed contract period there are also a child under 10 years contract and majority of the children are below 5 years contract. When the years of contract is compared with the age one can easily understand that the employers are traffickers are very much careful enough in establishing the contract as they reach adult stage by 18 years or so they will be relieved from the work.

This implies that the employers are in the advantage side of keeping only children with them so that they can be easily exploited. Once they become adult they may claim for more salary and other rights. The preferred year of recruitment is 13, 14 and 15 is an important factor in determining the contract and fixing the contract amount.

When the total amount of contract and the year of contract crossed it could be portrayed that concentration of respondents more in one year, three year and five year contract. The odd number of year of contract is the preferable year as it goes with the sentiment of the people.

This observation is in contraction with the views expressed by the NGO personnel that the normal period of contract is one year. When discussed with the NGO staff again with this findings it is opinioned that the business is so flourishing that the traffickers and recruiters now going for more years of contract so that they need not loose the experienced hands and search for new children is minimized.

Type of Industry

Murukku Company is nothing but preparing sweets, snacks and other eatable items in bulk and supply to the retailers and even directly to the customers. The people in the study area migrated to various other states such as, Andhra Pradesh, Karnataka, Kerala, Maharastra, Orissa, and to other far off places either alone or along with their families to do the murukku making business. As the business is flourishing more and more men and women fly to other states for this business.

Having Murukku Company is a money earning business as the local people, NGO and local representatives perceive. It is true as those who engage in such work proved by increasing their economic status in their own villages. It is a positive note as observed by the researcher and reported by the NGO and local representatives that the money earned in other states through this business are invested in local area or village in land, house and in other properties. This could also bring some employment opportunities to the local laborers as most of them invest in the lands and start doing agriculture in absentia.

On the other hand these business people find the children of their own local area as money earning machines as they are the cheap and hard working labour. Their property in terms of house, land, jewellery is the resultant factor of the hard bitter labour of these children.

Type of Work

There are fifty per cent of the respondents put into the production work means they are not directly involved in the production but help the other experienced and adult workers in the production area. The production here means making or preparing sweet and murukku (snacks) as most of the respondents are selected for this purpose. The murukku making working is popular among the people in the study area as it fetches lot of income to the entrepreneur. The children are put into various other works such as sales, packing, marketing, coolie work or helper. The coolie work implies any type of menial job assigned to the children then and there and there is no fixed work. They can be placed normally at the lower strata among the trafficked victims.

The children are placed in various categories of work according to their age, experience, physical nature and skills and talents. The experienced persons are placed in the marketing and sales especially in murukku making business.

Type of Work and Type of Industry

It is observed that 25.2 per cent of the respondents work in the production area of cotton mill represent that the children are put to work in the power loom frame and it is also to be remembered here that all the respondents are girls. With regard to murukku company there is a higher representation in the production (16.8%) area followed in the sales area (13.4%).

Normally children in the sales section are taken in a vehicle along with the produce to help the salesmen (the salesmen is either an adult men – the driver cum owner or the experienced trafficked children. Moreover the children in the hotel industry all of them (15.1%) work as helpers who do the work such as dish wash, servers, and cleaning work.

Type of Industry and Age

More than forty per cent (40.2%) of the samples belong to the age category of 13 and 14 is the most wanted category among the recruiters. As the labour involves hard work and manual labour; the children are selected based on the age and physical structure. The contract amount is fixed on these two criteria mainly apart from their experience in similar type of work or already been trafficked for similar work.

The distribution of the age group to various industry indicates that there is no trend as to what age group is most preferred to type of the industry rather every children is in need of every work. Depend upon their age the type of work is available from helper, menial work, production, sales, etc., and hence these industries can accommodate any age group of children even the below 10 years category is a very danger signal.

Type of Industry and Sex

It has been observed that there are 68.9 per cent of the respondents are male children and 31.1 per cent are female children and among the industry; Murukku company prefers only male members as it requires very hard labour in terms of manual work. More over the enterprises are located in far off places especially in other states and hence the employers select only male children. In the similar way Hotel business employed 18 children which constitutes 15.1 per cent of the total sample.

Among the 37 girl children 30 children (25.2%) per cent of them employed in the cotton mill. It is the trend in Tamilnadu that most of the cotton mills now opened their gate wide to unmarried young girls preferable in the age group of 14 to 19. Almost all the cotton mills sent off their permanent employees and these girls are recruited through various agents in almost all the parts of the state especially backward districts like viruthunagar, sivaganga, Ramnad, Madurai, Tirunelveli, etc.

Among the gaining districts Erode, Coimbatore, Salem districts find first birth followed by various other districts. In the name of training or apprenticeship these girls are recruited for a period of three years contract (normally) attracted with various schemes; placed them in the mill premises itself provided boarding and lodging – extract a work profit equalavent to many times than their payment (training stipend) It is an another trend to be probed into seriously.

Type of Work and Age

In the sales section more than half of the respondents' belong to the below 12 years category is observed is worth mentioning as these children are helpers taken in a vehicle along with the produce by a driver cum salesman cum owner. Helper is found to be another category where little less than one fourth (23.1%) belong to the more than 15 years category is understood that these children are with less skill and talent in other type of work and hence placed in the helper category. The helper category is one who are assigned specific work (in any type of work) and placed where ever they wanted.

The age group in the production work is more or less equally distributed and either no one age group is preferred or not preferred in the production work makes one to infer that the trend is not the one age group but any children. What ever be the age group of children there is bar as far as the trafficking phenomena for labour as far as this region is concerned. This table once again confirms the observation in tune with the earlier table on age and type of industry.

Caste Distribution and the Type of Industry

Majority 14.3 per cent of the respondents come under MBC who go to work in Cotton Mill. The other 10.9 per cent who fall under the group of SC also go to work in Cotton Mill as well as Sweet Companies. The predominant among the trafficked children belong to the Primalai Kallar community - a dominant caste in Usilampatty taluk; followed by scheduled caste children.

The Primalai Kallar community is listed as the Most Backward Community by the Government of Tamil Nadu. The Scheduled caste children are equally trafficked to work in these industries. The only positive aspect of the issue is that both the dominant caste and scheduled caste children are stay together, work together, eat together and live together in their trafficked destinations.

First Contact Person/Recruiter and Type of Industry

It is strange to observe that for 72 respondents the parents are the first contact person who motivated the children to take it work in these industries. In this study the researcher wanted to know the modus operandi of the trafficking phenomena and formulated as one of the objectives. It is strange to understand that the parents are very much convinced in sending their wards to work or put them in the trafficking chain. In other words this shows the unconsciousness on the part of the parents about the consequences or the impact of trafficking on the future life of the children.

Though parents are motivated through various sources such as relatives, neighbours, friends, local entrepreneur who has established units especially the Murukku company, etc., their attitude has been positive towards the trafficking business. Sending children to Murukku company is the trend recently been set in the study area Usilampatty Taluk and it is not considered as a negative phenomenon rather it is found as a boon during distress. Similarly there are 25 per cent of the parents' who contact their want or motivated them to join in the hotel industry.

Though the broker or agent contacted only 15 respondents in the study it should be understood that they have greater role in motivating or instigating or pressuring the parents in admitting their wards in the trafficking chain. The other contact persons are elders (29 respondents) and village leaders (3 respondents) suggest that it become community activity and all the sections of the population involve in one way or the other. The participation of the community is essential to curb the menace become evident by this observation.

Schooling and Type of Industry

The schooling years and the type of the industry are crossed in the above table. It has been observed that the schooling has nothing to do with the type of industry they were working. For instance in murukku company there are 53.3 per cent of the respondents belong to up to 3rd standard followed by middle schooling (41.7%), Primary schooling (39.1%) and 9th standard and above (25.0%). In the cotton mill the primary school category constitute 34.8 per cent followed by middle school (25%). It is to be understood these children are taken to work for manual and physical nature the education is not a consideration.

Schooling and Type of Work

When crossed the type of work with schooling of the respondents it has been found that among the primary educated (69) most of them found a place in production (53.6%); among the up to 3rd standard category (30) most of them found in sales (33.3%); among the middle school group majority placed in production followed by sales and helper category.

It is to be inferred that schooling has no relevance with the type of the work as though the categories of work are classified as production, sales, packing etc., their actual work is to assist them in the area of operation with the adult worker. It is also understood from the respondents during the data collection that because of the experience and skill developed during their work for number of years they would be allowed to do it independently. This status would take a minimum of 3 years to a maximum of 6 years depends upon the age, physical structure and the interest.

Causes and the Type of Industry

There are 24.4 per cent of the respondents work in Cotton Mill and 18.5 per cent of the respondents go to Murukku Company and 12.6 per cent of them go equally to sweet company and to hotel due to poverty. The 2.5 per cent go to work in Murukku Company due to Ignorance.

Though poverty is the predominant perceived cause expressed; the land holdings and income of the family shows a different picture. It is assumed that there are other reasons such as earn quick money, to meet the immediate needs, to get away from the clutches of greedy debtors are the factors hiding behind the cause poverty as observed through the local representatives and NGO's working in the area. It can also be predicted that 'poverty' is the big banner where in these people can conceal themselves behind so that the actual reasons need not be revealed. Nevertheless poverty can also be a dominant reason for a considerate population to send their wards to traffickers.

Duration of Work

Majority of the respondents (63%) are compelled to work from 11 to 15 hours per day with a mean hour of 12.30 hours; implies how these children are tasked. This over work would definitely lead to deterioration in the physical, mental and social development of the individual. There are also children who are working for 16 hours per day (7respondents) makes one to think that the greedy nature of the employer on one hand and the exploitation and vulnerability of the children on the other. There are 31.1 per cent of the children are put to work below 10 hours. Taking away their childhood is a curse and giving them such hours of work would doubly burden the children.

Type and Duration of Work

The bar chart shows the distribution based on the duration of work in each type of work. It is seen that 21.8 per cent of the respondents work for 11 to 15 hours at an average everyday in production and sales area. The duration of work falls between 11 to 15 hours for 10 percent of those who work in packing section which is a serious issue to be considered. Due to this the respondents are defenseless both physically and psychologically. Studies have shown that these types of people can have direct consequences on the child's development, both physical and mental. It shall be remembered that even for adult employees the working hours are regulated as eight hours. The pathetic condition of the children are that they are compelled to work on an average of 15 hours per day in most of the cases could really hamper their physical, mental and social development. It would definitely have its repercussions in their future life.

Production area mentioned in the table is nothing but the sweet making or mixture making and they are the helpers in the preparation of it. It is an odd job because the 'production' here means making children work through out the day starting at an early time of four or five O' clock in the morning and closing around 11 or 12 at midnight make the children miserable and they are expected to work on par with the adult workers.

Rest Time During Work

It is to be understood that hardly any rest is given to these children since they are under a period of contract and in most of the cases for a year. It should also to be remembered that working hours ranges from 11 to 15 hours per day. Apart from the sleeping hours, time for food and everyday needs they get hardly any rest in between the working hours. The rest time for the respondents means the time for break fast, lunch and dinner and not in between work.

It is seen that the mainstream of the respondents get time off only in the mornings. Their functioning hours commence from evening 4 to morning 2 by which they become free only in the morning.

Rest Timings and the Type of Industry

It is seen that the mainstream of the respondents get time off only in the mornings, predominantly those who work in Hotels (13%). Their functioning hours commence from evening 4 to morning 2 by which they become free only in the morning. The 12 per cent of those who work in Cotton Mill get rest in the evenings.

It is to be understood that hardly any rest is given to these children since they are under a period of contract and in most of the cases for a year. It should also to be remembered that working hours ranges from 11 to 15 hours per day. Apart from the sleeping hours, time for food and everyday needs they get hardly any rest in between the working hours. The rest time for the respondents means the time for break fast, lunch and dinner and not in between work.

Nature of Work, Manageability and Exposure to Extreme Climate

Majority of the children are unable to manage their work (78.2%). This may be due to the manual work (64.7%) they have to do. The children are exposed to various other factors like extreme hot climatic conditions (62.2%) and cold climates (37.8%) which make them unmanageable and tedious. Due to these deplorable conditions their health becomes worse gradually.

The children experienced lot of difficulties in the work field as perceived as manual and hard work and difficulties expressed by almost all the children. It is really a hard task loaded and over burdened with the tender children. It is inferred that lot of pressure and strain added with the work since it involves huge amount of labour and the resultant factor is fatigue which will make them more tiredness and stunned growth.

Details of Nature of Floor

It is apparent that the nature of flooring of the work spot for 23 per cent of the respondents is dangerous. They work in a very hazardous location which may cause serious injuries for the children. But all these are not considered by the supervisors or the owners. The floor is made up of cement which is not more serious. This is opting for those who work in murukku companies, cement industries. But for those who work in platform hotels the floor is muddy.

Ventilation and Lighting Requirements at the Work Spot

Fundamentally every work spot should have proper ventilation and lighting facilities. It is more vital for those who work. But here it is wretched to see that nearly 85 per cent of the work spots do not have proper ventilation facilities. Also it is to be noted that 89.1 per cent of the respondents are in need of lighting facilities to their work spot. This shows a clear picture about the tribulations; the respondents face.

Dangers in Work

It is alarming to note that majority of more than 88 per cent of the respondents experienced the dangers due to the trafficking they have undergone. The various dangers experienced are accidents, fire accidents, heavy work, injury, skin problem, and the like. Putting children is itself is dangerous to their life and personality and serious deterioration to the nation. Added to that exposing them to dangerous situations mentioned above apart from their child labour status make the condition more miserable and these children may go beyond repair if such situation continues.

Dangers Faced and the Type of Industry

The inventory of dangers the respondents faced is perceived that more number of accidents crop up in every industry especially in Hosiery companies (5.7%), Cotton Mill (3.8%) and in Murukku companies (3.8%). Mostly respondents are sent to work in these types of industries and they do not have any security in their life. The next form of hazard they face is fire accidents. It is high in Sweet companies (11.4%) and in Murukku companies (6.7%). They are also open to the elements of over heat in Hotels (12.4%). It shows a lucid picture about the type of surrounding they work.

Other Difficulties During Work

It has been observed that more than 75 per cent of the respondents experienced such intricacies in the work spot. Heavy work given to the children may deteriorate their health and it would have its consequences in the future life of the individual. Sometimes they may susceptible to serious health illness. Sleeping at late night (20.2%) and wake up early (15.1%) could cause sleeping problems and other complications to the children. It is to be understood that all the above mentioned factors are highly detrimental to the concept of childhood. The children also experienced other difficulties such as heavy work, sleep at late night, wake up too early and exposed to heavy heat and cold could cause serious damage to the children's health.

Other Difficulties Faced and The Type of Industry

It is apparent to make out that nearly 17 per cent of those who work in hotels suffer by sleeping late at nights. They have to work up to midnight and some go to work in the morning. They get drained due to lack of sleep. Some of those who work in Murukku Companies (11.8%) and Cotton mill (9.7%) have heavy work. They get totally exhausted each day. They are made as non stop machines.

As children coping up with the hard and continuous labour in hazardous working conditions adds aggravates their difficulties and put them in turmoil. The difficulties faced and the nature of the job they were doing is analysed to depict a concrete picture. Heavy work, sleep at late night, wake up early, no rest and over heat are reported by the respondents.

Met Accident and Wound/Scar Acquired

There are 23 respondents (19.3%) met with an accident in their work spot or in the course of employment and developed wound or scar (17.6%). The wound or the scar they have developed not only physically and also psychologically as depicted in the forth coming pages while analyzing the psychological problems of these children.

This is a serious factor taken into account how the care and protection of the children are at stake. It also speaks about the safety of the children and highly dangerous as to question of life is a serious matter to be considered immediately. It is worth noted that 21 per cent of the respondents have got any scar or wound during their work. They are more at peril of getting any such thing. The nature of work decides all those.

Occupational Diseases

The respondents are out in the open to work related diseases. Almost 12.6 per cent of the children have got occupational diseases and it is existed for 5 years for 1.7 per cent of the respondents. Other 5.9 of them have got it for 1 year. Due to the hot and cold conditions of the work spot they are at the risk of obtaining to various occupational diseases.

Types of Ill-Treatement Faced

The employers wanted most of the time from these children a high return by making them hard and continuous labour and wanted to extract the maximum essence out of them; hence the ill-treatment becomes predictable. The respondents underwent various types of ill-treatment such as oral, physical torture abuse and caste discrimination. It has been analysed in terms of their employment.

The ill-treatment is maximum in murukku making company followed by cotton mills. It should be understood that there are both and scheduled caste children are trafficked and put to work in the same place; but the Primalai Kallar caste is the dominant caste against the scheduled caste in their place of residence. The various reasons reported for such ill-treatments are being playful during work, Careless mistakes, Inability to work, Not punctual, Requesting for

REST, Sleeping due to over work, Talking during work and Working slowly. These reasons seem to be baseless as these are the characteristics feature of the childhood and manifestations of the inability to ascertain their childhood features. These evident behaviours pressurize the community to take steps to curb the menace as it indicates the seriousness of the problem.

Person Who Ill Treat

It is obviously seen that 47.1 per cent of the respondents are treated badly by the employers. It is due to the commitment of small mistakes, sleeping during work, talking during work, and working slowly. The respondents faced lot of ill-treatment. Some are severely punished by beating, increasing the work load, pouring cold or at times hot water on them. At times they provide no food. It is obvious to commit mistakes especially children, but the employers and supervisors doesn't consider and the respondents are severely ill treated which shows the cruelty of the employers.

Ill-Treatement and the Type of Industry

The murukku company children are the worst affected by the ill-treatment as more than one third of the respondents experienced the ill-treatment.

The respondents underwent various types of ill-treatment such as oral, physical torture abuse and caste discrimination. It has been analysed in terms of their employment. The ill-treatment is the maximum in murukku making company followed by cotton mills.

Ill-treatment is inevitable and unavoidable in the trafficking issue and it becomes part and parcel of the victims as depicted in the table. All the children in one way or the other faced ill-treatments in range of oral abuse, physical torture, abuse and caste discrimination. It is to be understood that the respondents faced multiple ill-treatments or a combination of ill-treatment. With each children the predominant ill-treatment experienced are taken for the study and compared with the type of work they underwent.

The employers wanted most of the time from these children a high return by making them hard and continuous labour and wanted to extract the maximum essence out of them; hence the ill-treatment becomes predictable. It should be understood that there are both and scheduled caste children are trafficked and put to work in the same place; but the Primalai Kallar caste is the dominant caste against the scheduled caste in their place of residence.

Psychological Problems

Nearly 31 per cent of the respondents are under severe depression. It is also understood that 15.1 per cent of the respondents have got the feeling of neglect where as 13 per cent of the respondents have felt under privileged.

The mental health is also very important for a person. This table shows the seriousness of the mental health of the respondents. It may be due to the work over load, ill treatment of the supervisors, and separation from their family members. Every thing has gone mechanical, in the sense that they have got no one to share their feelings.

Psychological Problems and the Type of Industry

Among the psychological problems it has been perceived by the respondents that they have feeling of depression (31.9%), feeling of under-privileged (13.4%), feeling of neglect (15.1%), hopelessness (7.6%) and having no self confidence (6.7%). Over loading of work, ill-treatment, bad habits and desperate future have contributed the feeling of depression which is found predominant among all the psychological troubles among the children in murukku making. These psychological issues may get aggravated if the children are not properly and appropriately rejuvenated.

Bad Habits Acquired Because of Trafficking

It seen that majority 68.1 per cent of the respondents have the habit of smoking and 34.5 per cent have drug habit. The respondents have acquired many bad habits due to trafficking. Some habits they have are smoking, drinking, tobacco, panparak, and drug habits. Since they are not monitored by any one, they easily attain all these habits.

Reasons for Bad Habits

The various reasons categorized are work pressure, ill treatment, feeling of loneliness, availability and enjoyment. It is obviously seen that nearly 35 per cent of the respondents get into bad habits due to the availability. They are easily exposed to these types of habits and due to this their physical as well as mental health goes worse.

Bad Habits Acquired and the Type of Industry

It is obviously seen that more than 29 per cent of the respondents who work in Murukku Company; 17 per cent of the respondents who work in cotton mill have the habit of smoking which shows that the respondents are easily in peril to grasp to various bad habits.

The various other bad habits such as drinking, tobacco, drug use and panparak (a new substance used to keep it in the mouth for a longer period of time to give a soothing effect and this habit has been identified as the prelude for cancer) The reasons are due to over load work, away from the parental care, influence of peer and ill-treatment of the employers; would make them indulge in such vices.

Reasons for Bad Habits and Type of Work

It exemplifies that there are 21.6 per cent of the respondents who work in the production section get in to bad habits due to work pressure. The heavy work leading to 11 to 15 hours per day could be one of the grounds to get in to these habits. They are hard-pressed. Friends are also one of the influencing factors for 16.7 per cent of hose who work in sales section.

The peer or friend's influence is the predominant factor attributed by the respondents as the dominant factor for their bad habit. The peer influence is dominant as they stay, work and live along with them in a new environment where they are away from their parental care. The neglected and depressed feeling could be an underlying factor for the high peer influence.

Work pressure is identified as an important factor that attributed for bad habits acquired by these children. The hard labour, ill-treatment, torture, no rest, hazardous working conditions, lack of proper ventilation and light and deplorable working condition are the contributory causes to aggravate the work pressure and in turn the children indulge in bad habits. It not only affects the physical and mental status but also the total personality of the children.

Future Plan

The major portion of two third of the respondents opting for employment is a dangerous signal that there are greater chances for fall prey to re-trafficked.

While asking about the future plan of the respondents' greater part of them have planned to get a good employment opportunity implies not only employment but also no other options left out. It may be that they might have not got good amount of money. Some have planned to get into business. Other part of the respondent's wished to go for vocational education. This could also be an indicator of vulnerability that they once again fall prey to the traffickers.

Suggestive Intervention Required

- Promoting employment and subsidiary opportunities especially during off seasons or hard seasons to parents and the family members
- Endorse alternative livelihoods and prevent them from falling a fry to the traffickers.
- Poverty, lack of education, low wages forces people to migrate and many a time in the realm of trafficking and hence initiatives taken to address these issues basically as prevention initially rather than rescue and rehabilitation.
- Priority should be given to rural related programmes in terms of poverty eradication, alternate livelihood, additional employment, dry land farming etc., so as to make the habitat self sustainable
- Committees at the village level and local level could be constituted to prevent as well as assist the vulnerable population
- Mobilizing people locally, nationally and internationally towards this cause
- Attitudinal change could be brought through proper awareness programme about the pros and cons and of trafficking among general masses and specifically the victims
- Trafficking legislations should be enacted making trafficking women ad children a felony instead of a misdemeanor.
- Public sharing of information in various forums such as conferences, workshops and seminars could be organized to sensitize and educate people.
- Involvement of NGO's for educating and piloting the community towards integrated action to combat the issue.
- State level network meetings should periodically be arranged to have a higher level of coordination
- Effective gender sensitization for women should be made more effective and strong.
- The influence of money lenders and the practice of borrowing to local lenders could be stopped by micro credit programmes in villages
- The intervention personnel should be given sensitization

training periodically and made compulsory before given charge.

- Multifaceted approach like health care, counseling, education, training and social integration shall be done with integral approach.
- The enforcement officials both at the centre and the state shall be trained and equipped with the objective of protecting the vulnerable group in to the web of trafficking
- Specific legislation is the need of the hour to promote anti-trafficking activities and to enforce specific measures.
- Strict implementation of recent amendment to the Child Labour Regulation Act to be done
- The rescue and rehabilitation measures shall be qualitatively improved so as to better reintegration of the victims shall be ensured.
- Traffickers must be put into task strictly using the legal provisions.
- The enforcement directorate must activate and book the culprits under any or all the laws applicable
- Participation of children should be ensured in various programmes of the Government especially compulsory primary education, SSA, nutritious meal programme, free text book etc., to increase their interest and aspiration towards eduation
- The child rights related issues are to be made known to the children who are supposed to be the stakeholders.
- Awareness programmes manner shall be given to the children in general and to children in distress in particular.
- They need to know the channels in which they can represent their case by themselves or with child rights activists to ensure less risk and danger.
- Educating the community and the parents is the need of the hour; as they are unconsciously participating in trafficking without fully understand the consequences on the children.
- Proper sensitization programmes should be planned by the Govt. and the NGO to enhance the capacity of the communities.

NGO Involvement and Intervention

The predominant cause found to be poverty and failure of monsoon and draught. Besides broken families, alcoholic father, dysfunctional and disorganized families, are the other attributed causes. There are about 22 NGO's working in the area to prevent and rehabilitate child trafficking. They are not able to do intensively because of lack of fund, infrastructure, lack of staff and the "**denial syndrome**" by the families themselves.

Suggestion During Discussion With NGO and Community

It is strongly recommended that the risk area identified and declare first. Then the intervention of Government agencies through NGO's with the active participation of local self Government and the community can prevent child trafficking.

An action plan should be evolved to focus on prevention, Awareness Generation, Mobilization of Community, Improving Health Care Services, Providing Educational Support within and outside the institution, providing housing shelter and other basic facilities.

More over providing economic empowerment to the families, legal awareness and gearing up law enforcement machinery, rescue operations by government having partnership with NGO's and rehabilitation in the form of Education, Vocational Training and Counseling, In the absence reliable data, the intervention strategies for the effective prevention is hampered.

There is also a need for Central Agency to Co-ordinate various activities towards prevention of trafficking and facilitating rescue and rehabilitation of the victims.

Trafficking in human beings is a social problem; hence the involvement of the entire community should be enlisted. The role of the voluntary organizations is very essential to effectively combat this menace. Lastly and not the least consciousness will go a long way in combating this modern day menace of trafficking in human beings.

- Inter State Co-ordination is lacking inadequate rehabilitation alternatives
- Inadequate networking with NGOs and amongst NGOs
- Lack of inter departmental coordination
- Lack of mechanism to monitor the activities of NGOs
- Insufficient financial resource

The need of the hour is to educate the communities in order to prevent and eradicate trafficking for child labour activities from

this area. The various stakeholders of the community in terms of trafficking such as the ward members, presidents, influential persons, elders, women and youth groups need to be sensitized by providing knowledge, skill and authority to respond to child right problems.

Appendix

Child trafficking –An Unconscious Phenomenon

Age : ***Education:*** ***Sex:***

I. Family details

S.No.	*Relation to Resp.*	*Age*	*Edn.*	*M.S.*	*Occn*	*Income*	*Caste*	*Religion*

Reason for school drop out if any :

II. Economic Status (to be asked to the Head/mother of the family)

A. Immovable property :

1. Do you have any I Wetland Yes/ No If yes area in acres: – – – –
2. Do you have any Dry land Yes/No If yes area in acres: – – – – –

Details of House: a. Hut b. Thatched c. Titled d. others

Rooms available in the house :

Details of other sources of income

(*a*) Land Rs.: ——————— /year

(*b*) Animals Rs.———————/year

(*c*) Others Rs.———————/year

B. Details of the movable properties

1. Do you have vehicles Yes/No Details :
2. Do you have Jewels Yes/No Details :
3. Do you have Television Yes/No Details :
4. Do you have the habit of saving: Yes/No
5. If yes mode of saving a. Post office b. Bank c. Private d. others:
6. Amount of Saving : Rs.
7. Do you have Debt Yes / No
8. Amount of Debt : Rs.
9. Source of Debt:

   a. b. c. d. e.
10. Rate of interest :
11. Purpose of which the loan is barrowed:

    (*a*) education (*b*) marriage (*c*) funeral (*d*) to repay old loans e. any other

C. EXPENDITURE PATTERN

How much do you spent every day/Month for the following:

(*a*) Food : Rs.
(*b*) Cloth : Rs.
(*c*) Medicine : Rs.
(*d*) Festivals : Rs.
(*e*) Repayment of loans : Rs.
(*f*) Agriculture Rs.
(*g*) Animals maintenance: Rs.
(*h*) Education: Rs.
(*i*) Others :

II. WORKING CONDITIONS FOR CHILDEN (to be asked to the children/Parents)

A.TYPE OF WORK

1. What is the type of work :

   a. b. c. d. e.
2. Type of Industry :

   a. b. c. d. e.
3. Whether the work is difficult to you : Yes /No
4. Whether it is a (*i*) manual work or (*ii*) hard work

5. Whether the work is manageable: Yes /No
6. Whether the work is exposed to Hot/Cold conditions
7. Whether the work involves risk factors: Yes /No
8. List down any dangers involved

   a. b. c. d. e. f.
9. What are other difficulties faced

   a. b. c. d. e. f.
10. Have you met with any accidents during the work Yes / No
11. Any wound or scar has been developed Yes / No
12. Do you got any occupational diseases Yes / No
13. For how many years :

B. TIME OF WORK

1. When you start the work :
2. When you finish the work :
3. What is the duration of work per day :
4. Is there any rest or interval during work :
5. If yes mention the timings : *(a)* Morning *(b)* Evening *(c)* Night

C. CONDITIONS OF WORK SPOT

1. What is the size or space of the work spot :
2. How many people were working :
3. Conditions of the floor a. Mud b. cement c other
4. Whether the floor is i) dangerous or ii)slippery
5. Whether there was enough ventilation Yes / No
6. Whether there was enough lighting Yes / No

III. WAGE AND SALARY/ STIPEND

1. Whether any advance amount paid for salary
2. How much is paid Rs. To whom:
3. How much per month Rs. Per Year Rs.
4. The amount is paid a) partial or b)full
5. How many years of contract:
6. Any bonus is paid Yes/No Give details :
7. Any daily allowance is paid :
8. The facilities like food or accommodation is given free

9. If no what is the charge *(a)* food *(b)* accommodation *(c)* other:

IV. CAUSES (Give the order of preference)

1. Poverty
2. Ignorance
3. Illiteracy
4. To earn more money
5. False promises
6. To pay the debt of the parents
7. To meet the expenses of the sibling
8. To meet the expenses for agriculture
9. Already there are role models
10. Brain washing by brokers/elders or others
11. Any other :

V. MODUS OPERANDI

1. Who contacted you for the first time for the work a. broker b. elder c. village leader d. parents e. others
2. Who took you to work place :
3. Do you aware the fact that you had been transported for work
4. How many accompanied along with you :
5. Where is your work place: State
6. Mode of traveling a. bus b. Train c. others

ILL-TREATMENT:

1. Have you undergone ill-treatment in the following form
2. Oral
3. Physical torture
4. Abuse
5. Caste discrimination
6. Sexual abuse
7. What are the general reasons for ill-treatment
8. Any scar or wound is found because of ill-treatment
9. Who do ill-treatment a. employer b. supervisor c. colleagues d. others :
10. Do you given punishment Yes / No
11. What type of punishment

12. Who give punishment
13. What are reasons for giving punishments

    a. b. c. d. e.

PSYCHO-SOCIAL ASPECTS

1. Do you feel depressed Yes / No
2. Do you feel under privileged Yes / No
3. Do you feel neglected Yes / No
4. Do you feel lost hope in life Yes / No
5. Do you loose self confidence Yes / No

DEVELOPMENT OF BAD HABITS

(1) Do you developed the following habits

  (a) Smoking Yes / No

  (b) Drinking Yes / No

  (c) Tobacco Yes / No

  (d) Drug addiction Yes / No

  (e) Panparak Yes / No

  (f) Others

(2) What are the reasons for developing such habits

  a. Friends b. work pressure c. ill-treatment d. lonely e. availability f. enjoyment g. others

FUTURE PROSPECTS

1. What is your future plan with regard to (order of preference)

   (a) Education

   (b) Vocational education

   (c) Skill development

   (d) Others

   (e) Employment

2. Do you confident that you gain status and recognition in the society Yes/ No
3. What type of employment you aim for :

   What are your suggestions to prevent children going for work.

Bibliography

ABC Nepal. 1996a. The Road to Bombay: Forgotten Women in Red Light Traffic. Kathmandu.

ABC, 2002. Combating Trafficking of women and Children in south Asia.(RETA-5948): Nepal Country Report.

Abraham, Shailaja.2001.Going Nowhere: Trafficking of Women and Children in International Sex Trade, Vols. I & II New Delhi: Dominant Publishers and Distributors/Asian Development Bank. 2002 a. Combating Trafficking of women and Children in south Asia : Regional Synthesis Paper for Bangladesh, India and Nepal. Manila.

Ach-review@ Achrweb. Org, "Trafficking: Beyond Gender".

Ahmed, Natasha. (2001),"In Search of Dreams: Study on the Situation of the Trafficked Women and Children from Bangladesh and Nepal to India", Dhaka International Organization for Migration.

Ali, Salma, 1997. Surveys in the Areas of Child and Women Trafficking. Dhaka. Bangladesh National Women Lawyers Association.

Amnesty Organization, (2003),"Trafficking and Prostitution in Asia and the Pacific." http://www.amnesty. org/worldwide.

Amnesty International. 2001. Claiming Women's Convention. London. International Publications.

Amnesty International. 2001. Claiming Women's Rights: The Optional Protocol to the UN Women's Convention. Amnesty International Secretariat.

Anand, V.S. Dravid, A. Wagh & A. Salvi. 1994. Study of Occupational Health Problems of Construction Workers in New Bombay. Mumbai: College of social work and society for Participatory

Research in Asia. Hazardous Industries of India. Baroda: Centre for Operation Research.

Asia Foundation / Population Council Horizons, (2001), Policy Analysis, Documentation of Current Intervention Models. Community _based Study of Trafficking, Prevention of Trafficking And care and Support of Trafficked Persons, Kathmandu.

ATSEC India. 2001. State Level Workshop held in Bihar. UNIFEM.

ATSEC India. 2001. Report on the National Consultation on Trafficking and sexual Exploitation of children. July 28-29 kolkata. ATSEC India.

Azad, Nandini(2000),"High Risk Children and Women Issues, Constraints and Strategies ", ICPRD, Delhi.

Bales, Kevin. 1999. Disposable people: New slavery in the Global Economy. California: University of California Press.

Bales, 2002. Keynote Address. Conference on Human Rights Challenge of Globalisation: Asia-Pacific-US: The Trafficking in persons, Especially Woman and Children 13-15 November. Honolulu, Hawaii: Globalisation Research Centre, University of Hawaii.

Bangladesh National Women Lawyers Association. 1998. Survey in the Area of Child and Women Trafficking Dhaka.

Bangladesh National Women Lawyers Association. 2002. Violence Against Women in Bangladesh, 2001. Dhaka.

Barse, Sheela. 1996. Child Victims Rights: International Conference on Child Sexual Abuse, Victim Protection, Investigation and Trial Procedure. February 22-24. Mumbai: Neel Foundation and New Delhi: Friedrich Naumanm Stiftung, India and South Asia region.

Bhoruka Public Welfare Trust. 2001. A Study on Cross-border Girl Trafficking Kolkata.

Blanchet, Therese. 2002. Beyond Boundaries: A Critical look at Women Labour Migration and the Trafficking Within Dhaka USAID.

Bhamathi, B. "Interstate trafficking of Women and Children-A SAARC perspective." CBI Bulletin VII, No 4. (April 1999).

Burra, Neera. 1995. Born work- Child Labour in India. New Delhi: Oxford University Press (Butterflies. Phenomenon of Substance Abuse and Sexually Transmitted Diseases among Street Children. New Delhi.)

Center for Development Population Activities. 1997. Girls' Rights: Society's Responsibility, Taking Action against Sexual Exploitation and Trafficking. New Delhi.

Chakma, Suhas. 2003. The status of children in India: An alternate report to the United Nations committee on the child on India's First Report (CRC | C\93 | Add. 5). New Delhi: Asian Centre for Human Rights.

Child Relief and You (CRY). 1999. "The Indian Child". Mumbai: CRY.

Centre for Women and Development 1996, Survey of Organisations Working on the Issues of Girl Trafficking. Kathmandu: The Asia Foundation.

Coomaraswamy, Radhika. 2000. Integration of the Human Rights of Women and Gender Perspective: Report on Trafficking by the Special Rapporteur on Violence against Women: Its Causes and Consequences. E | CN. 4 | 2000 | 68. 56th Session of the Commission on Human Rights. Economic and Social Council, United Nations.

CRS. 2001. Trafficking in Women and Children: The U.S. and International Response. Library of Congress: Congressional Research Service.

CWDS. 2002. Crimes Against Women: Bondage and Beyond-Revelation of Data. New Delhi: Center for Women's Development Studies.

Domestic work: The International Labour Organization (ILO) estimates that the majority of child domestics are girls. Parents and children are often lured by promises of education or a good job.

D'Cunha, Jean. 1998. "Prostitution and Sex Trafficking; A Review of Contemporary Feminist Perspectives and Strategies" in Violence Against Women, ed. Shirin Kudchedkar and Sabiha Al-Issa. New Delhi: Pencraft International.

Department of State, United States of America, 2001. Victims of Trafficking and Violence Protection Act, Trafficking in Persons Report, Washington D.C.

Department of Women and Child Development and UNICEF. 1996. A Report on the Six Regional Workshops on the Sexual Exploitation and Trafficking of Children. New Delhi: Department of women and Child Development, Ministry of Human Resource Development, Government of India.

Department of Women and Child Development 1998. Annual Report 1997-98, New Delhi Department of Women and Child Development, Ministry of Human Resource Development, Government of India.

Department of Women and Child Development. 1998. Report of the Committee on Prostitution, Child prostitutes and Children of Prostitutes Plan of Action to Combat Trafficking and Commercial Sexual Exploitation of women and Children. New Delhi: Department of Women and Child Development, Ministry of Human Resource Development, Government of India.

Department of Women and Child Development, Ministry of Human Resource Development and Government of India. 1998. Situational Report on the Trafficking of Children for Prostitution. New Delhi: New Concept Information Systems Pvt. Ltd.

Department of Women and Child Development. 2001b. Protecting Children from Trafficking and Sexual Abuse. New Delhi: Department of Women And Child Development, Ministry of Human Resource Development, Government of India.

Department of Women and Child Development. 2001c. SWADHAR-A Scheme for Women in Difficult Circumstances. New Delhi: Department of Women And Child Development, Ministry of Human Resource Development, Government of India.

Department of Women and Child Development. 2001f. National Charter for Children. New Delhi: Ministry of Human Resources Development, Government of India.

DePaul University and OAS. 2000. Sex Trafficking in the Americas. DePaul University: International Human Rights Law Institute.

D' Cunha, Jean. "Prostitution in a Patriarchal Society: A Critical Review of the SIT Act." Economics and political Weekly (7 November 1987).

ECPAT International. 2000. Looking Back-Thinking Forward. The Fourth Reporter on the Implementation of the Agenda for Action Adopted at the First World Congress Against the Commercial Sexual Exploitation of Children in Stockholm, Sweden, August 28, 1996. Bangkok.

ECPAT International. 2003. ECPAT Reports on the Implementation of the Agenda for Action Against the Commercial Sexual Exploitation of Children 2001-02. Bangkok. ECPAT International.

Equations, APSA, UNIFEM &USAID. 2004. Reusing Child labors: An Analysis of the Operation Undertaken to Rescue Children Trafficked to Lob our in the Jewellery Unit in Karnataka. Bangalore: Equations.

Equations. 2003. A Situational Analysis of Child Sex Tourism in India (Kerala and GAO). Bangalore: Equation.

ESCAP. 2003. Combating Human Trafficking in Asia: A Resource Guide to International and Regional Legal Instruments, Political Commitments and Recommend Practice. New York: United Nations.

Fernandez, G., F. Lambay, N. Mehta and H. Joseph. 1994. Study and Action Research on the Girl Child in Especially Difficult Circumstance, India Report-1994. Mumbai: College of Social Work, Nirmala Niketan.

Frederick, John & Thomas Likely, eds. 2000. Fallen Angels-The Sex Workers of South Asia. Delhi: Roil Books. Freidman, Report 1. (1996), "The Nation India's Shame: Sexual Slavery and Political Corruption are Leading to AIDS.

Friedman, Matt. 2001. Human Trafficking: Some International with the Present Definitions and Paradigm. Nepal: Technical Consultative Meeting on Anti-Trafficking: Programmes in South Asia.

GAATW. 1999. Human Right in Practice: A Guide to Assist Trafficked Women and Children. Bangkok: Global Alliance against Trafficking in women.

Gathia, Joseph. 1999. Child Prostitution in India. New Delhi: Concept Publishing Company.

Gathia, Joseph. 2003. Asia Me Deh Vyapar. New Delhi: Concept Publishing Company.

Ghosh S.K. 1993. Women and Crime. Delhi: Ashish Publishing House. pp. 131-136.

Ghosh. Neemai and Roop Sen. 2002. Barefoot Light. Kolkata: Sanlaap and UNIFEM.

Government of United States 2004 "Report on Trafficking in Persons", Office to Monitor and Combat Trafficking in Persons, Sexual exploitation: Children, especially girls, June.

Giri, Mohini. V. 1999. Kayana: Exploitation of Little Angels. New Delhi: Gyan Publishing House.

Ganguli, Geetanjali. "The Regulation of Women's Sexuality through the Law: Civil and Criminal Laws". Economic and Political Weekly (7March 1998).

HAQ Center for child Right. 2001. Chlid Trafficking in India. New Delhi: HAQ.

HAQ Center for Child Right. 2002. Children in Globalizing India: Challenging our Conscience. New Delhi: HAQ.

Haq Centre for Child Rights. Child trafficking in India. New Delhi.

Human Right Watch, July 2004, New Delhi.

Haq. K. 2000. Human Development in South Asia The Genter Question. Karachi: Oxford University Press.

Haque, Shadidul. 2002. Over view of Trends and patterns of Migration With Respect to Foreign Migrant.

Harvey J. P. & L. Riggin, 1994. Trading Away the Future: Child Labour In India 's Export Industries. Washington: International Labour and Research Fund.

Human Rights Watch. 1995. Rape for profit. Trafficking of Nepali girls and Women to India's Brothels, New York: Human Rights Watch.

Human, 1996, Small Hands of Slavery. New York: Human Rights Watch.

Human, 2003, Small Change: Bonded Child Labour in India's Silk Industry. New York Human Rights Watch.

Hughes, Donna, M. 2002. The Driving Force of Sex Trafficking: The Human Rights Challenge of Globalization in Asia-U.S: The Trafficking in persons, Specially among woman and Children November 13-15 2002, Honolulu, Hawaii: Globalization Research Centre, University of Hawaii.

International Labour Organization: Child Labour: Targeting the Intolerable. Targeting the Intolerable. Geneva: ILO, 1996.

International Labour Organization-IPEC.1999. Combating Sexual Exploitation of Children– Lesson Learned. Geneva: ILO- IPEC.

International Labour Organization. 2002. Every child Counts-New Global Estimates on Child Labour. Geneva: ILO-IPEC.

International Labour Organization. 2002. Stopping Forced Labour. Geneva: International Labour Organization.

International Organization for Migrants: IOM Policy and Activities: IOM, 1998.

ILO-IPEC. 1996. Convention Concerning the Prohibition and Immediate Action for the Elimination of the Worst of Child Labour : Targeting the Intolerable. Geneva: International Labour Organization.

ILO–IPEC. 2001a. Trafficking and Sexual Exploitation of Children: An Evaluation Trafficking and Sexual Exploitation of Children: An Evaluation of Programmers in Colombia, Caste Rica and Nicaragua, Thailand and Philippines. Geneva: International Labour Organisation.

Impulse NGO Network. 2002. Research on Girl Child Lobour in Shillong–Emergence of a New Socio–economic Problem. Shillong: Impulse NGO Network.

Indian Social Institute. 1993. The Tribal Domestic Worker at the Crossroads: A Search for Alternatives. New Delhi: Indian Social Institute.

Indian Social Institute. 1995. Women in the Inform anal Sector: Multi Disadvantages of Domestic Workers. New Delhi: Institute.

Iyer, G, ed. 2003. Migrant Labour and Human Rights. In India. Delhi: Kanishka Publishers.

India Human Right Report, 2004, Trafficking in Persons, July New Delhi.

Jagori. 2001. Migration. Trafficking and Sites of Work: Right and

Vulnerabilities, A Plan international Lobour Organization Study Report of Initial Finding in Rajasthan and Gujarat. New Delhi: Jagori.

Jayaweera, Swarna. 2003. Genter and Globalisation: Commemorating Beijing Fourth South Asia Regional Meeting Bhutan, 19-21 May Delhi UNFEM.

Jean , D'Cunha. The Legislation of Prostitution – A sociological Inquiry in to the Laws Relating to Prostitution in the West New Delhi: JOINT Women's Programme.

Johnston, Hugh and Sona Khan, eds., 1998, Trafficking in Persons in South Asia – Final Report of a workshop with Participants from Bangladesh, Sri Lanka, Nepal, Pakistan and Canada. New Delhi: Shastri Indo- Canada Institute.

Jorden, Ann. 2002. The Annotated Guide to the Complete UN Trafficking Protocol, Washington: International Human Rights Law Group.

Joint Women's Programme, (2002), Human Trafficking, How to Address the Issue?"

Joshi, Madhu, ed. 1997. Women and Children in Prostitution: Human Rights perception. Delhi: Joint Woman's Programme.

Karmakar, Sumari. 2001. Red Light Area: Social Environment of Sex Workers, New Delhi: Dominant Publishers and Distribution.

Kisan, M. 1995, Micro Studies of Child Labour: An Analytical Compilation of Micro Studies of Child Labour in Maharashtra: A report prepared for Action for the Rights of the Child (ARC) Pune: Action for the Rights of the Child.

Krishna, S. 1996. Restoring Childhood, New Delhi: Konark Publishers Pvt. Ltd.

Kumar K.C. Bal, Subedi, Govind, Gurung, Yogendra and Adhikar. 2001. Trafficking in Girls With Special Reference to Prostitution: A Rapid Assessment Geneva. International Labour Organisation/IPEC.

Lalita & Shalini. 1998 Women Soliciting Change. New Delhi: Indian Social Institute & Joint Woman's Programme.

Lichtenberger B. Joseph, (2002),"Combating Trafficking of Women and Children in South Asia."

Lim, Lin Lean, ed. 1998, The Sex Sector: The Economic and Social Bases of Prostitution in Southeast Asia. Geneva: International Labour Organisation.

Maiti Nepal 1999. Politics and TRAFFICKING: Role of Parliamentarians to combat Trafficking in Girls and Woman: Solution to the Problem

Commitment and Role of Parliamentarians. Report of the workshop Kathmandu: Maitri Nepal.

Maitri Nepal, 2001. Crusading for eight years 1993: Kathmandu : Maitri Nepal.

Manohar, Sujata. 2002. Trafficking in Women and Girls: Expert Group Meeting on Trafficking in Women and Girls. EGM/ TRAF/ 2002/ WP.I. New Delhi NHRC.

Manoj, Kavita and Jacob Thomas. 2002-2003. Trafficking of Women and Children for Tourism in Kerala, Cochin: DARSAN.

Marhur, K. et al. 1997. Violence Against Woman: The WDP perspective. Jaipur : Institute of Development Studies.

Mazumdar , Ishita, 'Widows of Vrindavan' in Living Death: The Trauma of Widowhood in India, ed. V. Mohini Giri. New Delhi: Manohar Publishers and Distribution. 77-81.

Mukherjee, K.K and Deepa, Das, 1996. prostitution in the six Metropolitan Cities of India. New Delhi: Central Social Welfare Board.

Mukherji, Santosh Kumar, 1986. prostitution in India. New Delhi: Inter-India Publication.

Murthy, Ranjan & Lakshmi Sankaran. 2001. Denial and Distress: Gender Poverty and Human Rights in Asia. Bangalore: Books for Change.

Mallick, Anupriya (2004), trafficking in persons: Facts and Facets." Social Change. Vol. 34, No. 3.

Myneni, S.R. 2002. Woman and the Law. Hyderabad: Asia Law House.

Nair, P.M. 2002. Combating Organised Crime. New Delhi: Konark Publishers.

Nair, P.M. & Poornima Advani. 2001. Report of the National Workshop on Gender and Law Enforcement. New Delhi: National Commission for Women.

National Commission For Woman. 1997, National Consultation on the Sexual Exploitation of children. July 23-24 New Delhi : National for Women.

National Crime Records Bureau, Crimes in India 1997, 1998, 1999, 2000, & 2002. New Delhi: NCRB, Ministry of Home Affairs, Government of India.

National Commission for Woman. 1997. The Velvet: Blouse: The sexual Exploitation of Children New Delhi National Commission for Women, Government of India.

National Commission for Women. 2001. Trafficking: A Socio-legal study. New Delhi: National Commission for Women.

Nirman- A Project for Construction Workers. 1993, A study of the Open Labour Market in Bombay, Mumbai: Nirmala Niketan College of Social Work.

O'Connsll, Davidson, Julia Sancher & Jacquelins Tailor, 1996 Child Prostitution and Sex Tourism: Goa. Bangkok: ECPAT International.

O'Connell Davidson, J. and Sanchej Taylor, J. 1996. Child Prostitution and Sex Tourism: Goa. Bangkok. ECPT International.

Pushpa Karuna, (1998), 'The Awesome Challenge of AIDS' Dominant Pocket Books (P) Ltd., New Delhi, p. 108.

Pandey, Balaji, Damodar Jena & Sugata Mohanty: 2002. Trafficking in Women in Orissa: An Exploratory Study. Bhubaneswar: Institute for Socio- Economic Development.

Patkar, Praveen & Priti Patkar. Frequently Asked Questions on Commercial Sexual Exploitation and Trafficking. Mumbai: Prerna.

Patkar, Praveen, Priti Patkar & Monica Sakhrani. E.d. Trafficking Commercial Sexual Exploitation: International Conventions, Laws and Policies. Mumbai: Prerna.

Patkar, Praveen, Priti Patkar & Monica Sakhrani. 2003. Child Traffcking. Issues and Concerns. Mumbai: Child line Indian Foundation.

Patkar, Praveen & Priti Patkar. 1999. Intervention in the Situation of Trafficking of Children for Prostitution and Children of Prostitution: A Six District Report of Rapid Assessment (Ahmednagar, Latur. Nasik, Sangli, Solapur and Thane) Mumbai: UNICEF.

Patkar, Praveen, Priti Patkar 2002 Tourism Related Commercial Sexual Exploitation of Children in the Western Coast—A Study for the National Commission on Women. Mumbai: Prerana.

Patkar, Praveen, Priti Patkar. 2003. Child Trafficking: Issues and Concerns. Mumbai: Child line Indian Foundation.

Patkar, Praveen, Priti Patkar. 2004. Home investigation Report: An Effective Guide in Post Operations in the fight against the Commercial Sexual Exploitation Trafficking of Children : Mumbai: Preana.

Penrose, Angela, Edda Ivan – Smith & Marilyn Thomson. 1996. Kids for Hire: A child's Right to Protection from Commercial Sexual Exploitation. London: Save the Children.

Penira, Faustian. 2002 The Fractured Scales: The Search for a Uniform Personal Code. Dhaka: The University Press Ltd.

Phinney, Alison. 2001. Trafficking of Women and Children for Sexual Exploitation in the Americas. Washington D.C.: Inter American Commission of Women (Organization of American States),

Women, health and Development Programme Pan American Health Organization and World Health Organization.

Prasad, K.J. 1996. Regional Profile on the Sexual Exploitation and Trafficking of Children. Hyderabad: SALT.

Prayas Institute of Juvenile Justice and UNIFEM.2001. From Darkness to Light: Regional Consultation on Institute of women and Children and Law Enforcement. Prayas Institute for Juvenile Justice.

Prayas. 2002. Issues and Concerns of Trafficking in Women and Children.

Razario, R. et al. 1988. Trafficking in Women and Children in Indian. New Delhi : Uppal Publishing House.

Ralph E. Regan. 2000. Background briefing International trafficking of women and Children . Testimony Before the Senate Committee on Foreign Relations Sub Committee on Near Eastern and south Asia Affairs. New York. Women's Right Division, Human Right Watch.

Roy, Sulagna. 1998. Situational Analysis of Child Prostitution in West Consultation Meeting for Combating Trafficking of Children and Child Prostitution. 'Kolkata: SLARTC.

Rozario S. R. et al., 1988. Trafficking in Women and Children in Indian. New Delhi: Uppal Publishing House.

Saarthak. 2002. The Sounds of Silence: A Manual for forming Therapeutic Relationships. New Delhi: Saarthak and UNIFEM.

Sanghera, Jyoti and Ratna Kapoor. 2000. Trafficking in Nepal: Policy Analysis: An Assessment of Policies and Legislative Measures for the Prevention and Control of Trafficking in Nepal. Kathmandu: The Asia Foundation and New Delhi: Population Council.

Sanghera, Jyoti. 1999. Trafficking of Women and Children in South Asia: A Review of Anti-trafficking Initiatives in Nepal, Bangladesh and India. New Delhi: UNICEF Regional Office and Save the Children Alliance.

Sanghera, Jyoti. 2000. Tracking of Women and Children in South Asia: Taking Stock and Moving Ahead: A Review of Anti-tracking Initiatives in Nepal, Bangladesh and India. New Delhi: UNICEF, ROSA and Mumbai: Save the Children Alliances, South and Central Asia Region.

Sangroula, Yubraj. 2001. Trafficking of Girls and Women in Nepal: Building a Surveillances System for Prevention. Kathmandu: Kathmandu School of Law.

Shalini, S.C.N. and Lalitha. 1996. Women Soliciting Change. New Delhi: Indian Social Institute & Joint Women's Programme.

Shamim, Ishrat. 1998. Trafficking and the Sexual Exploitation of Children: The Bangladesh Perspective Dhaka: Centre for Women and Children Studies.

Shamim, Ishrat. 2001. Mapping of Missing, Kidnapped and Trafficking Children and Women: The Bangladesh Perspective. International Organisation of Migration.

Sherwani, A. 1998. The Girl Child in Crisis. New Delhi: Indian Social Institute.

Sinha, Indrani. 1997. Princess of the Night. Kolkata: Sanlaap.

Skeldon, Ronald. 1999. Migration in the Context of Globalisation in the Asian Pacific Region.(Mimeograph) UNESCAP.

Social Alert. 2000. Invisible Servitude: An In-depth Study on Domestic Workers in the World. Belgium: Social Alert.

Society for Education, Research and Voluntary Effects (SERVE). 1996. Report on the Survey of Children of Prostitutes and Children Dependent on Prostitutes in Six Districts of Alwar, Baran, Bharatpur, Dausa, Dholpur and Sirohi in Rajasthan. Study sponsored by Government of Rajastan and UNICEF. Jaipur: SERVE.

Somerset, Caron, 2001. What the Professionals Know: The Trafficking of Children into, and through the UK for Sexual Purpose. London: ECPAT UK.

Sanghera, Jyoti. 2002."Trafficking of Children and Women in India: Thinking Through, Thinking Beyond-A Critical Framework of Analysis for Strategic Action." New Delhi. UNICEF.

Sanghera, Jyoti. 2002. "Trafficking of child and women in India New Delhi. UNICEF.

Shinha, Indrani (2004), "Women, Globalization, Malini Bhattacharrya (ed.) New Delhi, Tulika Books.

Sivadas, Meena M. (2000), Preliminary Analysis of Finding from Field Work in Nepal and Mumbai, Tata Institute (TISS), Child Prostitute in U.P.

Shilaja Abraham, 2002, 'Going Nowhere: Trafficking of women and children in International Sex Trade. Published by Dominant Published by Dominant Publishers and Distributors.

Subedi, Govind. 2002. Trafficking and Sexual Abúse among Street Children in Kathmandu.: ILO-IPEC.

Subedi, Pushp K.1995. Recent Migration in Kathmandu Municipality: Socio-demographic and Economic Correlates. Kathmandu: Central Department of Population Studies, Tribhuvan University.

Trafficking in women and Girls: Report of the Export of the Expert Group Meeting Glen Cove, New York, USA, 18-22. November, 2002.

Taylor, Ernest (2002), Trafficking in Women and Girls. "Paper presented in New York in an export group meeting on Trafficking in Women and Girls."

Tandon, R.K., and K.N. Sudarshan. 1997. Child Prostitution. New Delhi: A.P.H. Publications.

Terre des Hommes, Germany-India Programme. 2001. National Consultation on Trafficking in Children. 19-20 June at Atma Darshan Mumbai. Kolkata: Terre des Hommes Eastern Regional Office.

Truong, Thanh-Dam. 2002. The Human Rights Question in the Global Sex Trade', in Responding to the Human Deficit: Essays in Honour of Bas de eds. K.Arts and P. Mihyo. New York: Kluwer Law International.

Tumlin, Karen C. 2000. Trafficking in Children in Asia: A Regional Overview. Bangkok: Institute for Asian Studies, Chulalongkorn University.

UNDP. 2002. Layers of silence: Links Between Women's Venerability, Trafficking and HIVAIDS in Bangladesh, India and Nepal, Switzerland:.

UNESCO. 2000. passport to Equality. New Delhi: UNESCO.

UNESCO. 2001. A Cultural Approach to HIVAIDS Prevention and Care: A Handbook for India; Studies and Reports, Special Series No. 5, Division of Cultural Policies.

UNICEF. 2000. Trafficking of Women and Children in South Asia: Regional Strategy Framework for UNICEF's Work to Combat the Trafficking of Women and Children in South Asia. UNICEF.

UNIFEM 1998. A Life Free of Violence: It's our Right, For Women in the South Asian Region. New Delhi: UNIFEM.

UNIFEM. 2003. Information Dossier on Human Trafficking: Commemorating Beijing, Fourth South Asia Regional Meeting in Bhutan, 19-21 May. New Delhi: UNIFEM.

United Nations. 2000. Integration of the Human Rights of Women and the Gender Perspective: Violence Against Women. New York: United Nations.

United Nations, 2001. Integration of the Human Rights of Women and the Gender Perspective: Violence Against Women – Report of the Special Rapporteur on Violence of Women and Girls. UNESCAP.

Virani, Pinki. Butter Chocolate: Child Sexual Abuse in India. 2000. New Delhi: Penguin Books.

Vinay, Kumar. (2004) "India could lead the fight against human trafficking" Hindu Daily News paper on Globalization and Human Right.

Wickramasekara, Pryasini, 2002, Asian Labour Migration: Issues and Challenges in an Era of Globalisation. International Migration Papers No. 57, International Migration Programme, Geneva: International Organization for Migration.

Young, Richard, Sankar Sen and Helan Chernikoff. 1996. The Reality of Child profiting form Girl Child Vulnerability. New Delhi: UNICEF.

Zchariah, K.C, K.P. Kannan and Irudaya. S. Rajan. 2002. Kerala's Gulf connections: CDS Studies on International Labour Migrations from Kerala State in India: New Delhi: Centre for Development Studies.

U.S. Department of Labour, Bureau of International Labour Affairs. Consumer labels and Child Labour (Vol. IV). 1997. "By the Sweat and Toil of Children." Washington D.C. U.S Department of Labour, Bureau of International Labour Affairs.

Economic TIMES. "Children As Slaves," 9 April, 2002.

Ganguli, Geetanjali. "Prostitution, Legalization Decriminalization: Recent Debates." Economic and Political Weekly (7 March 1998).

Hezfeld, Beth. "Slavery and Gender". Gender Development 190, No. 1 March (2002): 50-55.

Hindu, "They have rights too," 18 April 1999.

Hindu, "Child Trafficking on the Rise,"6 February 1999.

Hindustan Times. "Goa is India's Bangkok: Major Destination for Sex Tourism," 20 March 1998.

Hindustan Times, "Father Sells Son for 10 kgs Rice," 22 March 1999.

Hindustan Times. "Where Parents Sell their Children for Paltry Rs. 1000 to Earn Rs. 50 a Month." 19 February 1999.

Hughes, Donna M. "The Natasha Trade: The Transnational Shadow Market of Trafficking in Women". Journal of International Affairs53, No. 2 (Spring 2000): 625-651.

Indian Express. "HC Orders Rehab Schemes for Reused Prostitutes", 23 June 1999.

Indian Express. "Inspect Rescue Homes for Prostitutes: HC " 24 April.

Kelly, Liz. " From Rhetoric to Curiosity: Urgent Questions from the UK about Responses to Trafficking in Women." Asian Women 13 (2001): 21.36.

Nair, P.M. "Combating Trafficking in Women and Children." CBI Bulletin 10, 4 (April 2002).

Nair, P.M. "National Centre for Missing and Exploited Children" CBI Bulletin (April 2001).

Sanlaap. 2000 'Child trafficking and prostitution.' Kolkata Newspapers: Anands Bazar Patrika, Bartaman, Aajaal and Ganashakti.

Bangladesh National Women Lawyers' Association. 2001. Movements against trafficking & sexual exploitation' Special Bulletin (October 2001).

Truong, Thanh-Dan. "Gender, Exploitative Migration, and the Sex Industry: A European Perspective." Gender, Technology and Development 7, No. 1 (2003): 31-52.

Wijers, Marjan , & Lin Lop -Chew (1997), "Trafficking in Women : Forced Labour and Slavery like Practices in Marriage, Domestic Labour, and Prostitution, Utrecht, Foundation Against Trafficking in Women.

Wadhwa, Soma (1998), "For sale Childhood," outlook, New Delhi.

Wennerholm, Caroline Johansson. "Crossing Border and Building Bridges: The Baltic Region Net working Project." Gender and Development 10, No. 1 (March 2002): 10-19. UNDP/South East Asia HIV and Development Project (2000), Land Transport &HIV Vulnerablity: A Development Challenge, Bangkok.

UNDP/UNIEF (1999), AIDS south and southwest Asia: A Development Challenge.

UNDP/UNOPS, Analytical and strategic Framework for Action: Prevention of Trafficking of women and Girls and HIV /AIDS in Asia.

UNDP, 2003.'From Challenge to Opportunities:

UN Report (2005), "Trafficking," http://www.hrw. oral/

UN Report (2005), "Trafficking", http://www.voucandaid, org/

www.imard.org

www.peacewomen. Org/news/Nepal/newsarchive01/will. Html

www.un.org/ women watch/dawn/egm/trafficking2002/reportes/ EP-Tailor. Pdf

www.crip. Org/pdf/pub-fac-adoles-trafficking. Pdf

Www. Socstats. Soton. Ac. Uk/ choic

Index